John Lubbock

On the Senses, Instincts, and Intelligence of Animals

With special reference to insects

John Lubbock

On the Senses, Instincts, and Intelligence of Animals
With special reference to insects

ISBN/EAN: 9783337240660

Printed in Europe, USA, Canada, Australia, Japan

Cover: Foto ©Andreas Hilbeck / pixelio.de

More available books at **www.hansebooks.com**

THE INTERNATIONAL SCIENTIFIC SERIES
VOLUME LXIV

THE INTERNATIONAL SCIENTIFIC SERIES

ON THE SENSES INSTINCTS, AND INTELLIGENCE OF ANIMALS

WITH SPECIAL REFERENCE TO INSECTS

BY

SIR JOHN LUBBOCK, BART.

M. P., F. R. S., D. C. L., LL. D.

AUTHOR OF "ANTS, BEES, AND WASPS;" "PREHISTORIC TIMES," ETC.

WITH OVER ONE HUNDRED ILLUSTRATIONS

NEW YORK
D. APPLETON AND COMPANY
1888

PREFACE.

In the present volume I have collected together some of my recent observations on the senses and intelligence of animals, and especially of insects.

While attempting to understand the manners and customs, habits and behaviour, of animals, as well as for the purpose of devising test experiments, I have found it necessary to make myself acquainted as far as possible with the mechanism of the senses, and the organs by means of which sensations are transmitted. With this object I had to look up a great number of memoirs, in various languages, and scattered through many different periodicals; and it seemed to me that it might be interesting, and save others some of the labour I had to undergo myself, if I were to bring together the notes I had made, and give a list of the principal memoirs consulted. I have accordingly attempted to give, very briefly, some idea of the organs of sense, commencing in each case with those of man himself.

Mr. John Evans, Dr. M. Foster, and my brother, Dr. Lubbock, have been so kind as to read through the proofs, and I have to thank them for many valuable suggestions.   Lord Rayleigh also has been so good as to look at the chapters on Hearing.

HIGH ELMS, DOWN, KENT.

CONTENTS.

CHAPTER I.

PAGE

Introductory remarks—Difficulty of the subject—The life of a cell—Possible modes of origin of sense-organs—Origin of eye and ear—The sense of touch—The organs of touch—Nerves of touch—Sense of temperature—Cold points—Heat points — Pressure-points—Organs of touch among lower animals — Medusæ — Annelides—Mollusca—Crustacea—Insects—Sense-hairs—Tactile hairs 1

CHAPTER II.

The sense of taste—Taste-organs of man—Mammalia—Birds—Reptiles—Taste-organs of the lower animals—Crustacea—Insects—Sense of taste in insects—Organs of taste in insects—The bee—Humble bee—Wasp—Fly—Individual differences 19

CHAPTER III.

The sense of smell—Protozoa and Cœlenterata—Worms—Mollusca—Insects—Seat of the sense of smell—Different theories as to the seat of the sense of smell in Insects—Experiments with Dinetus — Hydaticus — Silpha — Stag-beetle — Ants—Seat of the sense of smell partly in the palpi, partly in antennæ—Organs of smell—Leydig's olfactory cones—Organs of smell in Crustacea—Centipodes—Olfactory cones in insects—Olfactory hairs—Olfactory pits—Olfactory organs of fly—Antenna of Ichneumon—Olfactory organs of wasp—Antennal organs of insects—Complex structure of the antennæ—Various uses of antennæ ... 32

CHAPTER IV.

PAGE

The sense of hearing—Organs of sound—Mollusca—Crustacea—Insects — Locusts — Grasshoppers — Crickets — Cicadas — Beetles—The bombardier beetle—Paussus—Death-watch—Burying beetles—Weevils—Cockchafers—Variety of organs of sound among beetles—Diptera—Hymenoptera—Ants—Bees—Sounds produced in flight—Power of varying sound —Butterflies—Moths—Centipedes—Spiders—Power of hearing in insects—Sense of hearing in insects   60

CHAPTER V.

The organs of hearing—Structure of the human ear—The organ of Corti—Mode of action of auditory organs—Organs of hearing in the lower animals—Medusæ—Auditory hairs—Mollusca—Annelides—Crustacea—Use of grains of sand as otolithes—Ear in tail of Mysis—Mode of hearing—Organs of hearing in insects—Seat of the sense of hearing in insects —Different seats of organs of sense—Ears in legs of crickets —Ear of grasshoppers—Structure of ear—Auditory rods—Ear of locusts—Peculiar structure in leg of ant—Origin of ear—Ear of fly—Peculiar sense-organs—Auditory rods in beetles—Position of auditory rods—Chordotonal organs—Auditory hairs of antennæ of gnat—Sympathetic vibrations —Organs of hearing in various parts of body   77

CHAPTER VI.

The sense of sight—Three possible modes of sight—Different forms of eye—The vertebrate eye—Structure of the eye—The retina—The rods and cones—The blind spot in the eye —Inversion of the rods—The pineal gland—The rudimentary median eye—The median vertebrate eye—The organs of vision in the lower animals—Color-spots—Echinoderms—Worms—Molluscs—Cuttle-fish—Compound eyes in Molluscs —Arca—Spondylus—Pecten—Onchidium—Sense-organs of Chiton   118

CHAPTER VII.

The organs of vision in Insects and Crustacea—Ocelli—Compound eyes—Cornea—Crystalline cones — Retinula — Pigment—Different forms of eyes—Structure of the optic lobes—Eyes

of Crustacea—Structure of eye—Mysis—Corycœus—Copilia
—Calanella—Limulus—Scorpions—Light-organs of Euphausia—Mode of vision by compound eyes—Müller's theory
of Mosaic vision—Images thrown by the cornea—Objections
to other theories—Position of the image—Absence of power
of accommodation—Absence of retina—Summary—On the
power of vision in insects—Experiments on vision of insects
—On the function of ocelli—Difficulty of subject—Experiments—Short sight of ocelli—Ocelli of cave-dwelling spiders
—Probable function of ocelli   146

CHAPTER VIII.

On problematical organs of sense—Muciferous canals of fish—
Deep-sea fish—Light-organs—Living lamps—Problematical
organs in lower animals—Medusæ—Insects—Crustacea—
Difficulty of problem—Size of ultimate atoms—The range
of vision and of hearing—Unknown senses—The unknown
world   182

CHAPTER IX.

On bees and colors—Experiments with colored papers—Dr.
Müller's objections—Reply to objections—Preferences of
bees—The colors of flowers   194

CHAPTER X.

On the limits of vision of animals—Ants and colors—The
ultra-violet rays—The limits of vision in ants—Supposed
perception of light by the general surface of the skin—
Experiments with hoodwinked ants—Confirmation of my
experiments on ants—Experiments with Daphnias—Daphnias and colors—Preference for yellowish green—Experiments—Limits of vision of Daphnias—Perception of
ultra-violet rays—Objections of M. Merejkowski—Suggestion
that Daphnias perceive brightness, but not color—Further
experiments—Evidence that Daphnias perceive differences
of color   202

CHAPTER XI.

On recognition among ants—Experiments with intoxicated ants
—Evidence against recognition by means of a sign or pass-
word—Experiments with ants removed from the nest as

PAGE

pupæ and subsequently restored—Experiments with drowned
ants—Recognition after a year and nine months—Supposed
recognition by scent—Recognition by means of the antennæ   232

CHAPTER XII.

On the instincts of solitary wasps and bees—Instinct of rendering victims insensible—Origin of instincts—Habits not
invariable—Change of instincts—Bembex—Odynerus—Ammophila—Modifiability of instincts—Differences under
different circumstances—Origin of the habits of Sphex—
Race differences—Limitation of instinct—Toleration of para-
sites—Cases of apparent stupidity—M. Fabre's experiments
—Limitation of instinct—Instinct and habits—Inflexibility
of instinct—Different habits of males and females—Arrangement of male and female cells—Power of mother to regulate
the sex of the young   242

CHAPTER XIII.

On the supposed sense of direction—Experiments with bees—
Whirling bees—Behaviour of bees if taken from home—
Mode of finding their way—Experiments with ants—Mr.
Romanes' experiments—No evidence of separate sense
of direction   262

CHAPTER XIV.

On the intelligence of the dog—Education of the deaf and dumb
—Laura Bridgman—Application of the method followed
with the deaf and dumb to animals—My dog Van and his
cards—Use of cards with words on them, "food," "water,"
"tea," etc.—Recognition of the separate cards—Association
of the card with the object—Realization that bringing a
card was a request—Attempts to convey ideas—Arithmetical
powers of animals—Previous observations—Supposed powers
of counting—Mr. Huggins's experiments—Conclusion   ...   272

LIST OF ILLUSTRATIONS.

FIGURE   PAGE

1. Diagram to illustrate possible origin of a sense-organ. *c*, Cuticle; *h*, cellular or hypodermic layer   3

2. Diagram to illustrate possible origin of a sense-organ. *c*, Cuticle; *h*, cellular or hypodermic layer   3

3. Diagram to illustrate possible origin of a sense-organ. *c*, Cuticle; *h*, hypoderm; *n*, nerve   4

4. Diagram of further stage in the origin of a sense-organ   ..   4

5. Diagram illustrating a second possible origin of a sense-organ   5

6. Diagram of further stage in the origin of a sense-organ   ..   5

7. Section through the simple eye of a young Dytiscus larva. *h*, Hypoderm; *l*, lens; *o*, optic nerve; *g*, *p*, modified hypodermic cells; *r*, retina   6

8. Auditory vesicle of Ontochis   6

9. Pacinian corpuscle. *a*, Neurilemma; *b*, nerve-fibril; *c*, capsule; *d*, peculiar fibres; *e*, central cylinder   8

10. Papilla from the surface of the hand, × 350. *a*, Cone-like body; *b*, nerve; *c*, end of nerve   8

11. Portion of the skin of the back of the hand. The centre figure represents the arrangement of the hairs; *CP*, the cold-points; *WP*, the warmth-points   10

12. Half a cross section through the brain and hinder pair of eyes of *Nereis cultrifera*. 1, Hypoderm; 2, cuticle; 3, retina; 4, outer corneal cells; 5, inner corneal cells; 6, brain; 8, 8*a*, two places to which the brain sends large nerves, but where the cuticle is unaltered; *g*, gelatinous body   12

13. Part of upper nerve-ring and tactile epithelium of Lizzia. *a*, Tactile epithelium; *g*, ganglionic cell; *nr*[1], upper nerve-ring   12

14. Diagram of part of the skin of a sea-anemone (Actinia). *dz*, Glandular cell; *nz*, nervous cell   13

15. Anterior part of body of *Bohemilla comata*. *lb*, Tactile hair;

FIGURE   PAGE

hy, hypoderm ; *c*, cuticle ; *b*, anterior part of brain ; *a*, eye ;
ne, nerve-fibrils ; *v*, anterior blood-vessel   13

16. Diagrammatic section through a papilla of touch of Onchidium.
a', *a''*, two layers of the cuticle ; *a*, biconvex thickened portion
of the cuticle ; *b*, enlarged epithelial cells ; *b'*, ordinary epithelial cells ; *c*, cellular body ; *d*, cells ; *n*, nerve   14

17. Diagram of the structure of the soft and some of the hard parts
in the tegmentum of a shell of a Chiton (*Acanthopleura spiniger*),
as seen in a section vertical to the surface, and with the margin
of the shell bordering on the girdle lying in the direction of
the left side of the drawing. *f*, Calcareous cornea ; *h*, iris ;
g, lens ; *k*, pigmented capsule of eye ; *n*, optic nerve ; *r*, rods
of retina ; *n'*, branches of the optic nerve, perforating the capsule wall, and terminating in *b'*, *b'*, *b'*, ocular sense-organs ;
p, *p*, nerves to sense-organ ; *m*, body of sense-organ cut across ;
a, *p*, fusiform body of sense-organ entire ; *a*, obconical termination of sense-organ ; *e*, nerve given off by one sense-organ
to another, *b''*   15

18. Diagram of forms of hairs in insects. *a*, Ordinary surface hair ;
b, plumose natatory hair ; *c*, hair of touch ; *d*, auditory hair ;
e, olfactory hair ; *f*, taste hair ; *n*, nerve hair   16

19. Part of the proboscis of a fly (Musca). *n*, nerve ; *g*, ganglionic
swellings ; *s*, tactile hairs or rods ; *c*, cuticle   17

20. Right half of eighth segment of the body of the larva of a gnat
(*Corethra plumicornis*). *EG*, Ganglion ; *N*, nerve ; *g*, auditory
ganglion ; *gb*, auditory ligament ; *Ch*, auditory rods ; *a*, auditory
nerve ; *e*, attachment of auditory organ to the skin ; *b*, attachment of auditory ligament ; *hn*, *hn'*, termination of skin-nerve ;
tb, plumose tactile hair ; *h*, simple hair ; *tg*, ganglion of tactile
hair ; *lm*, longitudinal muscle   18

21. Taste-buds of the rabbit, × 450   20

22. *a*, Isolated taste-cells from the mouth of a rabbit ; *b*, two cover-
cells and a taste-cell in their natural position, × 600   ..   20

23. Termination of the nerves of taste in the frog, showing the
ramifications of the nerve-fibres and their connections with the
cells of taste, × 600   21

24. Inner layer of skin of the proboscis of *Asterope candida*, × 400.
a, Cuticle ; *b*, terminal (nerve) organs ; *c*, ganglionic cells ;
d, longitudinal muscle ; *e*, transverse muscle   22

25. Taste-organ of the bee. *B*, Horny ridge ; *R*, *R*, sensory pits ;
C, *C*, skin of the mouth ; *L*, muscular fibres ; *A*, *A*, muscular
fibres ; *S*, *S'*, *a b c d e f*, section of the skin of œsophagus   ..   26

FIGURE   PAGE

26. Shows three of Wolff's cups, each with a central hair, a chitinous ring, and a double ganglionic swelling terminating in a nerve-fibre, × 500 times. *R, R'*, Sensory pits and hairs; *G, G*, ganglionic swelling of nerve 27

27. Under side of left maxilla of Vespa. *Gm*, Taste-cups; *Shm*, protecting hairs; *Tb*, tactile hairs; *Mt*, base of maxillary palpus 28

28. Section through a taste-cup. *SK*, Supporting cone; *N*, nerve; *SZ*, sense-cell 28

29. Tip of the proboscis in the hive bee (Apis), × 140. *L*, Terminal ladle; *Gs*, taste-hairs; *Sh*, guard-hairs; *Hb*, hooked hairs .. 29

30. Organ of taste of fly (*Musca vomitoria*). *gn*, Nerve; *gg*, ganglion; *ax*, axe-cylinder; *gc*, terminal cylinder; *gk*, terminal cone .. 30

31. Epithelial and (B) olfactory cells of man.. 33

32. Cells from the olfactory region of a proteus (after Stricker). *a*, Epithelial cells; *b*, the apparent processes; *c*, olfactory cells. *A*, ciliæ 33

33. Section through the head segment of Polyophthalmus, × 300. *lmd*, muscle; *bo*, cup-shaped organ; *cu*, cuticle; *hp*, hypoderm; *lmd*, longitudinal dorsal muscle; *n*, peripheral nerve; *b*, cerebral ganglion; *cz*, commissure of brain; *mb*, membrane; *pmg*, pigment cells; *hpdz*, unicellular glands in the hypoderm; *gn*, brain; *k*, nuclei in the brain 34

34. Antenna of *Pontella Bairdii* (Lubbock) 47

35. Terminal segments of one of the smaller antennæ of the water-woodlouse (*Asellus aquaticus*), × 500. *a*, Ordinary hairs (not connected with a nerve); *b*, hairs of touch (with a nerve at the base); *c*, special cylinders (olfactory cylinders) 48

36. Tip of the antenna of a centipede (*Julus terrestris*), × 600. At the apex are four olfactory cylinders, a few of which are also seen on the following segment, among the ordinary hairs .. 49

37. End of a palpus of *Staphylinus erythropterus*, × 600. *a*, Olfactory pit 50

38. Part of antenna of *Callianassa subterranea*. *b*, Olfactory hairs; *g*, peculiar curved hairs 50

39. Terminations of olfactory hairs of Crustacea. *a*, Of larva of a Palæmon; *b*, of a Pagurus; *c*, of a Pinnotheres; *d*, of a Squilla; *e*, of a Pontonia 51

40. Antenna of blowfly. *a*, Enlarged third segment, showing pits; *c*, base of the antenna 53

41. One segment of the antenna of an Ichneumon 54

42. Section through part of the antenna of a wasp, × 430. *CH*, Chitinous skin; *Z*, olfactory cone; *G*, olfactory pit; *TB*, tac-

FIGURE   PAGE

tile hairs; *H*, hypodermic cells; *M*, the membrane surrounding
them; *K*, nuclei of the olfactory cell; *K,*, remains of the
earlier upper nucleus; *SK*, lower circle of rods; *RS*, olfactory
rod; *GZ*, Geisselzelle; *MZ*, membrane forming cell; *M*, membrane closing the pit   55

43. Diagram showing structures on the terminal segment of the
    antennæ of insects. *a*, Chitinous cuticle; *b*, hypodermic layer;
    c, ordinary hair; *d*, tactile hair; *e*, cone; *f*, depressed hair,
    lying over *g*, cup, with rudimentary hair at the base; *h*, simple
    cup; *i*, champagne-cork-like organ of Forel; *k*, flask-like
    organ; *l*, papilla, with a rudimentary hair at the apex   ..   56

44. Leg of *Stenobothrus pratorum*   62

45. Sound-bow of Stenobothrus   63

46. Diagram of human ear. D, Auditory canal; E, mouth of Eusta-
    chian tube; *cc*, tympanic membrane; B, tympanic cavity; *o*,
    fenestra ovalis; *r*, fenestra rotunda; *s*, semicircular canals;
    A, cochlea   78

47. Ossicles of the ear. H, Hammer; *Am*, anvil; *Am. k*, shorter
    process of the anvil; *Am. l*, longer process of the anvil; S,
    stirrup; S*t*, long process of the hammer   78

48. Section through the ampulla. *N*, nerve; *z*, terminal cells; *h*,
    auditory hairs   79

49. Tympanal wall of the ductus cochlearis, from the dog. Surface
    view from the side of the scala vestibuli, after the removal of
    Reissner's membrane, $\frac{300}{1}$. I. Zona denticulata Corti. II. Zona
    pectinata Todd-Bowman: 1, Habenula sulcata Corti; 2, Ha-
    benula denticulata Corti; 3, Habenula perforata Kölliker.
    III. Organ of Corti: *a*, portion of the lamina spiralis ossea
    (the epithelium is wanting); *b* and *c*, periosteal blood-vessels;
    d, line of attachment of Reissner's membrane; *e* and *e,*, epi-
    thelium of the crista spiralis; *f*, auditory teeth, with the
    interdental furrows; *g*, *g,*, large-celled (swollen) epithelium
    of the sulcus spiralis internus, over a certain extent shining
    through the auditory teeth; from the left side of the pre-
    paration they have been removed; *h*, smaller epithelial cells
    near the inner slope of the organ of Corti; *k*, openings through
    which the nerves pass; *i*, inner hair cells; *l*, inner pillars;
    m, their heads; *o*, outer pillars; *n*, their heads; *p*, lamina
    recticularis; *q*, a few mutilated outer hair cells; *r*, outer
    epithelium of the ductus cochlearis (Claudius's cells of the
    author's); removed at *s* in order to show the points of attach-
    ment of the outer hair cells   80

FIGURE   PAGE

50. *Eutima gigas* 83

51. Auditory organ of *Ontorchis Gegenbauri* 84

52. Auditory organ of Phialidium. d^1, Epithelium of the upper surface of the velum; d^2, epithelium of the under surface of the velum; *hh*, auditory hairs; *h*, auditory cells; *np*, nervous cushion; *nr'*, nerve-ring; *r*, circular canal at the edge of the velum 85

53. Auditory organ of Rhopalonema, still showing a small orifice. *kk*, Modified tentacle; *o*, auditory organ 85

54. Sense-organ of Pelagia. *o*, Group of crystals, *sk*, sense-organ; *sf*, fold of the skin; *ga*, gastro-vascular channel 86

55. Auditory organ of Unio. *a*, Nerve; *b*, cells; *c*, ciliæ; *d*, otolithe 87

56. Auditory organ of *Pterotrachea Friderici*. *Na*, Auditory nerve; *c*, central cells; *d*, supporting plate; *b*, outer circle of auditory cells; *a*, ciliated cells 87

57. Base of right antennule of lobster (*Astacus marinus*). *a*, Orifice; *s*, sac 88

58. Interior of auditory sac of lobster. *a*, Orifice; *h*, auditory hairs 88

59. Part of wall of auditory sac of lobster (*Astacus marinus*). *a*, Thickened bars in the membrane of the sac; *η*, first row of auditory hairs; *η'*, second row of auditory hairs; *η''*, third row of auditory hairs; *η'''*, fourth row of auditory hairs; *ε*, grains of sand, serving as otolithes 89

60. Auditory hair of crab (*Carcinus mænus*), × 500. *a*, Skin; *c*, nerve; *h*, delicate intermediary membrane or hinge 92

61. Mysis 92

62. Tail of *Mysis vulgaris*, showing the auditory organ 93

63. Part of the leg of a grasshopper (Gryllus). *o, t, n, b*, tympanum 98

64. Section through the tibia (leg) of a Meconema, × about 150. *tr, tr*, The two tracheæ; *ar*, the auditory rod 102

65. The tracheæ and nerve-end organs from the tibia (leg) of a grasshopper (*Ephippigera vitium*). *EBI*, Terminal vesicles of Siebold's organ; *HT*, hinder tympanum; *Sp*, space between the trachea; *hTr*, hinder branch of the trachea; *SN*, nerves of the organ of Siebold; *go*, supra-tympanal ganglion; *Gr*, group of vesicles of the organ of Siebold; *vN*, connecting nerve-fibrils between the ganglionic cells and the terminal vesicles; *So*, nerve terminations of the organ of Siebold; *vT*, front tympanum; *vTr*, front branch of the trachea 103

66. Auditory rod of a grasshopper (*Gryllus viridissimus*). *fd'*, Auditory rod; *ko*, terminal piece 104

67. Diagram of a section through the auditory organ of a grass-

FIGURE   PAGE

hopper (Meconema). *c*, Cuticle; *a.r*, auditory rod; *a.c*, auditory cell; *tr*, trachea   105

68. Outer part of a section through the tibia of a *Gryllus viridissimus*. *h*, Hard surface of leg; *tr*, trachea; *F*, fat bodies; *Su*, suspensor of the trachea; *vW*, tracheal wall; *TN*, nerve; *gz*, ganglionic cells; *rb*, tissue connecting the ganglionic cells; *E. Sch.*, end tubes of the ganglionic cells, each containing an auditory rod; *fa*, terminal threads of ditto   106

69. Tibia of yellow ant (*Lasius flavus*), × 75. *S, S*, Swellings of large trachea; *rt*, small branch of trachea; *a*, auditory organ   107

70. Part of the tibia of *Isopteryx apicalis*. *Sc*, Auditory organ; *ef*, terminal filament; *Cu*, cuticle; *G*, ganglionic cell; *Sc*, structure enclosing the auditory rod; *tr*, trachea; *n*, nerve   109

71. One of the halteres of a fly   110

72. Right half of eighth segment of the body of the larva of a gnat (*Corethra plumicornis*). *EG*, Ganglia; *N*, nerve; *g*, auditory ganglion; *gb*, auditory ligament; *Ch*, auditory rods; *a*, auditory nerve; *e*, attachment of auditory ligament to the skin; *hn, hn'*, termination of skin-nerve; *tb*, plumose tactile hair; *h*, simple hair; *tg*, ganglion of tactile hair; *lm*, longitudinal muscle   114

73. Head of a gnat   115

74. Diagram showing one possible mode of vision   119

75. Diagram showing a second possible mode of vision   119

76. Diagram showing a third possible mode of vision   120

77. Diagram of human eye. *G*, Vitreous humor; *L*, lens; *W*, aqueous humor; *c*, ciliary process; *d*, optic nerve; *e e*, suspensory ligament; *k k*, hyaloid membrane; *f f, h h*, cornea; *g*, choroid; *i*, retina; *l*, ciliary muscle; *mf, nf*, sclerotic coat; *p p*, iris; *s*, the yellow spot.   121

78. Section through the retina. 1, Limitary membrane; 2, layer of nerve-fibres; 3, layer of nerve-cells; 4, nuclear layer; 5, inner nuclear layer; 6, intermediate nuclear layer; 7, outer nuclear layer; 8, posterior membrane; 9, layer of small rods and cones; 10, choroid   123

79. *A*, Inner segments of rods (*s, s, s*) and cones (*z, z'*) from man, the latter in connection with the cone-granules and fibres as far as the external molecular layer, 6. In the interior of the inner segment of both rod and cone fibrillar structure is visible. × 800   124

80. Diagram to prove the existence of the blind spot in the eye   ..   125

81. Pineal eye-scale on the head of a small lizard (Calotis)   ..   127

FIGURE   PAGE

82. Diagram of a section through the skull and pineal eye of *Lacerta viridis*. *C*, Cuticle; *Pa*, parietal bone; *Ep*, epidermis; *L*, lens; *Pig*, Pigment; *R*, rete mucosum; *CH*, cerebral hemisphere; *N*, nerve; *Ep*, epiphysis; *OpL*, optic lobe of brain   128

83. *Englena viridis*. *e*, Eye-spot   130

84. Section through the simple eye of a young Dytiscus larva. *l*, Corneal lens; *g*, cells forming the vitreous humor; *r*, retina; *o*, optic nerve; *h*, hypoderm   131

85. Eye-spot of Lizzia. *oc*, Ocellus; *l*, lens   132

86. Eye-bulb of Astropecten   132

87. Eye of Asteracanthion. *c*, Cuticle; *e*, epithelium; *l*, lens; *p*, pigment   133

88. Anterior extremity of a freshwater worm (*Bohemilla comata*). *a*, Eye; *b*, brain; *c*, cuticle; *hp*, hypoderm; *lb*, tactile hair; *ne*, nerve; *v*, blood-vessel   135

89. Eye-dot of Nereis. In B the pigment is partly removed so as to show the lens   135

90. The first twelve segments of *Polyophthalmus pictus*, seen from below. The Roman numerals indicate the segments. *St*, Papillæ on the head; *KS*, head; *au*, head eye; *s.au*, side eyes; *Ol*, upper lip; *Ul*, under lip; *v.ph*, pharyngeal vein; *V.subinta*, anterior ventral vein; *V.d.l$^{1-4}$*, veins connecting the superior lateral and vessels; *sept$^{1-3}$*, intersegmentary membranes; *m.ocs.l*, lateral muscle of the œsophagus; *V.ann*, pulsating circular vessel; *Md.dr*, stomach-glands; *V.v-l*, vein connecting the inferior and lateral blood-vessels; *Md*, stomach; *Bm*, muscles of the hairs; *G*, brain; *fl.o*, ciliated organ; *qm*, transverse muscle   136

91. Alciope   137

92. Perpendicular section through the eye-pit of a limpet (Patella). 1, Epithelial cells; 2, retina cells; 3, vitreous body   ..   138

93. Eye of *Trochus magus*. *Gl*, Vitreous body; *No*, nerve   ..   138

94. Eye of *Murex brandaris*. *L*, Lens; *Gl*, vitreous body; *No*, nerve   139

95. Eye of *Helix pomatia*. *ct*, Cuticle; *a*, epithelium; *b*, cornea; *c*, envelope of the eye; *d*, cellular layer; *e*, fibrils of the optic nerve; *f*, feeler cell; *na*, nerve of the tentacle; *no*, optic nerve   140

96. Perpendicular section through an eye of *Arca noæ*. 1, Epithelium of the edge of the mantle; 2, cells of vision; 3, lens; 4, 5, connective tissue; 6, section of one of the cells   ..   142

97. Diagram of eye of Pecten. *a*, Cornea; *b*, transparent basement membrane supporting the epithelial cells of cornea; *c*, the

FIGURE   PAGE

pigmented epithelium; *d*, the lining epithelium of the mantle;
e, the lens; *f*, the ligament supporting the lens; *g*, the
retina; *h*, the tapetum; *k*, the pigment; *m*, the retinal
nerve; *n*, complementary nerve   143

98. Schematic representation of the soft and some of the hard parts
in a shell of a Chiton (Acanthopleura), as seen in a section
vertical to the surface, and with the margin of the shell lying
in the direction of the left side of the drawing. *a*, Conical
termination of sense-organ; *b*, *b'*, ends of nerve; *c*, nerve; *f*,
calcareous cornea; *g*, lens; *h*, iris; *k*, pigmented capsule of
eye; *m*, body of sense-organ cut across; *n*, nerve of eye; *p*,
nerve of sense-organ; *r*, rods of retina   145

99. Long section through the front (*A*) and hinder (*B*) dorsal eyes
of *Epeira diadema*. *A*, Anterior eye; *B*, posterior eye; *Hp*,
hypoderm; *Ct*, cuticle; *ct*, boundary membrane; *M*, muscular
fibres; *M*, *M'*, cross sections of ditto; *St*, rods; *Pg*, *P¹*, pigment cells; *L*, lens; *Gh¹*, vitreous body; *K*, nuclei of the cells
of the retina; *Kt*, crystalline cones; *Rt*, retina; *Nop*, optic nerve   147

100. Section through the eye of a cockchafer (Melolontha)..   ..   148

101. Section through the eye of a fly. *b.m*, Basilar membrane; *c*,
cuticle; *e.op*, epioptic ganglion; *n.c*, nuclei; *n.c.s.*, nerve-cell
sheath; *N.f*, decussating nerve-fibres; *op*, optic ganglion; *pc*,
pseudocone; *pg*, pigment cells; *p.op*, perioptic ganglion; *r*, retinula; *Rh*, rhabdom; *T*, trachea; *t.a*, terminal anastomosis;
Tt, trachea; *ti*, tracheal vesicle   149

102. Two separate elements of the faceted eye of a bee. *Lf*, Cornea;
n, nucleus of Semper; *Kk*, crystalline cone; *Pg*, *Pg¹*, pigment
cells; *Rl*, retinula; *Rm*, rhabdom   150

103. Eyelet of cockroach. *lf*, Cornea; *kk*, crystalline cone; *pg'*, pigment cell; *rl*, retinula; *rm*, rhabdom   152

104. Eyelet of cockchafer. *lf*, Cornea; *kk*, crystalline cone; *pg*, *pg'*,
pigment cells; *rl*, retinula; *rm*, rhabdom   152

105. Leptodora hyalina   156

106. Eye of Mysis. *n*, Nuclei; *Lf*, facets; *Kk*, crystalline cones;
n¹, cells of the retinula; *Rl*, retinula; *Rm*, rhabdom; *Cp*,
blood-vessels; *N*, fibres of the optic nerve; *N¹¹*, *N¹¹¹*, *N¹¹¹¹*,
decussations of the fibres of the optic nerve; *G*, *G¹*, ganglia;
M, muscles for the movement of the eye-stalk; *Km*, nuclei ..   157

107. Corycæus. *a*, *b*, The eye   158

108. Eyes of *Calanella Mediterranea*. *Pg*, pigment cells; *N.fr*,
frontal nerves; *N.op*, nervus opticus. The numbers show
the numbers of the cells   159

FIGURE   PAGE

109. Diagram of a vertical section through a portion of the lateral eye of *Limulus polyphemus*, showing some of the conical lenses, and corresponding retinulæ. *a*, Cuticle; *bb*, cuticular lens; *cc*, hypoderm; *Rn*, retinula; *n*, nerves 160

110. *Euphausia pellucida*. *l.o*, Luminous organ 161

111. Luminous organ of *Euphausia*. *f*, Fibres; *e*, lens 162

112. Eye-stalk of *Euphausia*. *lo*, Luminous organ; *a*, lower eye .. 162

113. One of the elements of the eye of a fly. *kk*, Crystalline cone; *x*, position of the image; *s*, rod; *sc*, sheath; *scm*, outer sheath; *r*, retina; *y*, seat of vision 166

114. *Photichthys argenteus* 185

115. *Ceratius bispinosus* 186

116. Edge of a portion of the mantle of *Aglaura hemistoma*, with a pair of sense-organs. *v*, Velum; *k*, sense-organ; *ro*, layer of nettle cells; *t*, tentacle 188

117. Sense-organ of leech. 1, Epithelium; 2, pigment; 3, cells; 4, nerve 189

118. *Daphnia pulex*. *a*, Antennæ; *b*, brain; *e*, eye; *h*, heart; *m*, muscle of eye; *n*, nerve of eye; *o*, ovary; *ol*, olfactory organ; *s*, stomach; *y*, three eggs deposited in the space between the back and the shell 211

LIST OF THE PRINCIPAL MEMOIRS, ETC., REFERRED TO IN THE PRESENT WORK.

Ahlborn, Zur Anat. und d. Ent. der Epi. b. Amphibien und Reptilien, *Zool. Anz.*, 1886.

Allman, Mon. of the Hydroids, Ray Society, 1871.

Becher, Zur Kenntniss der Mundtheile der Dipteren, *Denkschr. der Acad. d. Wiss. Wien.*, 1882.

Béla Haller, Untersuchungen über marine Rhipidoglossen, *Morphol. Jahrb.*, 1884.

Beraneck, Ueber d. Parietal Auge der Reptilien, *Jenaische Zeitschrift*, 1887.

Berger, E., Unt. ü. d. Bau d. Gehirns u. d. Retina d. Arthropoden, *Zool. Inst. Wien.*, 1878.

Bernstein, The Five Senses of Man.

Bevan, On the Honey Bee.

Blainville, De, Principes d'anatomie comparée.

Blix, Exper. Beit. z. Lösung d. Frage ü. d. Specif. Energie d. Hautnerven, *Zeit. für Biologie*, 1884.

——, Exper. Beit. z. Lösung d. Frage ü. d. Specif. Energie d. Hautnerven, *Zeit. für Biologie*, 1885.

Boll, F., Beiträge z. Phys. Optik, *Arch. für Anat. Phys. u. Wiss. Medicin*, 1871.

Bonnsdorf, Fabrica, usus, et differentiæ palparum in insectis. Dissertatio. Aboae, 1792.

Bourne, G. C., On the Anatomy of Sphærotherium. *Linnean Journal*, 1885.

Boyes, Capt., The Economy of the Paussidæ, *Ann. and Magazine of Natural History*, vol. xviii.

Brady, On the Copepoda of the *Challenger* Expedition, vol. viii.

2

Breitenbach, Beit. z. Kennt. d. Baues d. Schmetterling-Rüssels, *Jenaische Zeit.*, bd. xv.

Briant, T. T., On the Anatomy and Functions of the Tongue of the Bee, *Journal of the Linnean Society*, 1864.

Buchner, L., Mind in Animals.

Burmeister, Handbuch der Entomologie. 1885.

Carrière, J., Die Sehorgane der Thiere. 1885.

Claparède, E., Morphologie des zusammengesetzten Auges bei den Arthropoden. *Zeit. für Wiss. Zool.*, 1860.

——, Anat. and Ent. d. Retina, *Müller's Archiv*, 1857.

——, Sur les pretendus organes auditifs des Antennes chez les Coléoptères, *Ann. Sci. Nat.*, 1858.

Claus, Ueber den Acoust. App. im Gehörorgane der Heteropoden, *Arch. für Mic. Anat.*, 1878.

——, Ueber einige Schizopoden und niedere Malacostraceen, *Zeit. für Wiss. Zool.*, 1863.

Comparetti, Dinamica animale degli insetti. Padoue : 1800.

——, De aure interna comparata-Patavii. 1789.

Cornalia, Monografia del Bombice del Gelso, Mem. d. R. istit. Lombardo di science. Milano : 1856.

Dahl, Das Gehör-und Geruchsorgan der Spinnen, *Arch. für Mik. Anat.*, 1885.

Darwin, Descent of Man.

——, Earthworms.

——, Origin of Species.

Desvoidy, Robineau, Recherches sur l'organisation vertébrale des crustacés et des insectes.

Dönhof, Bienenzeitung, 1851 and 1854.

Dor, De la Vision chez les Arthropodes, *Arch. d. Sci. Phys. et Nat.* Genève : 1861.

Duméril, Considérations générales sur les insectes.

Du siège de la gustation chez les coléoptères, *Comptes rendus de.l'Acad. d. Sciences*, 1886.

Eimer, Dr. Th., Ueber Tast-apparate bei Eucharis multicornis, *Arch. für Mic. Anat.*, 1880.

Erichson, De fabrica et usu antennarum in insectis. Berlin : 1847.

Exner, S., Ueber das Sehen von Bewegungen und die Theorie des zusammengesetzten Auges. Sitzungsber, *Wien. Akad.*, 1875.

——, Die Frage der Functionsweise der Facettenaugen, *Biol. Centralblatt*, 1881, 1882.

Fabre, J. H., Souvenirs Entomologiques. Études et l'Instinct sur les Mœurs des Insectes, 1879.

——, Nouveaux Souvenirs Entomologiques. 1882.

——, Souvenir Entomologiques, troisième série. 1886.

Farre, On the Organ of Hearing in Crustacea, *Phil. Trans.*, 1843.

Forel, A., Les fourmis de la Suisse, Genève.

——, Expériences et Remarques Critiques sur les Sensations des Insectes, *Recueil Zool. Suisse*, 1887.

Fraisse, Ueber Molluskenaugen, *Zeit. für Wiss. Zool.*, 1881.

Gazagnaire, J., Orig. de la gust. chez les coléoptères, *Proc. verb. de la Soc. Zool. de France*, 1886.

Gegenbaur, Beit. zur Kennt. der Gastropodenaugen, *Gegenbaur's Morph. Jahrbuch*, 1885.

——, Elements of Comparative Anatomy.

Gerstäcker, Beschreibung neuer Arten der Gattung Apion, *Ent. Zeit.*, Stettin, 1854.

Goldschneider, Dr. A., Monath. für prackt. Dermatologie, 1884.

——, Die spezif. Energie der Temperaturnerven.

——, Die spezif. Energie der Gefühlsnerven der Haut. ibid.

——, Neue Thatsachen über die Hautsinnesnerven, *Zool. Anz.*, 1885, 1886.

Gottsche, C. M., Beitrag zur Anatomie und Physiol. des Auges der Fliegen und Krebse, *Müller's Arch. für Anat. und Phys.*, 1852.

Graaf, De, Zur Anat. und Ent. der Epi. b. Amphibien und Reptilien, *Zool. Anz.*, 1886.

Graber, Dr. V., Die Gehörorgane der Heuschrecken, *Arch. für Mic. Anat.*, 1875.

——, Die Tympanalen Sinnesapparate der Orthopteren, *Denkschr. d. Kais. Akad. Wiss. Wien.*, 1876.

——, Ueber neue otocystenartige Sinnesorgane der Insekten, *Arch. für Mic. Anat.*, 1879.

——, Ueber das unicorneale Tracheaten-und speciell das Arachnoiden-und Myriapoden Auge, *Arch. für Mic. Anat.*, 1879.

——, Die Chordotonalen Sinnésorgane und das Gehör der Insekten, *Arch. für Mic. Anat.*, 1882.

——, Morphologische Untersuchungen über die Augen der freilebenden Marinen Borstenwürmer, *Arch. für Mik.*, 1880.

——, Fundamental Versuche über die Helligskeits und Farben Empfindlichkeit augenloser und geblendeter Thiere, *Sitz. Kais Acad. d. Wiss. Wien*: 1883.

——, Vergleichende Grundversuche über die Wirkung und die Aufnahmestellen chemischer Reize bei den Thieren, *Biol. Centralblatt*, 1885.

Graber, Dr. V., Ueber die Helligkeits-und Farbenempfindlichkeit einiger Meerthiere, Sitzungs-Ber., *Akad. Wien.*, 1885.

Greeff, R., Untersuchungen über die Alciopiden ; *Nova acta Acad. Leopold. Carol*, 1876.

——, Untersuchungen über die Alciopiden. *Nova acta Acad. Leopold. Carol.*, 1878.

Grenacher, H., Zur Entwicklungsgeschichte der Cephalopoden, *Zeit. für Wiss. Zool.*, 1874.

——, Abhandlungen zur vergleichenden Anatomie des Auges. Das Auge der Heteropoden. Abh. Halle : 1886.

——, Untersuchungen über das Sehorgan der Arthropoden. Göttingen : 1879.

——, Ueber die Augen einiger Myriapoden, *Arch. für Mic. Anat.*, 1880.

Grobben, Ueber bläschenförmige Sinnesorgane u. eigenthümliche Herz-bildung der Larva von Ptychoptera contaminata, *Sitz. der K. Akad. der Wiss.* Wien : 1876.

Grube, E., Ueber Augen bei Muscheln., *Müller's Arch. für Anat. und Phys.*, 1840.

Günther, *Challenger* Reports, vol. xxvii.

——, Introduction to the Study of Fishes.

Haeckel, E., Ueber die Augen und Nerven der Seesterne, *Zeit. für Wiss. Zool.*, 1860.

Haller, G., Z. Kenntn. der Sinnesborsten der Hydrachniden, *Wiegmann's Arch. für Naturgesch.*, 1882.

Hauser, Physiologische und histol. Untersuchungen über d. Geruchsorgan der Insecten, *Zeitschrift für Wiss. Zoologie*, 1880 ; et *Bullet. de la Soc. des amis des Sci. Nat. de Rouen*, 1881.

Helmholtz, Sensations of Tone.

Hensen, V., Ueber das Auge einiger Cephalopoden, *Zeit. für. Wiss. Zool.*, 1865.

——, Ueber das Auge einiger Lamellibranchiaten, *Zeit. für Wiss. Zool.*, 1865.

——, Ueber das Gehörorgan von Locusta, *Zeit für Wiss. Zool.*, 1866.

——, Ueber den Bau des Schneckenauges, *Arch. für Mik. Anat.*, 1866.

Hertwig, O. und R., Das Nervensystem und die Sinnesorgane der Medusen. Leipzig : 1878.

——, R., Das Auge der Planarien., *Sitz. der Jenaischen Gesch. für Med. und Naturwiss*, 1880.

Hicks, On a New Structure in the Antennae of Insects, *Jour. Linn. Zool.*, 1857.

——, Further remarks on the organ found in the bases of the halteres and wings of Insects, *Trans. Linn. Soc. Jour.*, 1857.

——, On certain Sensorial Organs in Insects hitherto undescribed, *Ann. of Nat. Hist.*, 3rd ser., 1859.

Hickson, S. J., The Eye of Pecten, *Quar. Jour. Mic. Soc.*, 1880.
——, The Eye of Spondylus, ibid., 1882.
——, The Eye and Optic Tract of Insects, ibid., 1885.
Hoffmeister, Familie der Regenwürmer. 1845.
Houzeau, J. C., Études sur les Facultés Mentales des Animaux.
Huber, Obs. sur les Abeilles.
Huxley, T. H., On the Auditory Organs in Cruslacea, *Ann. Nat. Hist.*, 1851.
——, The Crayfish : An Introduction to the Study of Zoology.

Johnson, C., Auditory Apparatus of the Mosquito, *Quarterly Journal of Microscopical Science*, 1855.
Joseph, G., Zur Morphologie des Geschmacksorgans bei den Insekten, Tageblatt, der 50 Versammlung deutscher Naturforscher und Ärzte in München. 1877.

Keller, Geschichte der Gemeinen Stubenfliege. 1764.
Kingsley, On the Compound Eye, *Journal of Morphology*, 1887.
Kirbach, Mundwerkzeuge der Schmetterlinge, *Zool. Anz.*, 1883.
Kirby and Spence, Introduction to Entomology.
Kölliker, Ueber die Randkörper der Quallen, *Frorieps Neue Not.*, 1843.
Kraepelin, Phys. und Hist. über die Geruchsorgane der Insekten, *Zeit. für Wiss. Zool.*, 1880.
——, Ueber die Mundwerkzeuge der saugenden Insekten, *Zool. Anzeiger*, 1882.
——, Z. Kenntn. der Anat. und Physiol. des Rüssels v. Musca, *Zeit. für Wiss. Zool.*, 1883.
——, Ueber die Geruchsorgane der Gliederthiere, Osterprogr. d. Realschule des Johanneums. Hamburg : 1883.
Krohn, A., Ueber augenähnliche Organe bei Pecten und Spondylus, *Arch. für Anat. Phys.*, 1840 ; and *Müller's Arch.*, 1840.
——, Zool. und Anat. Bemerk. über die Alciopiden, *Wiegmann's Arch.*, 1845.
Künkel et Gazagnaire, Du siège de la gustation chez les Insectes diptères, *Comptes rendus des Sci. Nat.*, 1881.
Küster, Die Fühlhörner sind die Riechorgane der Insekten. Isis : 1844.

Landois, Das Gehörorgan des Hirschkäfers, *Arch. für Mic. Anat.*, 1868.
——, Die Ton. und Stimm. Apparate der Insekten, *Zeit. für Wiss. Zool.*, vol. xvii.
——, Thierstimmen.
Lange, W., Beit. zur Anat. und Hist. der Asterien und Ophiuren, *Morph. Jahrbuch*, 1876.

Langstroth, On the Honey Bee.

Lankester, E. Ray, Observations on the development of the Cephalopoda, *Quar. Jour. Mic. Soc.*, 1875.

—— and Bourne, A. G., The Minute Structure of the Lateral and the Central Eyes of Scorpio and of Limulus, *Quar. Jour. Mic. Soc.*, 1883.

Lebert, Hermann, Die Spinnen der Schweiz.

Lee, Bolles, Les Balanciers des Diptères, *Recueil Zool. Suisse*, 1885.

Leeuwenhoek, Select Works, Translated by H. Hoole.

Lehmann, De sensibus externis animalium exsanguium, insectorum scilic, ac vermium, commentatio. Goettingae : 1798.

——, De Antennis Insectorum Dissertatio prior, fabricam antennarum describens. Hamburgi : 1799.

——, De Antennis Insectorum Dissertatio posterior, usum antennarum recensens. Hamburgi : 1800.

Leroy, C. G., Intelligence and Perfectibility of Animals.

Lespès, Mém. sur l'appareil auditif des Insectes, *Ann. Sci. Nat.*, 1858.

Leuckart, R., Ueber muthmassliche Nebenaugen bei einem Fische, 39 Bericht Deutscher Naturforscher. Giessen : 1864.

——, Carcinologisches, *Wiegmann's Arch.*, 1859.

——, Organologie des Auges, in Graefe und Saemisch, Handbuch der gesammten Augenheilkunde, 1874.

Leydig, F., Carcinologisches, *Wiegmann's Arch*, 1858.

——, Zur Anatomie der Insekten, *Reichert's Archiv für Anat. und Phys.*, 1859.

——, Ueber Geruchs und Gehörogane der Krebse und Insekten, *Müller's Arch.*, 1860.

——, Die Augen und neue Sinnesorgane der Egel, *Reichert's Arch.*, 1861.

——, Das Auge der Gliederthiere. 1864.

——, Die Augenähnlichen Organe der Fische. 1881. Unt. z. Anat. und Hist. der Thiere. 1883.

——, Die Hautsinnesorgane der Arthropoden, *Zool. Anz.*, 1886.

Locy, W. A., Obs. in the Dev. of Agelena, *Bull. Mic. Comp. Zool. Harvard*: 1886.

Lowne, B. Thompson, On the Simple and Compound Eyes of Insects, *Phil. Trans.*, 1879.

——, On the Compound Vision and the Morphol. of the Eye in Insects, *Trans. of Linn. Soc. of London*, 1884.

Lubbock, *Ann. and Mag. of Natural History*, 1853.

——, On the Anatomy of Ants, *Microscopical Journal*, 1877.

——, On the Anatomy of Ants, *Trans. Linn. Soc.*, 1880.

——, Ants, Bees, and Wasps. 1886.

——, On the Sense of Color among some of the Lower Animals, *Jour. Linn. Soc.*, 1881.

Mark, E, L., Simple Eyes in Arthropods, *Bull. Mic. Comp. Zool.* Harvard : 1879.

Mayer, Dr. P., Sopra certi Organi di Senso nelle Antenne dei Ditteri, *Reale Acc. dei Lincei*, 1878–79.

——, A. M., Researches in Acoustics, *American Journal of Science and Arts*, 1874.

Meinert, Bid. til. de Danske Myrers Natur. Hist. 1860.

——, Die Mundtheile der Dipteren, *Zool. Anz.*, 1882.

Merejkowsky, M. C., Les Crustacés inférieurs distinguent-ils les couleurs?

Meyer, E., Zur Anat. und Hist. von Polyophthalmus Pictus, *Arch. für Mic. Anat.*, 1882.

Moseley, On the Presence of Eyes in Shells of certain Chitonidæ, *Quarterly Journal of Microscopical Science*, 1885.

Müller, Johannes, Zur Physiologie des Gesichtsinnes. Leipzig : 1826.

——, Phys. of the Senses, translated by Dr. Baly.

Newport, On the Uses of the Antennæ of Insects, *Trans. Ent. Soc.*, 1837–1840.

Notthaft, Ueber die Gesichtswahrnehmungen mittels des Facettenauges. Abh. Senkenberg. Naturf. Gesch. 1880.

Paasch, Ueber die Sinnesorgane der Insekten im Allgemeinen, von den Gehör und Geruchsorganen im Besonderen, *Troschel's Arch. für Nat.*, 1873.

Packard, First Annual Report of the United States Entomological Commission for 1877. Washington : 1878.

——, The Caudal styles of Insects, Sense-organs, *i.e.* Abdominal Antennæ, *American Naturalist*, 1870.

Patten, Eyes of Molluscs and Arthropods, *Mitt. Zool. Stat. Neapel*, 1886.

Pavesi, Pietro, Sopra una nuova Specie di Ragni, Alle callezioni del Museo Civico di Genova, *Ann. Mus. Civ.*, 1873.

Peringuay, Notes on Three Paussi, *Trans. Ent. Soc.*, 1883.

Perris, Ed., Mémoire sur le siège de l'odorat dans les Articulés, *Actes de la Société Linnéenne de Bordeaux*, 1850.

Plateau, F., Palpes des Insectes broyeurs, *Bull. de la Soc. Zool. de France*, 1885.

——, Rech. sur la perception de la lumière par les Myriapodes aveugles, *Jour. de l'Anat.*, etc., 1886.

——, Rech. Exp. sur la Vision chez les Arthropodes, *Comptes Rendus de la Soc. Ent. de Belg.*, 1887 ; Rech. Exp. sur la Vision chez les Arthropodes, *Bull. de l'Acad. Roy. de Belgique*, 1888.

Quatrefages, de, Études sur la Typ. Inf. de l'emb. des Annelés, *Ann. Sci. Nat.*, 1850.

Rabl-Rückhard, Entw. des Knochenfischgehirns, *Sitz. nat. urf. Freunde.* Berlin: 1882.

Ranke, Beit. zur Lehre von den Uebergangs-Sinnesorganen, *Zeit. für Wiss. Zool.*, 1875.

Réaumur, Mém. p. servir à l'Histoire des Insectes.

Report on the Locust Campaign, Parl. Paper, 5250 of 1888.

Roesel, Insectenbelustigungen.

Romanes, Mental Evolution in Animals.

——, Animal Intelligence.

Sars, On the Schizopoda, *Challenger* Reports, vol. xiii.

Sazepin, Ueber den histol. Bau und die Vert. der nervösen Endorgane auf den Fühlern der Myriopoden, *Mém. de l'Acad. Imper. de St. Petersbourg*, 1884.

Schiemenz, Ueber das Vorkommen des Futtersaftes, etc., der Biene, Dissertation der Univ. Leipzig: 1883.

Schmidt, Die Gehörorgane der Heuschrecken, *Arch. für Mic. Anat.*, 1875.

Schultze, Max, Untersuchungen über die zusammengesetzten Augen der Krebse und Insecten. 1868.

——, Die Stäbchen in der Retina der Cephalopoden und Heteropoden, *Arch. für Mic. Anat.*, 1869.

——, Zur Anat. und Phys. der Retina, *Arch. für Mic. Anat.*, 1866.

——, Ueber Stäbchen und Zapfen der Retina, *Arch. für Mic. Anat.*, 1867.

——, Ueber die Nervenendigung in der Netzhaut der Auges bei Menschen und Thieren, *Arch. für Mic. Anat.*, 1869.

——, Neue Beit. zur Anat. und Phys. der Retina, *Arch. fur Mic. Anat.*, 1871.

——, T. E., Ueber die Sinnesorgane der Seitenlinie bei Fischen und Amphibien, *Arch. für Mic. Anat.*, 1870.

Semper, Ueber Schneken Augen am Wirbelthier Typus, *Arch. für Mic. Anat.*, 1877.

Serres, Marcel de, De l'odorat et des organes qui paraissent en être le siège chez les orthoptères, *Annales du Muséum*, 1811.

Siebold, Ueber die Stimm und Gehörorgane der Krebse und Insekten, *Arch. für Mic. Anat.*, 1860.

Simroth, Ueber die Sinneswerkzeuge unserer einheimischen Weichthiere, *Zeit. für Wiss. Zool.*, 1876.

Slater, Ueber die Funktion der Antennen bei den Insekten, *Froriep's Notizen*, iii., 1848.

Spencer, The Pineal Eye in Lacertilia, *Quarterly Journal of Microscopical Science*, 1886.

Stricker, Manual of Histology.

Sulzer, Geschichte der Insekten. 1761.

Treviranus, Verm. Schriften Anat. und Physiol. Inhaltes, 1817.

Ussow, Ueber den Bau der sogenannten augenähnlichen Flecken einiger Knochenfische, *Bull. Soc. Imp. Moscow*, 1879.

Valentine, R., and T. T. Cunningham, "The Photospheria of *Nyctiphanes Norvegica*," in *Quarterly Journal of Microscopical Science*, 1888.
Vedjdovsky, Syst. und Morph. der Oligochoeten. 1884.

Wagner, Untersuchungen über die zusammengesetzten Augen der Krebse und Insekten. 1868.
Weissman, A., Die nachembryonale Entwicklung der Musciden, *Zeit. für Wiss. Zool.*, 1864.
Westwood, Modern Classification of Insects.
Will, F., Ueber die Augen der Bivalven und der Acidien, *Froriep's neue Notizen aus dem Gebiete der Nat. und Heilkunde*, 1844.
——, Das Geschmacksorgan der Insecten, *Zeit. für Wiss. Zool.*, 1885.
Wilson, The Nervous System of the Asteridæ, with Observations on the Structure of their Organs of Sense, *Trans. Linn. Soc.*, 1860.
Wolff, O. J. B., Das Riechorgan der Biene, Nova acta der K. L., *Arch. deutsch. Akad. d. Naturf.*, 1875.

ON THE

SENSES, INSTINCTS, AND INTELLIGENCE

OF

ANIMALS.

CHAPTER I.

INTRODUCTORY REMARKS.

THE organs of sense may be said to be the windows through which we look out into the world, and it has always been to my mind one of the most interesting problems of natural history, to consider in what manner external objects affect other animals, how far their perceptions resemble ours, whether they have sensations which we do not possess, and how we ourselves arrive at our own perceptions.

I propose to dwell in the present work especially on the senses of insects, partly because my own observations have been made principally on them, and partly because their senses have, perhaps, been on the whole more thoroughly and successfully studied than those of the other lower animals ; which again arises from the fact that no group offers more favourable opportunities for the study of these organs. The subject is no less vast than difficult, and I do not pretend in any way to give a complete view of the whole question, but have selected those cases which seemed to me the most suggestive, interesting, and instructive.

No one can doubt that the sensations of other animals differ in many ways from ours. Their organs are sometimes constructed on different principles, and situated in very unexpected places. There are animals which have eyes on their backs, ears in their legs, and sing through their sides. Nevertheless, in considering the different senses, it will probably be most convenient to begin by a short summary of our own organs, as affording the best clue to the purposes and functions of corresponding structures among the lower animals. The subject is one of very great difficulty. Even as regards our own senses, we are still in extreme ignorance. The clue afforded by anatomy is very imperfect, and sometimes almost misleading. No one can read the literature relating to the organs of sense without feeling how very little we really know on the subject. Even when, as especially in the cases of the organs of hearing and sight, we have careful and elaborate descriptions and figures of very complex structures, these relate rather to the separation and arrangement of the waves of sound or light, than to the actual manner in which they affect the nervous system itself; while as to the manner in which our perceptions are in turn created, we are almost absolutely ignorant. In the senses of taste and smell this becomes, perhaps, even more clearly evident.

Every cell, indeed, in the animal body is a standing miracle. Consider what it has to do. It must grow; it must assimilate nourishment; it must secrete; it must produce other cells like itself; and this often in addition to its own proper and distinctive function. The lowest animals consist but of a single cell. Yet they feed and digest; they grow and multiply; they move and feel. Their perceptions, indeed, are no doubt confused and undifferentiated, and perhaps devoid of consciousness. The soft protoplasm of which they consist is dimly affected by external stimuli, as, for instance, by the waves of light or of sound. These forms, however, are all minute, and, indeed, almost invisible to the naked eye. The larger animals are built up of a number of cells.

Let us, then, consider the possible modes in which an organ of sense, say an eye, may have originated.

In the simpler forms, the whole surface is more or less sensitive. Suppose, however, some solid and opaque particles of pigment deposited in certain cells of the skin

Fig. 1.—Diagram of skin. *c*, Cuticle; *h*, cellular or hypodermic layer.

(Fig. 1). Their opacity would arrest and absorb the light, thus increasing its effect, while their solidity would enhance the effect of the external stimulus. A further

Fig. 2.—Diagram of skin. *c*, Cuticle; *h*, cellular or hypodermic layer.

step might be a depression in the skin at this point, which would serve somewhat to protect these differentiated and more sensitive cells, while the deeper this depression the greater would be the protection.

The epithelial cells frequently secrete more or less matter, which may form a more or less solid ball. This might be set in vibration by the sound-waves, and would thus increase the effect on the epithelial

cells. Such a body is known as an otolithe. On the
other hand, it might serve as a lens, and by condensing

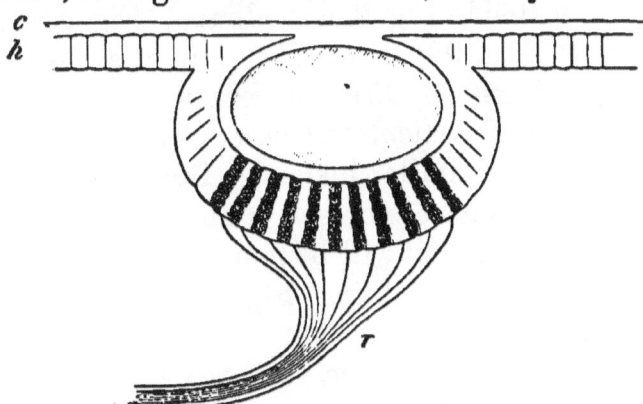

Fig. 3.—Diagram of origin of a sense-organ. c, Cuticle; h, hypoderm; * n, nerve.

the light would act like a burning-glass, and increase
its effect on the cells below. A further stage would be

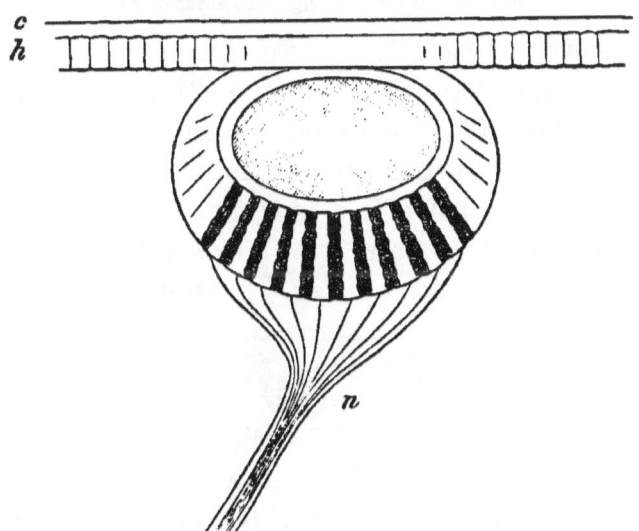

Fig. 4.—Diagram of further stage in the origin of a sense-organ.

that the immediately subjacent cells, acted on by the
increased stimulus, might (Figs. 3 and 4) develop into
special nerve-tissue.

* I.e. the cellular layer below the cuticle.

Nor is this a merely imaginary case. Each of the above stages may be found in actual existence—that, for instance, indicated in Fig. 2 in the limpet (Fig. 92); Fig. 3, in Trochus (Fig. 93); and Fig. 4 in the snail, Helix or Murex (Figs. 94, 95). Recent researches indicate that the eyes of Articulata (insects, etc.) have, in some cases at least, a similar history. But more than this, if the development of the eye of an individual snail be watched in the egg, it will be found to pass successively through stages resembling Fig. 2, then Fig. 3, and then Fig. 4.

In other cases, however, the organs of sense have a different origin and history. Suppose, for instance,

Fig. 5.—Diagram of origin of a sense-organ.

that the hypodermic layer were at any spot (Fig. 5) somewhat more strongly developed than elsewhere; in that case, the cuticle secreted by the hypodermic cells would tend to be rather thicker than usual. This would again (Fig. 6) constitute a lens, and serve to condense the light. That certain eyes have actually arisen in this way is indicated by Fig. 7, representing a section

Fig. 6.—Diagram of further stage in the origin of a sense-organ.

through the eye of the larva of a water-beetle (Dytiscus). Nor, as we shall presently see, do these two types of development by any means exhaust the ways in which eyes may originate. In the two cases given the eyes originate from the skin, but in others— for instance, in ourselves—the percipient elements are formed from the central nervous system.

The tissues of the lowest animals have not been shown to contain any special nerve-fibres, but underneath those

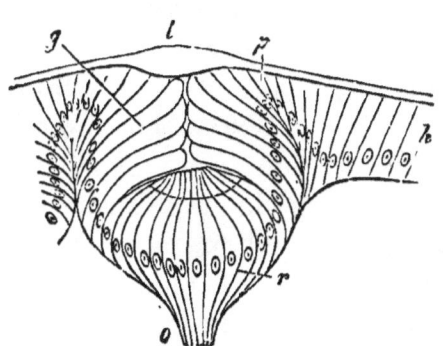

parts of the surface where, either in the manner indicated above, or in some other, the effects of external stimuli are heightened by any structural modifications, there would be a tendency to the specialization of an exceptionally sensitive tissue.

Fig. 7.—Section through the simple eye of a young Dytiscus larva (after Grenacher). *h*, Hypoderm; *l*, lens; *o*, optic nerve; *g*, *p*, modified hypodermic cells; *r*, retina.

Moreover, such an organ as that represented in Fig. 4 might serve either as a rudimentary ear or an eye. It might, indeed, be acted on by the waves both of light and of sound. Such organs—as, for instance, in the case of marginal bodies round the edge of certain jelly-fishes (Medusæ; see Figs. 8 and 50)—have been regarded by some naturalists

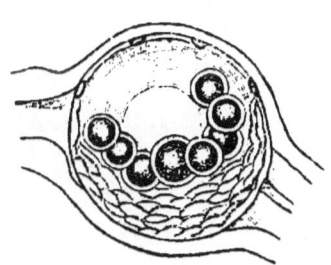

as eyes, and by others as ears. Haeckel suggests * that some may be warmth-organs.

Fig. 8 represents one of the marginal sense-organs of a Medusa (Ontochis), where we have a row of brilliantly refractive spherules, which from analogy are considered to serve

Fig. 8.—Auditory vesicle of Ontochis (after Haeckel).

as otoliths; but which, under other circumstances, might be, and in fact have been by some, regarded as the lenses of a simply constructed organ of vision.

* " Report on Deep Sea Medusæ," " *Challenger* Reports," vol. iv.

Even among the most highly specialized organs of sense, it is impossible not to be struck by the similarity between the cones in the retina (Fig. 79) and certain organs in the antennæ of insects (Fig. 42) which are generally considered as olfactory. It does not follow that an organ with a nerve, a lenticular body, and pigment, should necessarily be an eye. Nor, on the other hand, is there anything in the structure of the organs, for instance, of smell or taste which throws any light on the perceptions we receive from them. That there should be separate nerve-fibrils in our own skin, not only for the sensations of temperature and of touch, but, as appears from the researches of Blix and Goldschneider, even of heat and of cold, we had not anticipated *à priori;* and it would be difficult to prove in any animal but ourselves.

THE SENSE OF TOUCH.

I commence with the sense of touch, as being the one which is most generally distributed, and from which the others appear to have been in some cases developed. The senses are not, indeed, as already mentioned, always to be easily distinguished from one another; and it would seem that the same nerve may be capable of carrying different sensations according to the structure of the end organs.

The sensibility of our skin appears to be mainly due to a plexus of fine nerve-fibres, which end in free terminations between the cells of the skin (rete mucosum). There are also in some parts of the skin two sets of minute corpuscles, which are called after their discoverers, the first Vaterian, or more commonly Pacinian, corpuscles; the second, Meissner's or Wagner's corpuscles.

The Pacinian corpuscles consist of a capsule formed
of several layers, one enveloping the other. The
undulating nerve-fibres, after several windings, enter
the capsule, which, indeed, seems to be nothing
more than a much-thickened end of the outer nerve-
coat. These corpuscles measure from 1·1 to 4·5mm.
They occur principally on the hands and feet, and
in the flexures of the joints, but occasionally also
elsewhere.

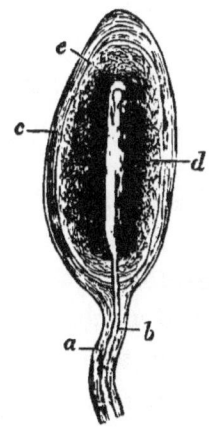

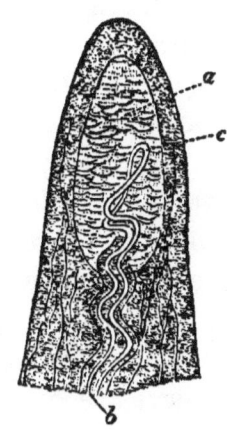

Fig. 9.—Pacinian corpuscle (after Leydig).
a, Neurilemma ; b, nerve-fibril ; c, capsule ; d, peculiar fibres ; e, central
cylinder.

Fig. 10.—Papilla from the surface of
the hand, × 350 (after Kölliker). a,
Cone-like body ; b, nerve ; c, end of
nerve.

Meissner's or Wagner's corpuscles are cone-like or
egg-shaped bodies, in each of which a nerve terminates, after several convolutions. They are especially
numerous at the tips of the fingers, where there may
be as many as a hundred in a square line. They
occupy the papillæ (which, however, do not always
contain one), which give the surface of the hand its
peculiar striped appearance. They also occur, though
less numerously, elsewhere, as on the feet, breast, and
lips.

It appears probable, however, that these are not really the organs of touch, but rather, perhaps, guards or protectors of the true and very sensitive organs within. They are, no doubt, most numerous on the more sensitive parts of the skin, such as the hands and tongue, and the sense of touch is most acute where they occur; but they appear to be absent in some places where the sense of touch certainly exists, and they are abundant again in the foot, which, though not especially sensitive, is particularly exposed.

The sensation of pressure is intimately associated with the hairs, which no doubt serve, at any rate in some cases, for protection, but which, in Blix's * opinion are in man probably all organs of touch.

We have still indeed much to learn as to the terminations of the nerves in the skin. It would seem that some are connected with cells, while others terminate in a free point. Merkel has suggested that those which end in cells are the true nerves of touch, while the free nerves record changes of temperature. Others, · perhaps with more probability, have supposed that the free nerves convey merely a general and undifferentiated sensation, while those which terminate in cells give the specific impressions of pressure, heat, cold, etc., any one of which may be intensified into pain.

However, this may be, Blix * and, shortly afterwards, Goldschneider † have made the interesting discovery that we do not feel changes of pressure and of

---

* "Exper. Beitr. zur Lösung der Frage über die Specif. Energie der Hautnerven," *Zeit. für Biologie*, 1885. Blix's previous papers in *Upsala Läkan-forenings Förhandlingar*, 1882, I have not seen.

† "Monatschr. für prakt. Dermatologie." 1884. "Neue Thatsachen ü. die Hauptsinnesnerven," *Zool. Anz.*, 1885 und 1886.

temperature at the same points of the skin or by the
same nerve-ends. The feeling of pressure seems to
be intimately associated with the hairs, which is not
the case with sensations of temperature. Even the
feelings of heat and cold are also separate. These
three sets of points, indeed, are so near together that
the separation had hitherto not been observed, especially as they are closely intermixed. They have a
tendency, however, to arrange themselves in more or
less curved lines. Goldschneider experimented with
a fine point, which he passed over the skin, thus
testing it sometimes for pressure, sometimes with
a warm point for heat, sometimes with a cold point for

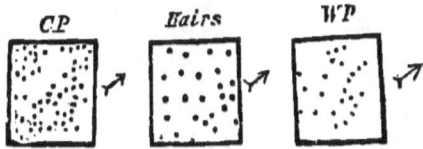

Fig. 11.—Portion of the skin of the back of the hand (after Goldschneider). The
centre figure represents the arrangement of the hairs; *CP*, the cold-points; *WP*.
the warmth-points.

cold. Moreover, if he raised the points thus determined
with a fine needle, and snipped off the fragment of the
skin, he found that the resulting sensation was quite
different in the three cases. If the point removed
was a "pressure-point" the sensation was one for the
moment of pain; while the temperature-points gave
one respectively of heat or cold. The terminations of
the temperature-nerves are, according to Goldschneider,
much finer than those of the pressure-nerves, and they
are also fewer in number. He cut out from his own
skin a large number of sensitive points, but, while he
found that each corresponded to a nerve-end, he has
not been able to discover any difference at or in the

termination of the nerves corresponding to these different sensations, though it may reasonably be expected that such must exist.

The question has arisen whether there are separate nerve-endings for pain, as apart from pressure, etc.; but the observations of Blix and Goldschneider appear to show that pain arises merely from the intensification of other impressions, and that it does not reside in any special organs.

SENSE OF TOUCH AMONG THE LOWER ANIMALS.

Among the lower animals the outer skin is often very sensitive, but we know scarcely anything as to the minute structure of the organs of tactile perception. In some cases they are, no doubt, very simple; but in others it will probably be found that the apparent simplicity is due to our deficient information and means of investigation, rather than to any want of complexity in the organs themselves.

In the Cœlenterata (zoophytes, etc.) certain setæ, especially on the tentacles and near the mouth, are generally regarded as organs of touch.

In the epithelium of many of the lower animals, two forms of cells may be detected. Some unmodified, or indifferent, which form the general substance of the epithelial layer; others more or less specialized, which are seldom absolutely contiguous, but generally separated by one or more of the indifferent cells.

In other cases, nerves may end abruptly at the cuticle without the latter presenting, so far as our present means of investigation have shown, any apparent change; as, for instance, in the following figure of a part of the skin of a small worm (Nereis).

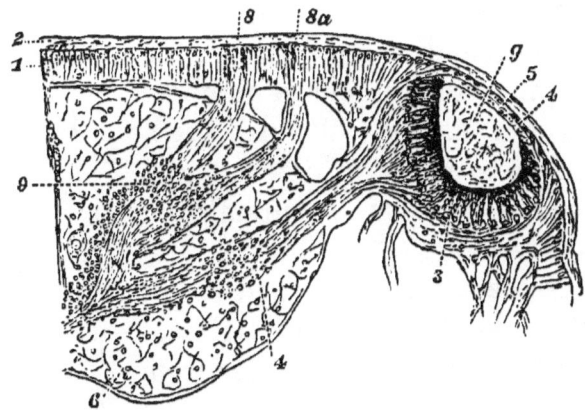

Fig. 12.—Half of a cross section through the brain and hinder pair of eyes of *Nereis cultrifera* (after Carrière). 1, Hypoderm ; 2, cuticle ; 3, retina ; 4, outer corneal cells; 5, inner corneal cells; 6, brain ; 8, 8*a*, two places to which the brain sends large nerves (9), but where the cuticle is unaltered ; *g*, gelatinous body.

Among the Medusæ (jelly-fishes), also, the supposed tactile organs are ciliated cells (Fig. 13), which scarcely differ from the other epithelial cells, but which terminate externally in a cilia, and internally in a nerve-fibril.

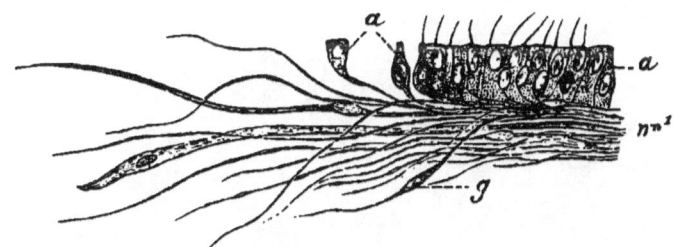

Fig. 13.—Part of upper nerve-ring and tactile epithelium of Lizzia (after Hertwig). *a*, Tactile epithelium ; *g*, ganglionic cell ; *nr'*, upper nerve-ring.

In other cases, the tactile hairs scarcely differ from those covering the general surface. Fig. 14 represents part of the skin of a sea-anemone, the long cylinders are nematocysts, or thread-cells—elastic sacs, in the

interior of which lies coiled up a long filament, which
is often serrated at the end. Even a
very slight pressure causes this thread
to spring out, and these little darts,
which are present in immense numbers
in the skin of Hydrozoa (jelly-fish, etc.),
serve both as weapons of defence and
also to wound the small animals on
which they feed.

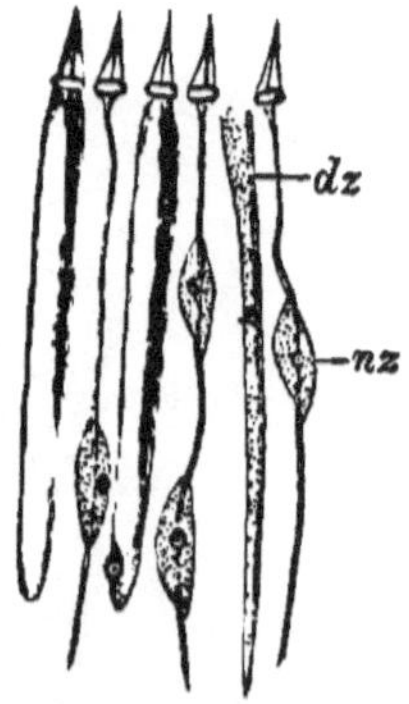

nz represents a nerve-cell, and it will
be seen that the hair in which it terminates does not materially differ from
the rest.

In the Annelides, also, the general
surface of the integument (Fig. 15)
presents tactile setæ or ciliæ, which are scattered over

Fig. 14.—Diagram of
part of the skin of
a sea-anemone (Ac-
tinia); after Korot-
neff. *dz,* Glandular
cell; *nz,* nervous
cell.

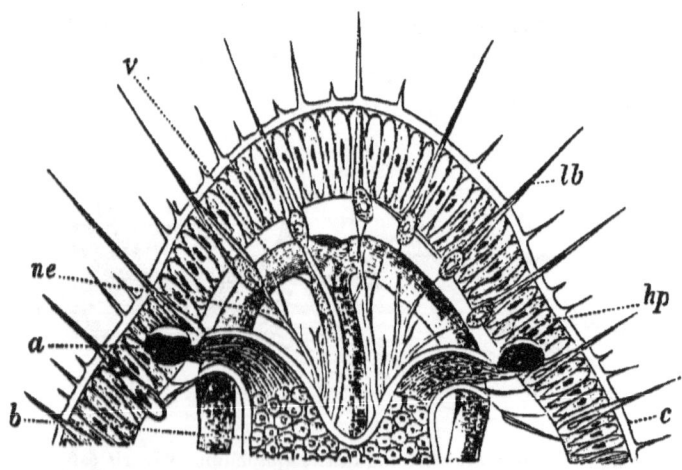

Fig. 15.—Anterior part of body of *Bohemilla comata* (after Vejdovsky *). *lb,* Tactile
hair; *hp,* hypoderm; *c,* cuticle; *b,* anterior part of brain; *a,* eye; *ne,* nerve-
fibrils; *v,* anterior blood-vessel.

the surface, and especially on the head. In some cases

* "Syst. und Morph. der Oligochœten." 1884.

these setæ are collected into special groups, either situated in cup-shaped depressions of the skin, or on more or less elevated papillæ. Fig. 15 represents the anterior part of the body of a small fresh-water worm (Bohemilla), and shows clearly the small cuticular, and the larger tactile, hairs. In other cases, as in the feelers and cirri of the Alciopidæ, there are short, shining, ovoid rods, to the base of which runs a nervous fibril.

In the Mollusca, also, the surface of the skin is very sensitive, and is generally provided with minute setæ, especially on the tentacles, or as in Lameliibranchiata (mussels, etc.), on the edge of the mantle. In some, the snail for instance (Helix), the nerves, on approaching the skin, have been ascertained to divide into a plexus of fibrils.

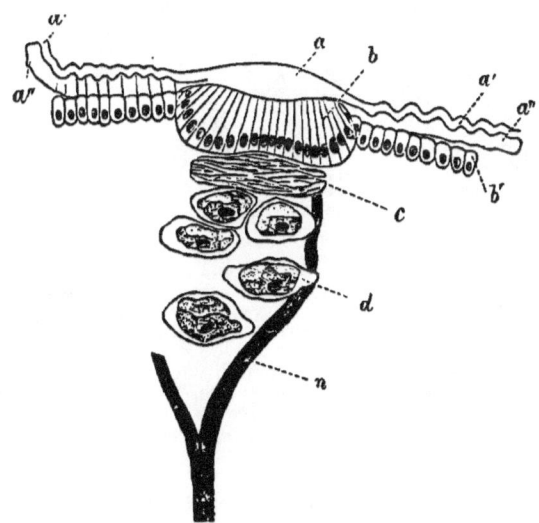

Fig. 16.—Diagrammatic section through a papilla of touch of Onchidium (after Semper).
a', a'', Two layers of the cuticle; a, biconvex thickened portion of the cuticle; b, enlarged epithelial cells; b', ordinary epithelial cells; c, cellular body; d, cells; n, nerve.

In Onchidium, a genus of slugs, Semper describes as organs of touch (Fig. 16) certain slight elevations of the skin caused by the cuticle being somewhat thickened. Beneath these the epithelial cells are larger than usual; and under them, again, lies a cellular mass, the minute structure of which he was not able to determine, but which is connected with a nerve.

On the mantle of the Chitons are also certain well-defined organs, probably of touch. They occupy pores in the shells, and resemble obconical or somewhat dice-box shaped plugs of transparent, highly refracting

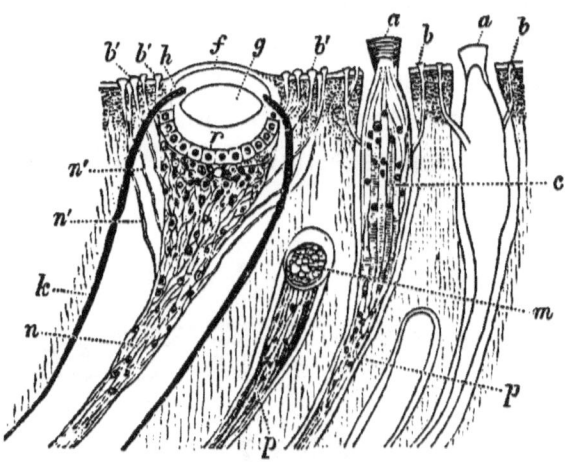

Fig. 17.—Diagram of the structure of the soft and some of the hard parts in the tegmentum of a shell of a Chiton (*Acanthopleura spiniger*), as seen in a section vertical to the surface and with, the margin of the shell bordering on the girdle lying in the direction of the left side of the drawing. *f*, Calcareous cornea; *h*, iris; *g*, lens; *k*, pigmented capsule of eye; *n*, optic nerve; *r*, rods of retina; *n'*, branches of the optic nerve, perforating the capsule wall, and terminating in *b'*, *b'*, *b'*, ocular sense-organs; *p. p*, nerves to sense-organ; *m*, body of sense-organ cut across; *a. p*, fusiform body of sense-organ entire; *a*, obconical termination of sense-organ; *e*, nerve given off by one sense-organ to another, *b''*.

tissue. The terminal knobs end in flat discs, which show a series of concentric rings, as if composed of a series of concentric layers or inverted cones fitted one within the other.* Each one terminates in a nerve-

* Moseley, *Quarterly Journal of Microscopical Society*, 1885.

fibre. They are of two distinct sizes, which Moseley
proposes to call macrœsthetes and microœsthetes.

In many animals, as in ourselves, the outer skin is
soft and susceptible to external impressions. In Insects
and Crustacea on the contrary, the inner skin, or hypoderm, is covered with a more or less thick layer of
horny substance known as chitine; and, from the
nature of their chitinous integument, it naturally
follows that the sensations of insects, excepting that
of sight, are effected by means of variously modified
hairs. We know, however, so little, in the first place,
as to the real means by which animals, including
man, hear, smell, or taste, and, in the second, as to the
intimate structure of their minute organs, that we are
often in doubt, and there are still great differences of
opinion whether a given sense-hair serves for hearing,
smell, or touch.

The hairs of Arthropods belong to very different

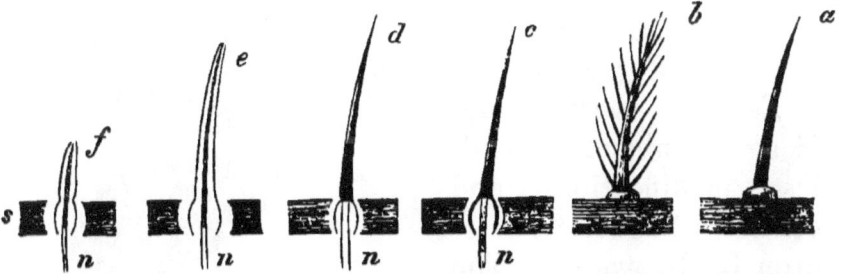

Fig. 18.—Diagram of forms of hairs in insects. *a*, Ordinary surface hair; *b*, plumose
natatory hair; *c*, hair of touch; *d*, auditory hair; *e*, olfactory hair; *f*, taste hair;
n, nerve hair.

categories, some of which we may perhaps distinguish
as follows:—

Those under which the chitinous integument is entire.

1. Ordinary surface hairs (Fig. 18, *a*).
2. Plumose natatory hairs (Fig. 18, *b*).

Those under which the chitinous integument is perforated, and a special nerve-fibre runs to the base of the hair.

1. Hairs solid.

    (1) Hairs attached stiffly; organs of touch (Fig. 18, *c*).

    (2) Hairs attached by means of a thin membrane, sometimes plumose; organs of hearing (Fig. 18, *d*).

2. Hairs hollow, and either open at the end, or closed by an extremely delicate membrane.

    (1) Hairs containing a continuation of the nervous plasma; organs of smell (Fig. 18, *e*).

    (2) Hairs generally very short, and situated in the mouth or on the mouth part; organs of taste (Fig. 18, *f*).

Each of these classes is again subject to endless modifications, and others will doubtless hereafter be discovered. The sense-hairs are also often more or less completely sunk in the chitinous integument.

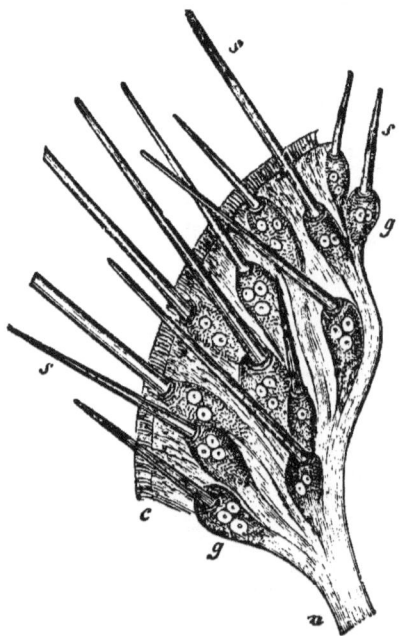

Fig. 19.—Part of the proboscis of a fly (Musca); after Leydig. *n*, Nerve; *g*, ganglionic swellings; *s*, tactile hairs or rods; *c*, cuticle.

Fig. 19 shows some of the tactile hairs on the proboscis of a fly (Musca), each seated on a ganglion and connected with a nerve (*n*).

The tactile hairs—as, for instance, those on the upper side of the proboscis of the fly—are delicate, hollow, tapering, pointed organs, inserted on a chitinous ring, and connected with a nerve which immediately below the skin swells into a multicellular ganglion.

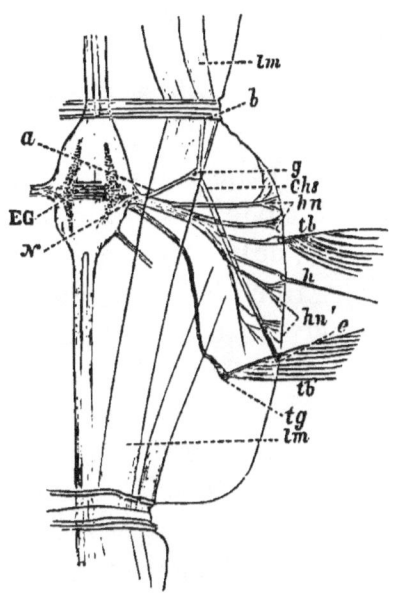

Fig. 20.—Right half of eighth segment of the body of the larva of a gnat (*Corethra plumicornis*); after Graber. *E, G*, Ganglion; *N*, nerve; *g*, auditory ganglion; *gb*, auditory ligament; *Ch*, auditory rods; *a*, auditory nerve; *e*, attachment of auditory organ to the skin; *b*, attachment of auditory ligament; *hn, hn'*, termination of skin-nerve; *tb*, plumose tactile hair; *h*, simple hair; *tg*, ganglion of tactile hair; *lm*, longitudinal muscle.

The terminations of the nerves and their connection with the sensitive hairs are also beautifully shown in some of the transparent water-insects. Fig. 20 represents part of one segment of the glassy larva of a gnat (*Corethra plumicornis*), showing the tactile hairs (Fig. 20, *h, tb*), and the nerves connecting them with the central ganglion (Fig. 20, *EG*).

CHAPTER II.

WHILE the organs of touch are spread more or less over the whole surface, and those of sight and of hearing may be, and in fact are, situated in very different parts of the body in different animals, the sense of taste is naturally confined to the mouth or its immediate neighbourhood.

In the case of Man, it resides especially in the tip, the edges of the upper surface, and the back part of the tongue, and (probably) the inferior portion of the soft palate. The actual mode of termination of the nerves of taste has, however, only recently been discovered.

Loven and Schwalbe detected, independently and almost simultaneously, in the epithelium of the papillæ of the tongue, many small budlike groups of cells (Fig. 21) which are probably connected with the ultimate fibres of the glosso-pharyngeal nerves. These have been supposed to be the special seats of the sense of taste, and thence termed "taste-buds;" they are in man shaped like a flask, in some other animals they are more slender. In the dog, they are ·072 of a millimeter in length, and ·03 in breadth.

In the pig the number is estimated at 9500: in the sheep, at 9600; in the rabbit, at 1500; in the cow, at

35,000. In man they almost touch each other on some parts of the tongue, and their number is very great.

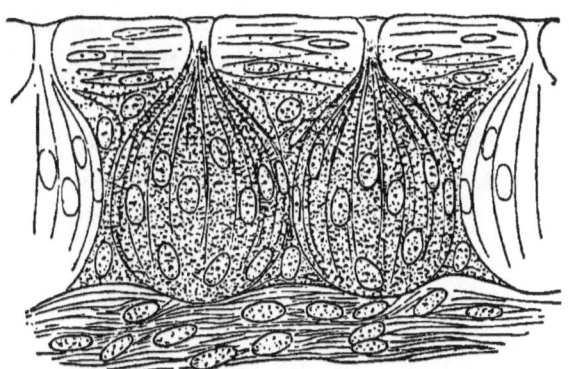

Fig. 21.—Taste-Buds of the rabbit (after Engelmann in Stricker's "Handbook"), × 450.

The "taste-buds" consist of from fifteen to thirty long narrow cells, arranged almost like a circular bundle. Those on the outside lie in close contact with the walls of the cavity. The cells appear to be of two kinds:

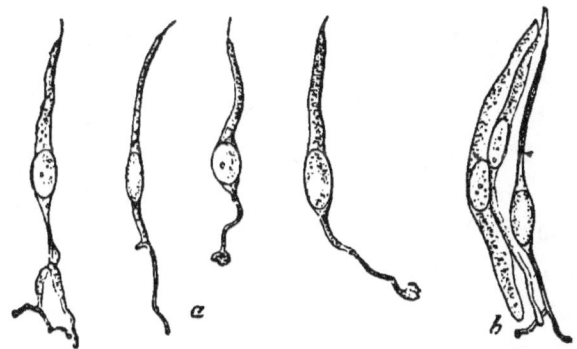

Fig. 22.—a, Isolated taste-cells from the mouth of rabbit; b, two cover-cells and a taste-cell in their natural position (after Engelmann), × 600.

the outer ones do not differ markedly in appearance— at least, with our present magnifying powers—from ordinary epithelial cells, and have not been shown to be connected with nerves. Those in the centre are more highly organized. Each consists of an ellipsoidal nucleus surrounded by a thin layer of protoplasm, continued downwards into a fine fibril, which sometimes branches, and which—though this is not clear—probably joins the nervous fibres. The upper process of the protoplasm is a narrow cylinder, in some cases prolonged at the end into a very delicate hair or rod.

Schwalbe thought he could distinguish in man and the sheep, two kinds of taste-cells—firstly, needle cells, in which the cell appears to terminate in a narrow, brilliant needle, abruptly cut off at the end; and, secondly, staff cells, which are less numerous, shorter, of uniform breadth, and without any terminating needle. It is still unknown whether there are different classes of taste-cells for different tastes, and whether one taste-bud can distinguish more than one taste.

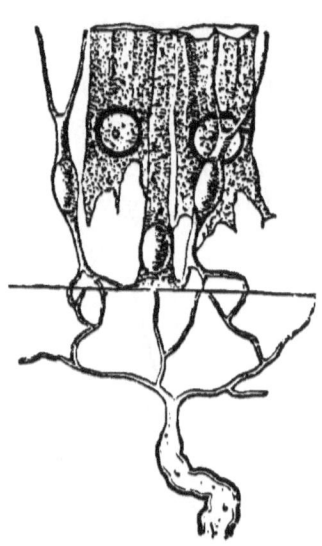

I know of no detailed description of the organs of taste in birds and reptiles. In the frog the taste-organs are not flasklike, but are flat disks. They occur in hundreds on the tongue and soft palate. These taste-disks are composed of several forms of cells. Those which are supposed to be especially connected with the sense

Fig. 23. — Termination of the nerves of taste in the frog, showing the ramifications of the nerve-fibres and their connection with the cells of taste (after Engelmann), × 600.

of taste terminate in a fork, sometimes, though rarely, of three prongs. The taste-organs of fishes are shaped like beakers.

It will be observed that these structures give us no help to realize in what actually consists the sense of taste. We know that we possess it ourselves. We perceive that other animals can select, and appear to enjoy, their food, and hence we ascribe to them a similar faculty. We know that in our own case this sense resides in the mouth, and we assume that it must do so in other animals; we find in the mouth certain structures, and we infer that to them is due the sensation of taste. Even in our own case the inferences are, perhaps, not very clear, and certainly the facts, as yet known, aid us but little in framing any definite idea of the process.

But if our knowledge is so imperfect in the case of the higher animals, it becomes much more so in the lower groups.

In the Mollusca, Annelida, and lower groups, we know scarcely anything of the organ of taste, though we can hardly doubt that such exists.

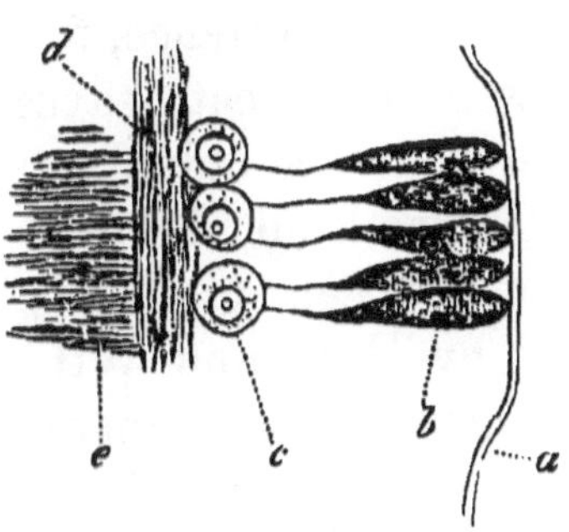

Medusæ (jelly-fishes) are very sensitive to any change in the composition of the sea-water; for instance, they sink below as soon as it begins to rain. It is difficult, however, to say which sense is affected.

In Asterope (a marine worm belonging to the Alciopidæ), Greef has described, in the skin of the proboscis, certain peculiar club-shaped, ringed bodies, which taper into a thread connected with a nucleated cell. These he

Fig. 24.—Inner layer of the skin of the proboscis of *Asterope candida*, × 400 (after Greef). *a*, Cuticle; *b*, terminal (nerve) organs; *c*, ganglionic cells; *d*, longitudinal muscle; *e*, transverse muscle.

suspects to be ganglionic cells, and he suggests that the organ is one of taste.

Even in the Crustacea (crabs, lobsters, etc.), though we can scarcely doubt that they possess the sense of taste, no organs have been yet described to which it can be with any confidence ascribed. Huxley, for instance, in his work on the Crayfish,* says, "It is probable that the crayfish possesses something analogous to taste, and a very likely seat for the organ of this function is in the upper lip and the metastoma, but if the organ exists it possesses no structural peculiarities by which it can be identified."

As regards insects, the possession of the sense of taste cannot be questioned, though, except perhaps in many Hymenoptera and certain phytophagous insects, it may not be of great importance. No one who has ever watched a bee or a wasp can entertain the slightest doubt on the subject. It is, again, probably by taste that caterpillars recognize their food-plant. Moreover, this is partly the effect of individual experience, for, when first hatched, caterpillars will often eat leaves which they would not touch when they are older, and have become accustomed to a particular kind of food.† Special experiments, moreover, have been made by various entomologists, particularly by Forel and Will. Forel mixed morphine and strychnine with some honey,

---

* "The Crayfish: an Introduction to the Study of Zoology."

† A remarkable case is afforded by those species in which the food of the larva and perfect insect is different, so that the mother has to select and find for her offspring food which she would not care to touch herself. Thus while butterflies and moths themselves feed on honey, each species selects some particular food-plant for the larvæ. Again, flies, which also enjoy honey themselves, lay their eggs on putrid meat and other decaying animal substances.

which he offered to his ants. Their antennæ gave them
no warning. The smell of the honey attracted them,
and they began to feed; but the moment the honey
touched their lips, they perceived the fraud. Will tried
wasps with alum, placing it where they had been accustomed to be fed with sugar. They fell into the trap,
and ate some, but soon found out their error, and began
assiduously rubbing their mouth parts to take away the
taste.

Will found that glycerine, even if mixed with a large
proportion of honey, was avoided; and to quinine they
had a great objection. If the distasteful substance is
inodorous and mixed in honey, the ant or bee commences to feed unsuspiciously, and finds out the trick
played on her more or less quickly according to the
proportion of the substance and the bitterness or
strength of its taste.

The delicacy of taste is, doubtless, greater in bees
and ants than in omnivorous flies or in carnivorous
insects. At the same time, the sense of taste in ants is
far from perfect, and they cannot always distinguish in-
jurious substances. Forel found that if he mixed
phosphorus in their honey, they swallowed it unsus-
pectingly, and were made very unwell. Some workers,
he says,[*] " de *Formica pratensis* se gorgèrent de miel au
phosphore que je leur donnai. Après cela elles
demeurèrent pendant de nombreuses heures immobiles,
les mandibules écartées, la bouche ouverte, avec l'air
très obsédées. Celles qui en avaient le plus mangé
périrent, les autres guérirent peu à peu." It cannot,
then, be doubted that insects possess a sense of taste,
the seat of it can hardly be elsewhere than in the

[*] "Receuil Zool. Suisse." 1887.

mouth or its immediate neighbourhood; and in all the orders of insects there are found on the tongue, the maxillæ, and in the mouth, certain minute pits which are probably the organs of taste. In each pit is a minute hair, or rod, which is probably perforated at the end. On this point there is, indeed, some difference of opinion. Will, for instance, maintains that to convey the sense of taste the food must come into direct contact with the termination of the nerve of taste, so that those hairs, or bristles, on the mouth parts which present no perforation cannot be regarded as true taste-organs, and probably serve rather as guards. Forel, on the contrary, considers this as an error. He observes, with justice, that the secretions are able to pass through the chitinous membrane which terminates the excretory canals of the glandular cells, and he maintains that the chitin is so thin and delicate—as well on the surface of the taste cones and hairs as on the olfactory hairs and plates of the antennæ of bees and other insects—that endosmosis through this fine membrane may sufficiently explain the sensation.

In 1860 Meinert* described, on the maxillæ and tongue of ants, a series of chitinous canals, connected with ganglion cells, and through them with the nerves, and suggested—though with a note of interrogation—that they might be the organs of taste. Forel, in 1874, confirmed these observations of Meinert's, and described, at the point of the tongue of *Formica pratensis*, a series of seven such chitinous tubes. In the following year Wolff published his work, "Das Riechorgan der Biene," which contains a number of valuable observations,

* "Bid. til. de Danske Myrers Natur Hist." 1860.

though I am unable altogether to concur in his conclusions. He described a group of minute pits at the
base of the tongue of the bee, and considered them
as the organs of smell. It seems to me, however, more
probable that they serve as organs of taste. Forel *
also is disposed to regard these as constituting, perhaps,
the most important part of the organ of taste, but considers that this sense resides also in certain organs
scattered over the tongue and the maxillæ. Will
regards the maxillæ and tongue as the only organs of

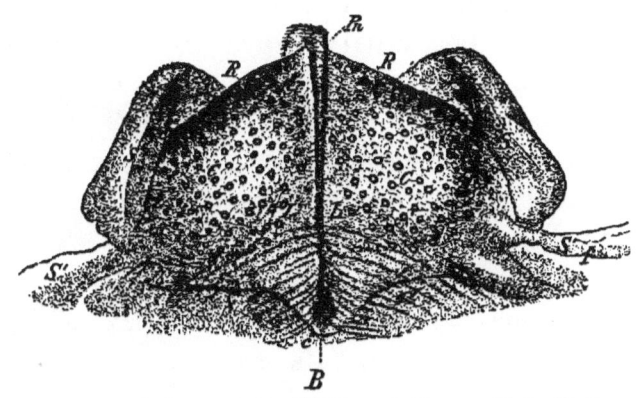

Fig 25 —Taste-organ of the bee (after Wolff). *B*, Horny ridge; *R, R*, sensory pits,
C, C, skin of the mouth; *L*, muscular fibres; *A, A*, muscular fibres; *S, S', a b c
d e f*, section of skin of œsophagus.

taste in the bee. He maintains † that the organs of
Wolff are deficient in the first requisite of an organ of
taste, for that there is no orifice through which the food
could directly enter into relation with the nerve.

No doubt, moreover, the taste-organs on the
tongue and maxillæ might be of themselves sufficient, so that *à priori* we need not seek for any
others. At the same time, as to the existence of the

* " Sensations des Insectes," *Receuil. Zool. Suisse*, 1887. Kraepelin
also regards them as the organ of smell.

† Will, " Das Geschmacksorgan der Insekten," *Zeit. für Zool.*, 1855.

organs described by Wolff there is no doubt, and their position certainly seems to indicate that they are organs of taste. Moreover, we are not, I think, sufficiently acquainted either with the essential requisites of an organ of taste, on the one hand, or, on the other, with the minute structure of these organs, to feel justified in concluding that this is impossible. It must be remembered that these pits are very minute, being only from ·003 to ·006 of a millimetre in diameter, so that it is hazardous to assert that they are certainly imperforate, while even if they are, this would not necessarily prove that they cannot be organs of taste.

Fig. 26 shows three of Wolff's cups, each with a central hair, a chitinous ring, and a double ganglionic swelling terminating in a nerve-fibre, magnified 500 times.

An additional reason for supposing that the Wolffian pits are really sense-organs arises from the fact that they are fewest in those insects which we may reasonably

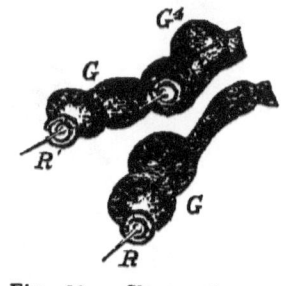

Fig. 26. — Shows three of Wolff's cups, each with a central hair, a chitinous ring, and a double ganglionic swelling terminating in a nerve-fibre, × 500 times. R, R', Sensory pits and hairs; G. G, ganglionic swelling of nerve.

suppose to have the sense of taste least developed, and increase in number where, on other grounds, we may fairly regard it as being probably more highly developed. Thus the Chalcididæ have often only one or two; the Evaneadæ, seven; the Proctotrupidæ, fifteen; the Tenthredos, twelve to twenty-four; the common wasp, twenty : some of the great tropical wasps, forty; while in the hive bee, the drone has fifty, the queen about one hundred, and the worker rather more still, say one hundred and ten.

Kraepelin has described at the end of the proboscis in the humble bee (Bombus), besides the hairs of touch, certain peculiar club-shaped hairs, which he believed were perforated at the end, and which he considered to be taste-hairs; and Haller has ascribed the same function to some very similar hairs which he found on the under lip of the Hydrachna.

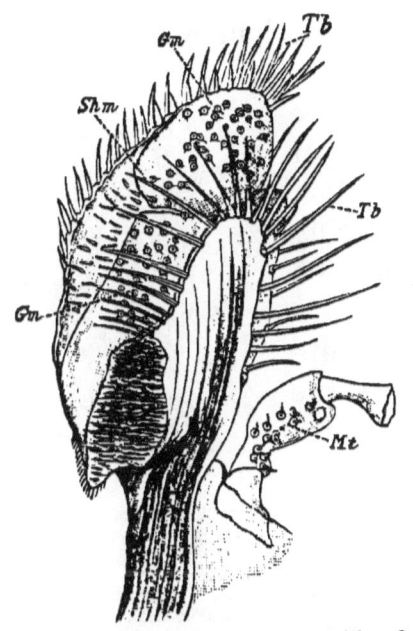

Fig. 27.—Under side of left maxilla of Vespa (after Will). *Gm*, Taste-cups; *Shm*, protecting hairs; *Tb*, tactile hairs; *Mt*, base of maxillary palpus.

Fig. 28.—Section through a taste-cup (after Will). *SK*, Supporting cone; *N*, nerve; *SZ*, sense-cell.

Fig. 27 represents the under side of the left maxilla of a wasp (*Vespa vulgaris*), after Will, magnified 55 times. *Gm* are the taste-cups; *Shm*, the protecting hairs; *Tb*, the tactile hairs.

Fig. 28 represents a section through one of the taste-cups, *Sk* is the taste-cone contained in the cup; it is perforated and continuous at the base with a nerve-fibre.

Similarly, in the wonderfully beautiful and complex proboscis of the hive bee there is, between each of the trachea-like ducts, a row of minute pits (Fig. 29, *Gs*), with a central papilla, which have been described by Leydig, Meinert, Lowne, Kraepelin, and others, and are probably organs of taste.

Kraepelin * distinguishes four kinds of hairs on the proboscis of the fly:

1. Ordinary hairs, which are not hollow, and do not stand in connection with a nerve.

2. Hairs of touch. These are principally situated on the upper side. They are delicate, hollow, pointed organs, situated on a ring of the integument, and connected with a nerve.

3. Glandular hairs. These are larger than the former, and the chitinous ring is sometimes so much developed as to form a short cylinder surrounding the base of the hair. The principal characteristic is, however, that the hair presents along one surface a deep furrow,

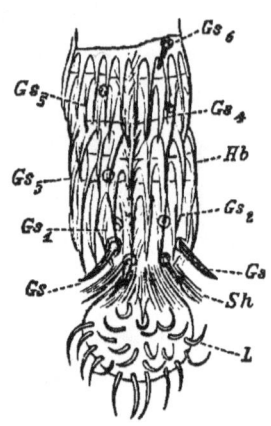

Fig. 29.—Tip of the proboscis in the hive bee (Apis), × 140. *L*, Terminal ladle; *Gs*, taste-hairs; *Sh*, guard-hairs; *Hb*, hooked hairs.

and is connected at the base with a cellular organ. Kraepelin therefore considers that this is a gland, and that the secretion passes outwards along the furrow. Kunckel and Gazagnaire, however, regard these also as sense-hairs. The supposed gland they consider to be a ganglion.

4. Taste-organs (Fig. 30). These lie in a row between

* Kraepelin, "Zur Anat. und Phys. des Rüssels von Musca," *Zeit. für Wiss. Zool.*, 1883.

the trachea-like channels, and correspond to the similar organs in the bee (Fig. 29, *Gs*). Each of these resembles a double circle, which scarcely projects, if at all, beyond the general surface, and which he regards as a metamorphosed, hollow, perforated hair. At the base of each organ is a nerve, which at some little distance forms a multicellular ganglion, and the sheath of which, immediately below the skin, forms a delicate and short, but well-marked, chitinous, cylinder.

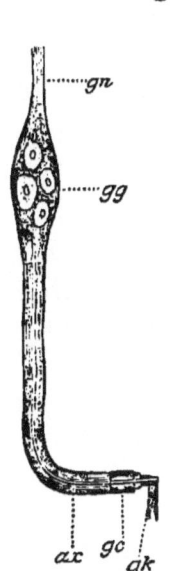

It may also be observed, at any rate in most insects, that while they are feeding the palpi hang down motionless, and evidently take no part in the operation.

In reference to the sense of taste, I may also mention that an additional complexity arises from the fact that many insects possess more than one kind of salivary gland, and it is possible, as Wolff suggests,[*] that the secretions may have different properties. In addition to this, Wolff thinks he has proved that the character of the secretion differs at different ages; that for many days after the bee has arrived at its imago condition, the glands are still imperfect and gradually increase to their full size. In old bees, again, according to him, the secretion diminishes in quantity. This, perhaps, throws some light on the division of labour. Forel has observed among ants that they remain for some days engaged in indoor

Fig. 30. — Organ of taste of fly (*Musca vomitoria*); after Kraepelin. *gn*, Nerve; *gg*, ganglion; *ax*, axe-cylinder; *gc*, terminal cylinder; *gk*, terminal cone.

---

[*] "Das Riechorgan der Biene."

duties, and do not leave the nest till some time after they have arrived at maturity.

I have noticed, also, that some individuals seem to possess a finer sense of taste than others, and some light seems to be thrown on this difference by the fact that the number of the taste-pits is not the same in all individuals. Thus Will observed that the number on the tongue of *Lasius flavus* (our common yellow ant) varies from twenty to twenty-four, and in Atta from forty to fifty-two. The number of pits on the maxillæ is subject to still greater variations, and is not even always the same on the two sides of the same insect.

On the whole, then, we may conclude that the organs of taste in insects are certain modified hairs situated either in the mouth itself or on the organs immediately surrounding it.

CHAPTER III

THE organ of smell is, in vertebrate animals, embedded in the mucous membrane of the nostrils, and in mammalia can generally be distinguished by its yellow or brownish colour. In birds, on the contrary, it presents hardly any peculiarity to the naked eye. For our knowledge of the minuter structure we are mainly indebted to Max Schultze. The cylindrical epithelial cells in the olfactory organs of man (Fig. 31) terminate in broad flat ends. Between them are rod-like filaments, which are supposed to expand into a ganglionic cell, terminating in a nerve-fibre. Schultze terms these olfactory cells.

In other cases, as in birds, Amphibia (Fig. 32), etc., the olfactory cells terminate in fine ciliæ, or olfactory hairs, either one or many to each cell. These hairs are sometimes motionless, sometimes have a slight movement of their own. It is obvious that no one from the structure alone could have predicated the function; nor can we, I think, form to ourselves any satisfactory conception how such a structure conveys the impression of smell, or in what consist the differences between different odours.

If, then, we know really so little as to the mode, or organs, by which the sense of smell is induced among the higher animals, we cannot wonder that in the lower groups our knowledge is still less.

In the Protozoa and Cœlenterata no organs have yet been met with to which this function can with any confidence be ascribed.

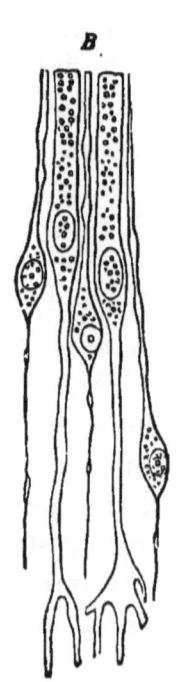

Fig. 31.—Epithelial and (B) olfactory cells of man (from Stricker, after Schultze).

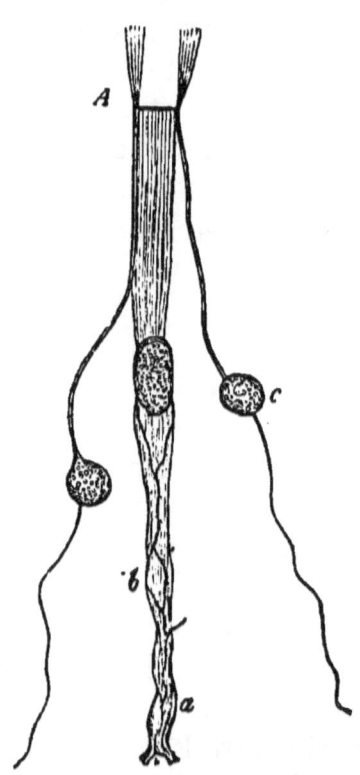

Fig. 32.—Cells from the olfactory region of a proteus (after Stricker). *a*, Epithelial cells; *b*, the apparent processes; *c*, olfactory cells. *A*, Ciliæ.

Meyer has described,* in Polyophthalmus (a small marine worm), on each side of the head, two ciliated organs (Fig. 33), which have been supposed to be organs of smell. These had been already mentioned by

* "Zur. Anat. und Hist. von Polyophthalmus," *Arch. für Mic. Anat.*, 1882.

De Quatrefages, who compared them with the ciliated wheels of Rotifers, and thought that they produced currents in the water, thus urging microscopic algæ, infusoria, etc., to the mouth of the worm. Meyer, on the contrary, with more probability, regards them as olfactory organs. They are slight depressions (Fig. 33) in the general surface, lined with peculiar long ciliæ, supplied with a large nerve coming from

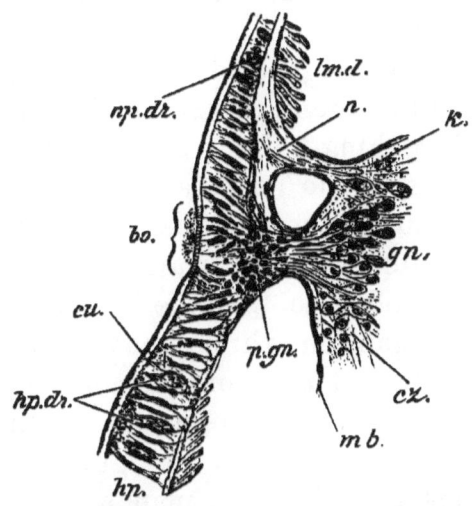

Fig. 33.—Section through the head segment of Polyophthalmus. × 300 (after Meyer). *lmd*, muscle; *bo*, cup-shaped organ; *cu*, cuticle; *hp*, hypoderm; *lmd*, longitudinal dorsal muscle: *n*, peripheral nerve; *cz*, commissure of brain; *mb*, membrane; *pgn*, pigment-cells; *hpdz*, unicellular glands in the hypoderm; *gn*, brain; *k*, nuclei in the brain.

the cerebral ganglion *gn*. Similar pits occur in many other Annelida. They differ in number; Polyophthalmus having only a pair, the Capitellidæ several.

In the Mollusca, the hinder pair of tentacles have been supposed by some to serve as olfactory organs. In the cuttle-fish (Cephalopoda) there are certain pits, at the base of which is a papilla, supplied with a nerve, which is perhaps olfactory.* The true function of the

* Leydig, "Histologie."

organs described by Hancock in Gasteropods, and by Leuckart in Pteropods, as olfactory, seems very doubtful.

As regards the seat of the sense of smell in insects, there have been four principal theories. It has been supposed to reside—(1) In the spiracles, or breathing holes; (2) in the neighbourhood of the mouth; (3) in the antennæ; (4) in different parts of the body. The history of the question has been well given by Kraepelin in an admirable memoir, "Ueber die Geruchsorgane der Gliederthiere." *

Sulzer, in 1761,† suggested that the organ of smell was probably to be found in the neighbourhood of the spiracles, or breathing-holes. It is hardly necessary to observe that insects do not breath as we do, through their mouths, but through a series of orifices along the sides, leading into tracheæ, or air-tubes, which ramify throughout the body; so that the blood is aerated, not in one special organ, but throughout its course. Now, it is important that a more or less continuous current of air should pass over the surface of the organ of smell, as it is in this manner brought in contact with the odoriferous particles. In man and the other air-breathing vertebrates, the combination of the entrance to the lungs with the nose and mouth offers great advantages. The olfactory organ is brought close to the mouth, where it is especially useful in the examination of food; while the continuous current of air necessary to respiration is utilized in the production of sound, on the one hand, and in bringing odoriferous particles to the organ of smell, on the other.

* Separat Abdruck aus dem Osterprogramm der Realschule des Johanneum." 1883.
† "Geschichte der Insekten."

In insects the separation of the mouth from the respiratory orifices is, in this respect, a manifest disadvantage. Still, it was not unnatural to look for the organ of smell in the neighbourhood of the spiracles, Sulzer's view was supported by Von Reimarus, Baster, Dumeril, Schelvir, and especially by Lehmann,* who lays it down as a general proposition that every organ of smell is to be sought near the orifices through which animals breathe: "Omnibus olfactus organon in iis locis quærendum est, per quos inspirent."

The most careful observations, however, have failed to detect in the neighbourhood of the spiracles any special supply of nerves, or any organ which could be supposed to serve for the perception of odors, and I believe this view may be said to be now generally abandoned.†

Treviranus ‡ suggested that the organ of smell was situated in the mouth, and he has been followed by Newport, Wolff, Kirby and Spence, and Graber. The descriptions they have given may be accepted as correct, but the organs they describe in the mouth itself are rather, I think, to be ascribed to the sense of taste than to that of smell.

Lyonnet, Bonsdorff, Marcel de Serres, Newport, and others, believed that the sense of smell resides in the

---

* Lehmann published three memoirs on the subject: "De Sensibus Externis Animalium Exsanguium," 1798; "De Antennis Insectorum Dissertatio," 1799; and "De Antennis Insectorum Dissertatio Posterior," 1800.

† Joseph, indeed ("Bericht der 50 Vers. Deutscher Nat. und Aerzte. München," 1877), supported this view in a short communication, and has promised fuller details. These, however, have not, I believe, yet appeared.

‡ "Ueber das Saugen und das Geruchsorgan der Insekten," *Ann. der Wetter Ges.*, 1812.

palpi, although the experiments of Perris, Plateau, Forel, and others, have conclusively proved that it is not situated exclusively in them.

The credit has been ascribed to Réaumur of having been the first to suggest that the sense of smell is seated in the antennæ. This view has been adopted by Lesser, Roesel, Lyonnet, Bonnet, Sulzer, Latreille, Burmeister, Lefevre, Erichson, Dugès, Perris, Dufour, Slater, Vogt, Forel, Lowne, Hauser, Kraepelin, Schiemenz, and other observers, and my own observations lead me to the same conclusion.

Many entomologists, indeed, including Scarpa, Schneider, Bolkhausen, Bonsdorff, Carus, Strauss-Durckheim, Oken, Kirby and Spence, Newport, Landois, Hicks, Wolff, and Graber, have considered that the antennæ serve as ears. These two views are, however, not irreconcileable, and the truth seems to be that, while organs of smell and of hearing, when present, may be both situated in the antennæ, they are not in all cases confined to them.

Comparetti* seems to have been the first to suggest that the organ of smell might not be seated in the same part of the body in all insects; he suggested the antennæ in certain beetles (Lamellicornia), the proboscis in butterflies and moths (Lepidoptera), and certain frontal cellules (the existence of which has, however, not been confirmed) in locusts, etc. (Orthoptera), as the probable seats.

The real manner in which odors are perceived, and the structure of the olfactory organs, is still so little understood, that experiments are perhaps more conclusive than anatomy.

* "De aure interna comparata-Patavii." 1789.

The oldest experiments of importance are those of Lehmann. He bored holes through bottles, and then inserted into them the abdomen of various insects, filling up the interspace with wax, and leaving the head and thorax outside. He then introduced into the bottle various powerful odors, such as burnt feathers, assafœtida, burnt sulphur, etc., and as these caused obvious movements of the body, he concluded that the insects perceived the smell by the membrane surrounding the tracheæ. The facts have been verified by subsequent observers, and are themselves doubtless correct. They do not, however, prove Lehmann's case, for similar fumes would, as Dugès and Perris justly observe, produce an irritation in our throat, where there is certainly no sense of smell. On the other hand, when substances which have no such irritating properties are used, as, for instance, honey in the case of a bee, decaying meat with a carrion-eating beetle (Silpha), and so on, no reaction has been perceived. On the whole, experiments lend no countenance to Sulzer's theory (see p. 35), and, in the absence also of any anatomical evidence in its support, it has, I believe, now no advocates.

I pass, then, to the second theory—that which considers that the organ of smell is situated in the mouth parts, either in the mouth itself according to some authors, or the palpi according to others. We have, I think, no clear evidence that the mouth itself possesses any organ of smell. Huber, however, observed that while, if he brought close to the mouth of bees substances which were repulsive, or others which were acceptable to them, such as honey, they were evidently affected; this was, on the other hand, no longer the case if the mouth parts were stopped up with paste.

Perris, on the contrary, found that even when the whole of the mouth parts were enclosed in gum, insects still retained the power of smell. These observations have been entirely confirmed by Forel and other observers. The explanation, I believe, is that Comparetti was right, and that the sense of scent is not confined to one part of the body; that, while it is possessed by the palpi, it is not confined to them.

It has long been observed that insects use their antennæ to examine and test their food. This is clearly not an act of hearing; nor has any one suggested that the antennæ are organs of sight or taste. It is obviously more than mere touch—indeed, they do not need to come into actual contact—and is, therefore, probably that of smell.

This conclusion has been confirmed by many experiments. Among those of the older observers some of the most important were made by Perris.* In Dinetus, a genus of the solitary wasps, the female, when absent in search of prey, covers over the orifice to her nest with a little sand. Perris selected two nests, and while the wasps were absent he disturbed the surface round one nest with a piece of stick, and laid his hand (which was rather warm) over the other. The first Dinetus was a little disturbed. She ran about, rapidly vibrating her antennæ, and was, perhaps, rather longer than usual in finding the entrance, but lost very little time. The other, he says, "Se trouva de prime abord, beaucoup plus embarrassé: ma main, dont l'état de moiteur avait rendu les émanations beaucoup plus actives, avait laissé sur le sable une odeur qui semblait l'étonner, et

---

* "Sur le siège de l'odorat dans les articulés," *Ann. Sci. Nat.*, 1850.

qu'il cherchait à reconnaître : car lorsqu'il arrivât à l'endroit que ma main avait couvert, il ralentissait sa marche, et ses antennes palpaient rapidement le sable. Le pauvre insecte s'épuisait en marches et contre-marches ; il passait par dessus son nid sans s'en douter ; il creusait çà et là avêc ses pattes de petites fosses, dans lesquelles il plongeait ses antennes pour explorer les couches inférieures ; il s'arrêtait pour brosser ses antennes, comme on se frotte les yeux quand on se sent ébloui : rien n'y faisait. Découragé, il prit son vol ; mais il revint quelques instants après et recommença ses recherches. Cette fois, soit qu'il fût mieux disposé et que les antennes qui étaient évidemment l'agent explorateur, fussent plus perspicaces, soit plutôt que le soleil qui était ardent eût fait évaporer les émanations de ma main, il parvint retrouver son nid, mais il y mit bien du temps et de la patience."

Perris also repeated Lehmann's experiment, only that he inserted the head of the insects into the bottles instead of the body ; he then satisfied himself that they perceived odors, and hence concluded that the sense of smell resides in the head, partly in the antennæ, and partly in the palpi.

Newport, on the contrary, maintained that the antennæ possess no sense of smell. He experimented on a water-beetle, *Hydaticus cinereus*, which, he says, " I had purposely confined for three days without food in a cup about half filled with water, and, at the expiration of that time, attached a small piece of raw flesh to the end of a wire, and carried it several times along the sides of the insect, particularly near the spiracles, where it was suffered to remain for a short time. The insect, however, did not appear to perceive it, but during the whole time remained in the water perfectly undisturbed. The flesh was then carried very near to one of the antennæ, but without exciting the slightest motion in that organ, while the insect began to move its palpi very briskly, as if it detected the presence of something; but continued, in other respects, motionless as before. The flesh was then brought in direct contact with the antennæ, and the insect immediately withdrew them as if annoyed, as in the experiment with the Silpha. It was then carried exactly in front, and at about the distance of an inch. The palpi were instantly in rapid motion, and the creature, darting forward, seized the flesh, and began to devour it most voraciously. The following day the experiment was repeated several times, and with precisely the same result; but on this occasion the antennæ were so repeatedly touched with the flesh, that the annoyed insect kept them at last beneath the sides of the thorax. Hence I think it must appear that, from there being no alterations in the motions of the insect when the food was held near the sides of its body, the sense of smelling does not reside in the spiracles, nor, for like reasons, in the antennæ; while, from the motion of the palpi and the avidity with which the insect darted upon the food when held in front of it, it seems but fair to conclude that the sense of smelling must certainly reside in the head, as above suggested." *

Again, he took a Silpha (one of the carrion-eating beetles), and, "placing it in a glass, attached a small piece of flesh within half an inch of it. The antennæ, as is usual with these insects, continued to

* Newport, "On the Antennæ of Insects," *Transactions of the Entomological Society*, 1837–1840.

be moved about on either side, but with nothing
remarkable in their motions, while the head of the
insect was a little elevated and carried forwards, as if it
perceived the flesh, and the palpi were in rapid vibra-
tory motion. It soon approached very near to the food,
and at length touched it three or four times with the
antennæ, but each time suddenly withdrew them as if
they had fallen unexpectedly on something obnoxious,
the palpi during the whole time continuing their motion.
The insect at length reached the food, and, after having
touched it once or twice with the extremities of the
palpi, their motion ceased, and it commenced feeding,
while the antennæ were occasionally in motion as
before." It would certainly seem, therefore, that in
these insects, at any rate, the sense of smell resides
principally in the palpi.

Newport made certain other experiments on the
powers of hearing of insects, which I shall mention in
the next chapter, and he concludes, "These facts,
connected, with the previous experiments, have convinced me that the antennæ in all insects are the
auditory organs, whatever may be their particular
structure, and that, however this is varied, it is appropriated to the perception and transmission of sound."

Newport was an excellent observer and profound
entomologist, and I see no reason to doubt the correctness of his observations ; nor, indeed, of his inferences,
so long as we confine them to the species on which the
observations were made. They may prove that some
insects possess no sense of smell, or that, at any rate,
it does not reside in the antennæ.   On the other
hand, they cannot disprove the positive results obtained
by other observers, that in other species the opposite is

the case, and that in them the sense of smell does reside in the antennæ.

That the stag-beetle can smell seems clearly proved, but Landois found * that, after the removal of the terminal plates of the antennæ, the insect still possessed this faculty, whence he concluded that the sense of smell must reside in some other part of the body, and that the antennæ probably serve as organs of hearing. This does not, however, prove that the sense of smell does not reside partly in the antennæ.

Forel removed the palpi and mouth parts of a wasp, and she appeared to perceive the presence of honey as well as before.

I myself took a large ant (*Formica ligniperda*), and tethered her on a board by a thread. When she was quite quiet, I tried her with tuning-forks; but they did not disturb her in the least. I then approached the feather of a pen very quietly, so as almost to touch first one and then the other of the antennæ, which, however, did not move. I then dipped the pen in essence of musk and did the same; the antenna was slowly retracted and drawn quite back. I then repeated the same with the other antenna. I was, of course, careful not to touch the antennæ. I have repeated this experiment with other substances with several ants, and with the same results. Perris also made the same experiments with the palpi, and with the same result; but if the palpi were removed, the rest of the mouth gave no indications of perceiving odours.

Graber † also has made a number of experiments, and

* "Das Gehörorgan des Hirschkäfers," *Arch. für. Mic. Anat.*, 1868.

† "Vergl. Grundversuche über die Wirkung und die Aufnahmestellen chemischer Reize bei den Thieren," *Biol. Centralblatt*, 1885.

found that in some cases (though by no means in all), insects which had been deprived of their antennæ still appeared to possess the sense of smell. But if, as we have, I think, good reason to suppose, the power of smell resides partly in the palpi, this would naturally be the case.

He also tested a beetle, *Silpha thoracica*, with oil of rosemary and assafœtida. It showed its perception by a movement in half a second to a second in the case of the oil of rosemary, and rather longer—one second to two seconds—in the case of the assafœtida. He then deprived it of its antennæ, after which it showed its perception of the oil of rosemary in three seconds on an average of eleven trials; while in no case did it show any indication of perceiving the assafœtida even in sixty seconds.

This would seem to indicate a further complication—not only that both the antennæ and the palpi may possess the sense of smell, but also that certain odours may be perceived by the former, and others by the latter.

Graber questions some of the experiments which seemed to me * to demonstrate the existence of a sense of smell in ants.†

* "Ants, Bees, and Wasps."

† He says, "Da Lubbock noch hinzufügt, dass keiner, der das Benehmen der Ameisen unter diesen Umständen beobachten würde, den geringsten Zweifel an ihrem Geruchsvermögen haben könnte, wählte ich auch diese Methode, um zu erforschen, wie sich etwa der Fühler beraubte Ameisen verhalten würden. Ich war nicht wenig überrascht zu finden, dass auch diese (es handelt sich um *Formica rufa*) vor dem Riechobjekt umkehrten. Um ganz sicher zu gehen, versuchte ich's aber noch mit dem gleichen Arrangement aber *mit Weglassung* des *Riechstoffes*, und siehe da! sie kehrten auch jetzt noch um! Bei genauerer Beobachtung der von einer Ameise vom Anfang an auf dem Papiersteg zurückgelegten Strecke stellte sich auch bald

I fastened a strip of paper in the air by means of two pins, suspended over it a camel's-hair brush containing scent, and then put an ant at one end. She ran forward, but stopped dead short when she came to the scented brush. Graber suggests that she did so from giddiness, but I am satisfied that this is not so. Ants which habitually climb trees are not likely to be affected by any such sensation. In my experiments, whether the bridge was high or low, broad or narrow, made no difference to them. Moreover, in each case they stopped exactly when they came to the scented pencil. Again, Graber has not observed that I expressly stated that "after passing two or three times, they took no further notice of the scent;" nor did they notice the camel's-hair pencil unless it was scented.

As regards flies (Musca), Forel removed the wings from some bluebottle flies and placed them near a decaying mole. They immediately walked to it, and began licking it and laying eggs. He then took them away and removed the antennæ, after which, even when placed close to the mole, they did not appear to perceive it.

Plateau also* put some food of which cockroaches are fond, on a table, and surrounded it with a low

---

heraus dass es sich bei dem gewissen Umkehren lediglich um ein versuchsweises Abschreiten oder Ausprobiren des unbekannten Weges handelte, oder das sich die Ameisen ähnlich benehmen wie wir selbst, wenn wir etwa auf einem schwanken Brette eine tiefe Gebirgskluft überschreiten sollen."

Graber's observation is, I doubt not, quite correct; but his inference is not, I think, well founded, nor was his experiment the same as mine.

* *Bull. de la Soc. Ent. Belgique*, 1876.

circular wall of cardboard. He then put some cockroaches on the table: they evidently scented the food,
and made straight for it. He then removed their
antennæ, after which, as long as they could not see the
food, they failed to find it, even though they wandered
about quite close to it.

On the whole, then, the experiments which have
been made seem clearly to prove that in insects the
sense of smell resides partly in the antennæ and partly
in the palpi. This distribution would be manifestly
advantageous. The palpi are more suited for the examination of food; while the antennæ are more conveniently situated for the perception of more distant
objects.

We will now glance at the antennæ and palpi
themselves, and consider briefly the structures which
are supposed to give the sensation of smell. For
this three conditions are requisite: (1) an appropriate
nerve; (2) free access to air; and perhaps, though
this is not so clear, (3) a fluid which can dissolve the
odoriferous substance.

The olfactory organ in Vertebrata consists, as already
mentioned, of a mucous membrane containing (1)
cylindrical epithelial cells, with a broad, flat termination
at the free end; and (2) of rod-like filaments which,
some little distance below the surface, swell out into
a nut-shaped expansion, and then contract again into a
fine thread, which is probably continuous with the
fibrils of the olfactory nerve.

In Insects and Crustacea the conditions are different.
The cellular "underskin," or hypoderm, secretes a hard,
horny envelope, and the terminations of the olfactory nerves are enclosed in a horny tube with a

terminal perforation, or project as free threads. They differ, again, between themselves, Insects being as a general rule aerial, and Crustacea aquatic.

Erichson * has the merit of having been the first to support this theory by anatomical examination. Newport had previously mentioned the existence in many insects of certain pits, or "pores," closed by a delicate membrane, and which he regarded as the seat of hearing. Erichson extended his observations, and suggested that the pits were rather to be regarded as organs of smell. His descriptions were confirmed by

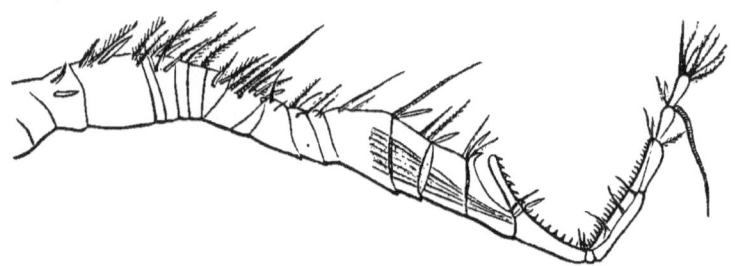

Fig. 34.—Antenna of *Pontella Bairdii* (Lubbock).

Burmeister, who, moreover, detected in some of these "pits" the presence of a small knob, or hair.

In 1853 I called special attention to the antennæ of certain Crustacea, distinguishing five kinds of hairs—(1) short, downy hairs; (2) plumose hairs; (3) cylindrical, tapering hairs; (4) flattened, lanceolate hairs; (5) wrinkled hairs—and pointed out that they were by no means scattered indiscriminately, but arranged in definite situations, indicating special functions. The two last I was disposed to regard as sense-organs. The above is a figure of the right male antenna of Pontella Bairdii, one of the Cope-

* " De Fabrica et usu Antennarum in Insectis." 1847.

poda, from one of my memoirs in that group,* and
shows the curious clasping organ.

Leydig, in his beautiful work on the Daphnidæ, and
more fully·in a special memoir on the subject,† described certain organs which had been also mentioned
by La Vallette. I give below his figure of the
terminal segments of one of the smaller antennæ of
the water-woodlouse (*Asellus aquaticus*) magnified 500
times. It will be seen
that there are three
kinds of appendages—1.
Ordinary stiff, cylindrical,
tapering, pointed hairs,
which are not connected
with any nerve. 2. Pale,
cylindrical hairs, with a
blunt termination and a
tuft of fine setæ. These
hairs are connected with a
nerve, and Leydig regards
them as organs of touch.
3. Peculiar cylinders, of
which there is one to each
segment. They are com-
posed of three parts,
the middle one somewhat

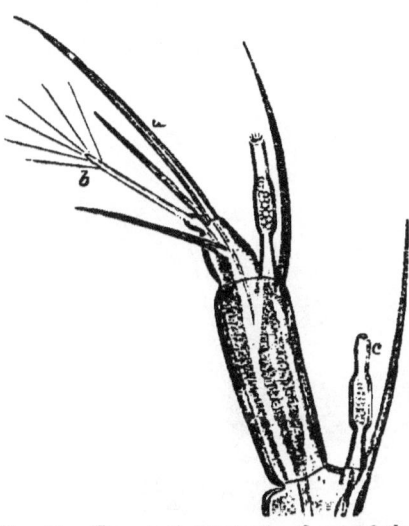

Fig. 35.—Terminal segments of one of the
smaller antennæ of the water-woodlouse
(*Asellus aquaticus*), × 500 (after Leydig).
a, Ordinary hairs (not connected with a
nerve); *b*, sensitive hairs (with a nerve at
the base); *c*, special cylinders (olfactory
cylinders).

wider than the others. The lower third is strongly chiti-
nized, like the ordinary hairs; the other two are more
delicate. At the free end he observed, in some cases,
a group of very fine, short hairs. At the base of

* *Ann. and Mag. of Natural History*, 1853.
† "Ueber Geruchs und Gehörorgane der Krebse und Insekten,"
Müller's Ar.. 1860.

each cylinder is a nerve, which apparently swells into a ganglion.

Leydig described similar organs on the antennæ and palpi of various other Crustacea. They have obviously some special function, and he suggests that they are olfactory organs. It is interesting that, in certain species which live in subterranean waters and have lost their eyes, these olfactory cones are unusually developed. They are much larger, for instance, in *Asellus cavaticus* and *Gammarus*

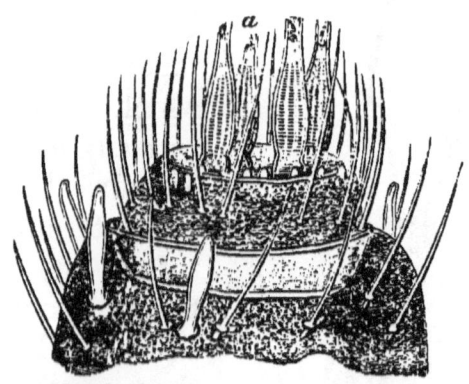

Fig. 36.—Tip of the antenna of a centipede (*Julus terrestris*), × 600 (after Leydig). At the apex are four olfactory cylinders, a few of which are also seen on the following segment, among the ordinary hairs.

puteanus, which live in the dark and are blind, than in *Asellus aquaticus* and *Gammarus pulex* or *G. fluviatilis*.

Fig. 36 represents the end of the antenna of a centipede (*Julus terrestris*). There are four olfactory cylinders at the tip, and several are also seen on the following segment among the ordinary hairs. In this species the cuticle of the cylinder appeared sometimes as if wrinkled, and Leydig believes that the end is open.* Similar cylinders occur in Scolopendra, Glo-

* *Loc. cit.*, p. 286.

meris, and other centipedes. He also described similar cones in certain insects.

Further details with reference to the structure and arrangement of these bodies have been given by Claus, Sars, Weissman, Rougemont, Gamroth, Heller, Hensen, Hauser, and others, who have also ascribed to them this function. In Claus's opinion, the nerve itself enters these bodies. On this point, however, there is

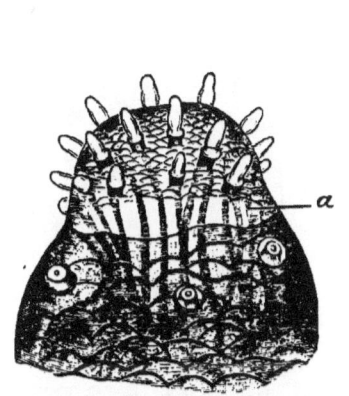

Fig. 37.—End of a palpus of *Staphylinus erythropterus*, × 600 (after Leydig). *a*, Olfactory pit.

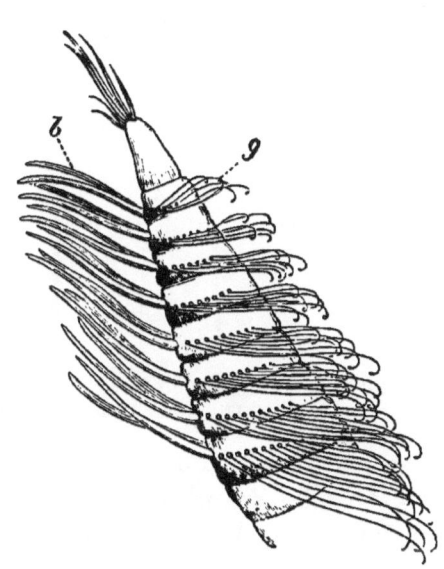

Fig. 38.—Part of antenna of *Callianassa subterranea*. *b*, Olfactory hairs; *g*, peculiar curved hairs.

still much difference of opinion. At any rate, it seems to be established, by the most recent observations, that even if the cones are in some cases closed at the end, they certainly remain open in others. Similar organs also occur in the palpi (see Fig. 37).

Kraepelin describes other peculiar forms of hairs to which he ascribes the perception of smell, as occurring in all the stalk-eyed Crustacea (Podophthalmata).

These olfactory hairs are partly round (Pontonia), partly flat (Pagurus); the end is described as being sometimes simply open (Fig. 39, *a, b*), sometimes provided with a small cone (Fig. 39, *c, d, e*). The number of these hairs is often very considerable. Moreover, they themselves sometimes bear, near the base, a number of very fine bristles (Pagurus). There can, I think, be no doubt that these hairs are organs of sense, and it is probable that they are olfactory. The antenna of Callianassa (Fig. 38) also bears another remarkable series of long,

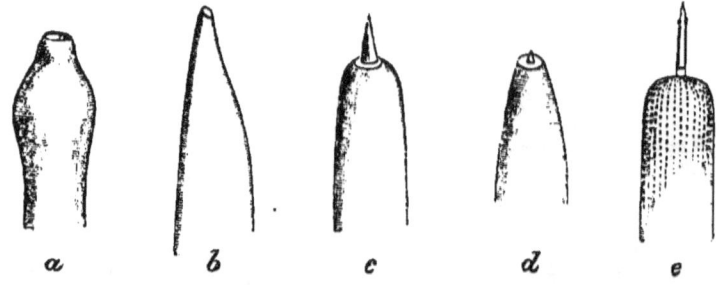

a   *b*   *c*   *d*   *e*

Fig. 39.—Terminations of olfactory hairs of Crustacea. *a*, Of larva of a Palœmon; *b*, of a Pagurus; *c*, of a Pinnotheres; *d*, of a Squilla; *e*, of a Pontonia.

thin, movable, but stiff and hooked hairs (Fig. 38, *g*), which also stand in direct connection with the nerve, and have probably some sense-function.

In many cases the sense of smell is connected with minute depressions in the integument. In spiders Dahl has described a structure in the maxilla which he believes to be olfactory. The skin presents a number of minute orifices, under which lie elongated cells, each terminating in a nervous fibril.[*]

Leydig also mentions[†] the existence of small pits on

* "Das Gehör-und Geruchsorgan der Spinnen," *Arch. für Mic. Anat.*, 1885.

† "Ueber Geruchs und Gehörorgane der Krebse und Insekten," *Müller's Arch.*, 1860.

the antennæ and mandibular palpi of the crayfish (*Astacus fluviatilis*) but I do not find any further description of them. On the other hand, in insects they play a more important part, and it will be convenient to describe here very briefly the various structures occurring on and in the antennæ of insects, although it is not to be supposed that they all serve for the sense of smell. Newport * alludes to the " pits "; but they were first described by Erichson †; while Burmeister ‡ suggested that there are two classes—those containing a hair, and those in which there is none. The pits are only found in certain regions, and have certainly some specific function. In the stag-beetle (*Lucanus cervus*) the terminal plate of the antenna shows two large pits, one on each side, and nearly opposite one another. In other Lamellicorn beetles, as, for instance, in the cock-chafer (*Melolontha vulgaris*), they are very numerous. Lespès§ supposed them to be closed sacs, each containing an otolithe. They certainly do present this appearance, but the existence of any otolithe has been conclusively disproved by Claparède,∥ Claus, Hicks, and others.

Graber thought ¶ that he had discovered an organ of hearing containing an otolithe in the antennæ of certain Diptera. Mayer,** however, has since examined

* *Transactions of the Entomological Society of London*, vol. ii.

† " De Fabrica et usu antennarum in Insectis." 1847.

‡ " Beob. über den feineren Bau der Fühlerfachur der Lamelli-cornier." 1848.

§ " Mém. sur l'appareil auditif des Insectes," *Ann. Sci. Nat*, 1858.

∥ "Sur les prétendus organes auditifs des Antennes chez les Coléoptères," *Ann. Sci. Nat.*, 1858.

¶ " Ueber neue otocystenartige Sinnesorgane der Insekten," *Arch. für Mic. Anat.*, 1879.

** "Sopra certi organi di Senso nelle Antenne dei Ditteri," *Reale Acc. dei Lincei*, 1878–79.

them, and it appears to be really a sac lined with sense-hairs.

Hicks * described the structure of the antennæ in a

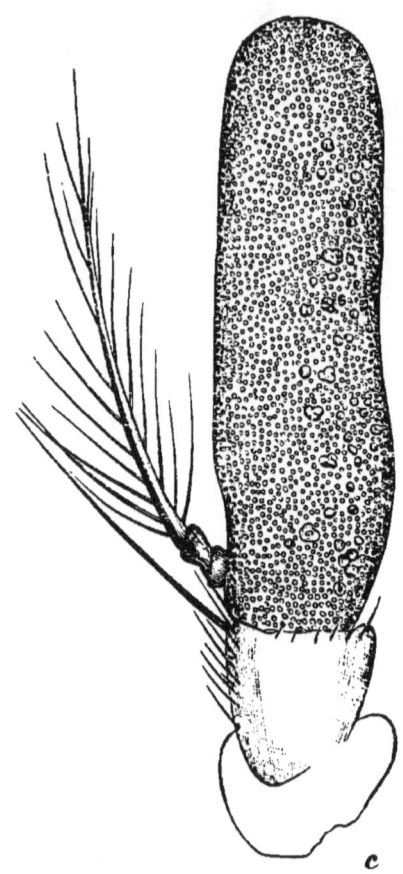

Fig. 40.—Antenna of blowfly (after Hicks). *a*, Enlarged third segment, showing pits; *c*, base of the antenna.

considerable number of insects. On the antenna of the blowfly (Musca; Fig. 40) he found no less than 17,000 perforations, each leading into a small sac, besides which

* *Transactions of the Linnean Society*, 1857–1859.

there are larger orifices leading into more complex depressions, apparently arising from the confluence of a number of the simple sacs. At the base of these large sacs are a number of papillæ, or small hairs. In the dragonfly, each segment of the antenna contains a large convoluted sac. The sacs, in fact, vary much in number, size, and form, but Hicks considered that "they all possess the same elements, and are formed on the same principle." In many cases he traced a nerve to the base of the pits. He considered that they were generally, if not always, closed in by a delicate membrane, which, indeed, sometimes projected in a hemispherical, conical, or even hair-like form.

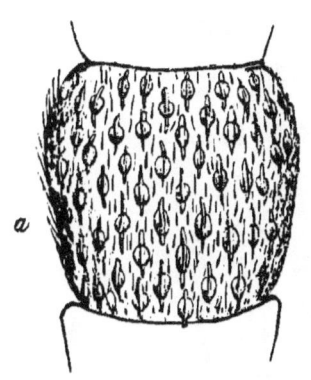

Fig. 41.—One segment of the antenna of an Ichneumon (after Hicks).

The minute structure of the pits was further studied by Leydig in 1860. He describes them as parts of the integument in which the chitine is very thin, and more or less depressed, with a hair in the centre. This hair may be even reduced to a mere ring.

Hicks also called attention to a remarkable speciality in the antennæ of the Ichneumons, the true nature of which he did not, however, correctly ascertain. He describes the appearance presented as that of a great number of narrow inverted canoes, with a keel-like ridge, and each inverted over an oval perforation. He regarded these as consisting of a thin transparent membrane. Subsequent observations, however, have shown that each supposed canoe-shaped membrane is, in fact, a fine hair, inverted over one of the usual pits.

In 1880 Hauser published an excellent memoir * on the olfactory organs of insects, from which I have taken Fig. 42, representing a section through part

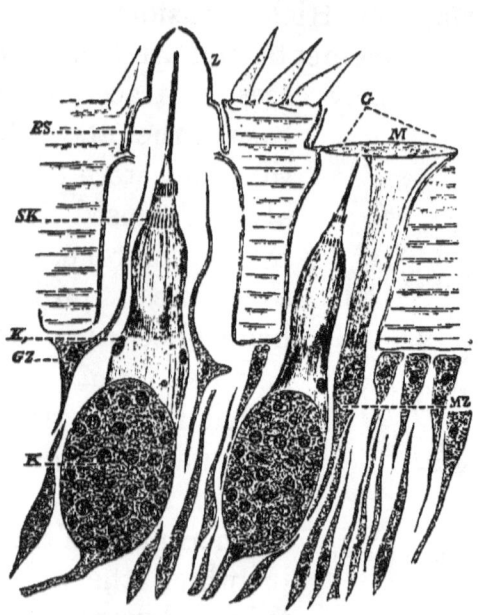

Fig. 42.—Section through part of the antenna of a wasp (after Hauser), × 430. *CH*, Chitinous skin; *Z*, olfactory cone; *G*, olfactory pit; *TB*, tactile hairs; *H*, hypodermic cells; *M*, the membrane surrounding them; *K*, nuclei of the olfactory cells; *K₁*, remains of the earlier upper nucleus; *SK*, lower circle of rods; *RS*, olfactory rod; *GZ*, Geisselzelle; *MZ*, membrane forming cell; *M*, membrane closing the pit.

of the antenna of a wasp, showing two of the olfactory cones, one projecting beyond the general surface. They terminate above in a fine rod, below in a nerve-thread, and present a double series of ridges.

* "Phys. und Hist. Unt. ü. die Geruchsorgane der Insekten," *Zeit. für Wiss. Zool.*, 1880.

Kraepelin* and Sazepin† have also published valuable memoirs containing many interesting details.

The hairs of the antennæ, then, serve some for touch and some for smell, while there is, as we shall presently see, strong reason for supposing that the sense of hearing is also in some insects seated in the antennæ.

The greatest variety of antennal organs, so far as we yet know, occurs in the Hymenoptera (ants, bees, and wasps). Of these I give a diagrammatic figure. There are at least nine different structures.

1. Ordinary hairs (Fig. 43, c).

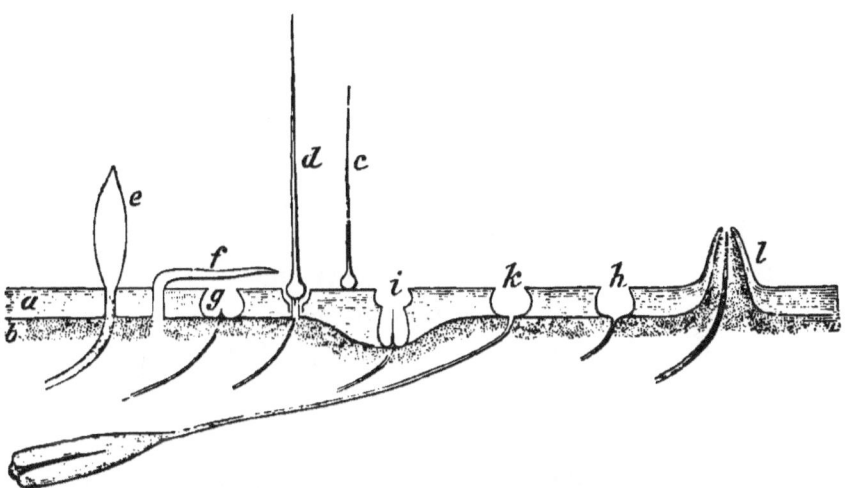

Fig. 43.—Diagram showing structures on the terminal segments of the antenna of insects. *a*, Chitinous cuticle; *b*, Hypodermic layer; *c*, ordinary hair; *d*, tactile hair; *e*, cone; *f*, depressed hair, lying over *g*, cup, with rudimentary hair at the base; *h*, simple cup; *i*, champagne-cork-like organ of Forel; *k*, flask-like organ; *l*, papilla, with a rudimentary hair at the apex.

2. Hairs of touch (Fig. 43, d).

* " Phys. und Hist. Unt. ü. die Geruchsorgane der Insekten." *Zeit. für Wiss. Zool.*, 1880; and " Ueber die Geruchsorgane der Gliederthiere," 1883.

† " Ueber den histol. Bau und die Vert. der nervösen Endorgane auf den Fühlern der Myriopoden," *Mém. de l'Acad. Impér. de Sc. de St. Petersburg*, 1885.

3. Flattened hairs (Fig. 43, *e*).

4. Depressed hairs (Fig. 43, *f*).

5. Pits with a minute hair at the base (Fig. 43, *g*).

6. Pits without a hair at the base (Fig. 43, *h*).

7. Cones containing a nerve (Fig. 43, *l*).

8. The champagne-cork-like organs of Forel (Fig. 43, *i*). These consist of a pit, with a constriction about halfway up. They differ, in fact, from the second sort mainly in the presence of this constriction.

9. The curious flasks (Fig. 43, *k*) first observed and described by Hicks.* "They consist," he says, "of a small pit leading to a long delicate tube, which, bending towards the base, dilates into an elongated sac having its end inverted." † Of these remarkable organs there are about twelve in the terminal segment, and one or rarely two in the others. Similar structures have since been found in other Hymenoptera; but not, I believe, as yet in any other order of insects. I have ventured to suggest that they may serve as microscopic stethoscopes. Kraepelin was disposed to regard them as glands, but I agree with Forel that there is no sufficient reason for doing so.

There may, moreover, be a distinctly characterized sense-organ without any alteration of the actual surface, as shown in some of the figures given by Kraepelin, and also by that from Hauser given above (Fig. 42).

These are, perhaps, the principal types, but there

---

* *Transactions of the Linnean Society*, vol. xxii. p. 39. Kraepelin attributes the observation to Forel, but this is an error. Forel had overlooked Hicks's description and figure.

† Hicks, "On the Organs of the Antennæ of Insects," *Transactions of the Linnean Society*, vol. xxii.

are many modifications; for instance, complex pits often arise from the confluence of several small ones. The structure of the antennæ is then very complex, and increases with the importance of the antennæ in the life of the insect. Among the Hymenoptera, Lyda has about 600 pits; Tenthredo, 1200; Sirex, 2000; Pompilus, 3000; Paniscus, 4000; Ichneumon, 5000; Hylœus, 6000; the wasp (Vespa), about 13,000 pits and 700 cones; the blowfly, 17,000; the hive bee, according to Hicks, about 20,000 pits and 200 cones. Among beetles (Coleoptera) the numbers are generally small, but the cockchafer (Melolontha) possesses, according to Hauser, on each antenna as many as 35,000 in the female, and 39,000 in the male. Moreover, it is significant that in those species where the females are quiescent and are actively sought out by the males, the antennæ are much less highly developed in the female sex than in the male.

As already mentioned, the antennæ probably serve partly as organs of touch, and in some cases for smell.

On the other hand, I do not believe that touch and smell are the only two senses possessed by the antennæ. Forel and I have shown that in the bee the sense of smell is by no means very highly devel·ped. Yet their antenna is one of those most highly organized. It possesses, as I have just mentioned, besides 200 cones, which may probably serve for smell, as many as 20,000 · pits; and it would certainly seem unlikely that an organization so exceptionally rich should solely serve for a sense so slightly developed.

Much as these antennal structures differ from one another in form, arrangement, and structure, they are all reducible to one type—to a hair—more or less developed, more or less deeply seated, standing in connection with the ganglionic cells, and so with the cerebral ganglia. Even the long-necked "bottles" (Fig. 43, k) may be regarded as an extreme form of this type, especially if the inversion at the end can be, as seems probable, regarded as a hair.

All entomologists are agreed that some of the antennal hairs serve as organs of protection, and others as organs of touch. The evidence is, as we have seen, very strong, that some of them serve as organs of smell. They fulfil, therefore, at least three different functions, and when we consider their manifold variety, there is not only no *à priori* improbability, but, on the contrary it seems very probable that some of them, at least, perform some other function in the animal economy.

There is, indeed, strong reason, as we shall see in the next chapter, to believe that, in some cases at any rate, the antennæ act also as ears; while some of these peculiar antennal organs, though obviously organs of sense, seem to have no special adaptation to any sense of which we are cognisant.

CHAPTER IV.

THE sensation of sound is due to vibrations of the air striking on the drum of our ear. The intensity of the sound depends on the extent or amplitude of the sound-wave; while the pitch of the tone depends on the frequence of vibration, and consequently on the number of waves which strike the ear during a given interval. The fewer the number of vibrations in a second, the deeper the sound; the more numerous, the shriller it becomes. Our pianos generally begin with the C of 32 vibrations in a second, and extend to A'''' of 3520 vibrations. The number of vibrations for the tone A', which is that of the hum of a bee, is about 440 in a second. If the vibrations are fewer than 30 in a second, they produce only a buzzing and groaning sound, while the shrillest sound we can hear is produced by about 35,000 vibrations in a second.

It may seem curious that there should be any difficulty in ascertaining whether an animal can hear. But, in the first place, in order to experiment on them, we are often obliged to place them in situations very unlike those to which they are accustomed; and, secondly, it is by no means always easy to say whether they are affected by a real noise, or whether they are merely conscious of a concussion or vibration.

As regards the lower animals, it appears to me, I confess, that many organs have been described as auditory, on grounds which are anything but satisfactory. At the same time, it cannot be doubted that many of the lower animals do possess the power of hearing, especially as some have elaborate organs for the production of sound.

Among the lowest groups, none of the Protozoa or Cœlenterata are known to produce sounds, and in the Mollusca, also, the power is very rare. The Pectens, which are the most lively of bivalves, moving actively by the sudden opening and closing of their valves—as Pliny says, "Saliunt Pectines et extra volitant seque ipsi carinant"—also produce in the same way a certain sound, which Aristotle * gives as an exceptional case among the Mollusca.

Nor is the production of sound much more frequent among the Crustacea. In one genus of crabs (Ocypoda), the claw bears a rasp, or file, which can be rubbed against a ridge on the basal segment of the limb, and thus produces a harsh, jarring sound. Some of the lobsters also (Palinurus) make a noise by rubbing one segment of the antennæ against another; but, considering that the ear is well developed in this group, it is rather remarkable how few of them are known to possess the power of producing sounds.

Passing on to the insects, the song of the Cicada has been celebrated from time immemorial; the chirping of the crickets and grasshoppers is also familiar to us all.

For the reasons, however, already alluded to in the

* " Historia Animalium."

preceding chapter, no insect possesses a true voice. The sounds they make are produced in various ways—for instance, by the wings or the spiracles, by rubbing one part of the body against another, etc.

The power of producing sounds audible to us is possessed by many insects scattered sporadically through all the great groups.

In many of these cases, the power of producing sound is confined to the males. Their sounds are really love-songs.*

In Locusts, as Westwood says,† "The stridulating powers of these insects must have attracted the notice of every one who has walked through the fields in the autumn. Unlike the insects of the two preceding families, it is owing to the motion of the hind femora, either conjointly or alternately rubbed against the sides of the wing-covers, that the sound is produced, the insects resting on their four anterior legs during the operation; the veins of the wing-covers being considerably elevated, so as to be easily acted upon by the rugose inner edge of the thigh. Some species, according to Goreau, may be observed to execute this movement without producing any sound perceptible to our ears, but which he thinks may be perceived by their companions."

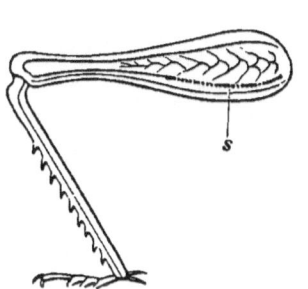

Fig. 44.—Leg of *Stenobothrus pratorum* (after Landois).

* The females are not, however, invariably dumb. In Ephippigera both sexes are able to produce a sound, which, however, is not very loud.

† Westwood, "Modern Classification of Insects."

Fig. 44 represents the leg of a grasshopper (*Steno-bothrus pratorum*). On the inner side of the thigh, at *s*, is a file, consisting of a row of fine teeth (Fig. 45, *z*), which rub against the wing-covers, and thus produce the well-known sounds.

Lehmann states that Brunelli " kept and fed several males of *Gryllus viridissimus* in a closet, which were very merry, and continued singing all the day ; but a rap at the door would stop them instantly. By practice he learned to imitate their chirping ; when he did this at the door, at first a few would answer him in a low note, and then the whole party would take up the tune and sing with all their might. He once shut up a male of the species in his garden, and gave a female her liberty ; but when she heard the male chirp, she flew to him im-mediately." *

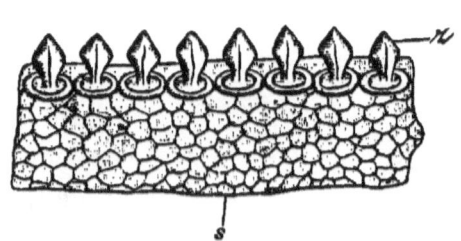

Fig. 45.—Sound-bow of Stenobothrus (after Landois). *s*, Surface of the skin ; *z*, teeth.

In the males of the house and field crickets, the source of the sound is different. On the inner margin of the left wing-cover, about one-third of its length from the base, a thickened point is observed, from which several strong veins diverge. The strongest of these veins, that running towards the base of the wing-cover, is regularly notched on the under side trans-versely, like a file. When the wing-covers are closed, this oblique bar of the wing-cover lies upon the upper surface of the corresponding part of the right wing-

* " De Sensibus externis Animalium exsanguinium." Göttingen: 1798. I give Kirby and Spence's translation.

cover, and when a tremulous motion is imparted to the wing-covers, this bar rubs against the corresponding bar of the right wing-cover, and thus produces the familiar chirping sound.

The song of the Cicadas is produced, again, in a different manner. The musical organs are internal, are placed "at the base of the abdomen beneath, and are covered by two large flat plates attached behind the place of insertion of the hind legs, varying in form in the different species, being, in fact, the dilated sides of the metasternum. . . . The sound issues out of two holes beneath the above-mentioned plates, in a manner somewhat analogous to the action of a violin."[*]

Many beetles have special organs for the production of sounds. A remarkable case is that of the so-called "bombardier beetles," which, when attacked, discharge at the enemy, from the hinder part of their body, an acrid fluid which, as soon as it comes in contact with air, explodes with a sound resembling a miniature gun. Westwood mentions, on the authority of Burchell, that on one occasion, "whilst resting for the night on the banks of one of the large South American rivers, he went out with a lantern to make an astronomical observation, accompanied by one of his black servant boys; and as they were proceeding, their attention was directed to numerous beetles running about upon the shore, which, when captured, proved to be specimens of a large species of Brachinus. On being seized, they immediately began to play off their artillery, burning and staining the flesh to such a degree that only a few specimens could be captured with the naked hand, leaving a mark which remained a considerable time. Upon ob-

* Westwood, "Modern Classification of Insects," vol. ii. p. 42.

serving the whitish vapour with which the explosions were accompanied, the negro exclaimed in his broken English, with evident surprise, 'Ah, massa, they make smoke!' " *

A similar means of defence is possessed by beetles belonging to a very different family—the Paussidæ. Captain Boyes mentions † that on one occasion, having captured a *Paussus Fichtelii* " it immediately emitted two loud and very distinct crepitations, accompanied with a sensation of heat, and attended by a strong acidulous scent. It left a dark-coloured stain on the fingers resembling that produced by caustic, and which had a strong odour something like nitric acid. A circumstance so remarkable induced me to determine its truth, for which purpose I kept it alive till the next morning, and, in order to certify myself of the fact, the following experiments were resorted to. Having prepared some test-paper by colouring it with a few petals of a deep red oleander, I gently turned the Paussus over it, and immediately placed my finger on the insect, at which time I distinctly heard a crepitation, which was repeated in a few seconds on the pressure being renewed, and each discharge was accompanied by a vapour-like steam, which was emitted to the distance of half an inch, and attended by a very strong and penetrating odour of nitric acid."

I do not, however, refer to these cases as affording any evidence that the insects themselves possess the power of hearing, but merely on account of their

* Westwood, "Modern Classification of Insects," vol. i. p. 76.
† "The Economy of the Paussidæ," *Ann. and Magazine of Natural History,* vol. xviii.; see also Péringuay's "Notes on Three Paussi," *Transactions of the Entomological Society,* 1883, p. 133.

intrinsic interest. The following instances, however, do seem to imply a power of hearing.

A well-known case is that of the death-watch, associated with so many superstitions, and supposed in old days to be a certain indication of approaching death. In this case the insect produces the sound by tapping with its head or abdomen, or, according to Doubleday, with its thorax. If a male death-watch ticks, and there be a female even within several yards, she returns the tap, and they approach one another slowly, tapping at intervals, until they meet. The male Ateuches stridulates to encourage the female in her work, and also, according to Darwin, " from distress when she is removed." *

It has long been known that among the Longicorn beetles many of the species, when alarmed, " produce a slight but acute sound by the friction of the narrowed anterior part of the mesothorax, or rather a polished part of the scutellum, against the edge of the prothoracic cavity, by which motion the head is alternately elevated and depressed. It has been generally stated that it was by the friction of the hind margin of the thorax against the base of the elytra that this sound was produced, but this is not the case."† The burying beetles (Necrophorus) produce a sound by rubbing the abdomen against the hinder edges of the wing-cases.

Wollaston, in a short paper on certain musical Curculionidæ,‡ describes a species of Acalles, which he found in Teneriffe. A number of specimens were in a hollow stem, and when it was shaken " the whole plant

* " Descent of Man," vol. i.
† Westwood, " Modern Classification of Insects," vol. i.
‡ *Ann. and Magazine of Natural History*, 1860.

appeared musical." In this genus the sound is produced by rubbing the tip of the abdomen, so rapidly that the movements were scarcely visible to the eye, against the under surface of the ends of the elytra, or wing-cases. The tip of the abdomen, though roughened, is not conspicuously so, the ends of the elytra are shagreened, though very finely, and Wollaston expresses his surprise that so small an instrument could produce so loud a noise. He describes a similar structure in other species of the group.

The cockchafers (Melolontha), besides the humming of the wings, produce a sound which may almost be called a voice. In the large trachea, immediately behind each spiracle, is a chitinous process, or tongue, which is thrown into vibration by the air during respiration, and thus produces a humming noise.

In the beetles, then, the sounds produced may be divided into three classes :

1. Incidental, such as those produced during flight.

2. Defensive.

3. For signals, as in Longicorn beetles, Ateuches, Anobium, etc.

Laudois gives the following summary of the different modes in which sounds are produced by the Coleoptera :—

1. Tapping sounds (Bostrychidæ, Anobium).

2. Grating sounds (Elaterida).

3. Friction without rasping organs (*Euchirus longimanus*).

4. Rasping sounds produced by friction, viz.—

    (1) Pronotum on Mesonotum (Cerambycida, with the exception of Spondylis and Prionus).

  (2) Prosternum on Mesosternum (*Omaloplia brunnea*).

  (3) Elytra with rasp at the end (Curculionida; Dytiscida, Pelobius).

  (4) Coxæ with rasp (Geotrupes, Ceratophyus).

  (5) Cover-margin rasp rubbing against the thigh (*Chiasognathus Grantii*).

  (6) Pygidium with two rasps in the middle (Crioceris, Lema, Copris, Oryctes, Necrophorus, Tenebrionida).

  (7) Abdomen with a grating-ridge and four grating-plates (*Trox sabulosus*).

  (8) Abdomen with two toothed ridges rubbing on cover-margin rasp (Elaphrus, Blethisa, Cychrus).

  (9) Elytra rubbing with under-wing rasp (*Pelobius Herrmanni*).

  (10) Wings rubbing against abdominal ringlets (*Melolontha fullo*).

  5. Exploding sounds from the tail (Brachinus).

  6. Sounds produced by the spiracles (Melolontha).

Graber, moreover, has shown by a number of interesting experiments * that the power of hearing is by no means confined to those beetles which are known to produce sounds themselves.

Passing on to other groups of insects, flies and gnats, besides the humming of the wings, produce sounds, like the cockchafer, through the spiracles, some of which are especially arranged for this purpose. If a fly be caught and held between the fingers, it will generally make a loud and peculiar sound. The hum of the mosquito is only too familiar to most of us.

* "Die Chordotonal Sinnesorgane der Insekten," *Arch. für Mic. Anat.*, 1882.

Landois, mentions that he has heard species of Eristalis and Syrphus sing while they have been sitting quietly. The dragon-flies (Libellulina) also produce a sound by means of their spiracles.

Among Hymenoptera, the hum of an angry bee is proverbial. Nor must I omit to mention the piping noise made by young queen bees. It is well known that there is only one queen in a hive, and that working bees never turn their back on her; as she moves among the combs, they all turn towards her. If there has been a swarm led by the old queen, the young queen who has succeeded often makes a piping noise, first noticed by Huber, whose statements are generally recognized as correct.* While "singing" the queen assumes a particular attitude, and the other bees all lower their heads and remain motionless until she begins to move again. In the mean while, if there are any other young queens which have not yet left the cells, they answer the old one, and their notes seem to be sounds of challenge and defiance.

Other bees also produce a sound by means of their spiracles quite different from the humming of their wings. *Mutilla Europæa*, a wingless species, related to and not unlike the ants, makes, when alarmed, a rather sharp noise by rubbing one of the abdominal rings against the other.

Under these circumstances, Landois asked himself whether other genera allied to Mutilla might not possess a similar organ, and also have the power of producing sound. He first examined the genus Ponera, which, in the structure of its abdomen, nearly resembles

* Huber, "Obs. sur les Abeilles;" Bevan, "On the Honey Bee;" Langstroth, "On the Honey Bee."

Mutilla, and here also he found a fully developed stridulating apparatus.

He then turned to the true ants, and here also he found a similar rasp-like organ in the same situation. It is indeed true that ants produce no sounds which are audible by us; still, when we find that certain allied insects do produce sounds appreciable to us by rubbing the abdominal segments one over the other, and when we find, in smaller species, an entirely similar structure, it certainly seems reasonable to conclude that these latter also do produce sounds, even though we cannot hear them. Landois describes the structure in the workers of *Lasius fuliginosus* as having twenty ribs in a breadth of ·13 of a millimeter. In *Lasius flavus* I found about ten well-marked ribs, occupying a length of $\frac{1}{100}$ of an inch. Similar ridges also occur between the following segments.

In the flies (Diptera) and dragon-flies (Libellulina), the four thoracic spiracles produce sounds; while in Hymenoptera, as, for instance, in the humble bee (Bombus), the abdominal spiracles are also musical. The sounds produced by the wings are constant in each species, excepting where there are (as in Bombus) individuals of very different sizes. In these the larger specimens give generally a higher note. Thus the comparatively small male of *Bombus terrestris* hums on A', while the large female hums a whole octave higher. There are, however, small species which give a deeper note than larger ones, on account of the wing-vibrations not being of the same number in a given time. Moreover, a tired insect produces a somewhat different note from one that is fresh, on account of the vibrations being slower.

Indeed, from the note produced we can calculate the
rapidity of the vibration. The slow flapping of a
butterfly's wing produces no sound, but when the movements are rapid a noise is produced, which increases
in shrillness with the number of vibrations. Thus the
house-fly, which produces the sound of F, vibrates its
wings 21,120 times in a minute, or 335 times in a
second; and the bee, which makes a sound of A', as
many as 26,400 times, or 440 times in a second. On
the contrary, a tired bee hums on E', and therefore,
according to theory, vibrates its wings only 330 times
in a second.

Marey has succeeded in confirming these numbers
graphically. He fixed a fly so that the tip of the
wing just touched a cylinder which was moved by
clockwork. Each stroke of the wing caused a mark,
of course very slight, but still quite perceptible, and
he thus showed that there were actually 330 strokes in
a second, agreeing almost exactly with the number
inferred from the note produced.

The sound emitted from the spiracles bears no relation to that produced by the wings. Thus, according
to Landois, the wing-tone of the hive bee is A'; its
"voice," if we may call it so, on the contrary, is an
octave higher, and often goes to B" and C". In one of
the solitary bees, *Anthidium manicatum*, the difference
is still greater; the wing-tone is G', and the "voice"
nearly two octaves higher, reaching to F'".

The wing-tone is constant, at least with the exceptions just alluded to. The "voice," on the contrary,
appears to be to some extent under the control of the
will, and thus offers another point of similarity to a true
"voice." Thus a bee in the pursuit of honey hums

continually and contentedly on A', but if it is excited
or angry it produces a very different note.   Thus,
then, the sounds of insects do not merely serve to bring
the sexes together; they are not merely "love-songs,"
but also probably serve, like any true language, to
express the feelings.

Landois also describes the muscles by means of
which the form of the organ, the tension of the drum,
etc., is altered, and the tone thus, no doubt voluntarily,
affected.* We can, indeed, only in few cases distinguish
the differences thus produced; but as even we, far
removed as we are in organization, habits, and sentiments, from a fly or a bee, can yet feel the difference
between a contented hum and an angry buzz, it is highly
improbable that their power of expressing their feelings
should stop there.   One can scarcely doubt but that
they have thus the means of conveying other sentiments
and ideas to one another.

Butterflies and moths do not habitually produce any
sound in flight. The texture of their wings is comparatively soft, and they are generally moved slowly.
Still, they are not altogether silent.

The death's-head moth (*Sphinx atropos*) emits a
mournful cry, first noticed by Réaumur. This moth,
he says, "dans le temps qu'il marche, a un cri qui a
paru funébre; au moins est-il le cri d'une bonne âme
de papillon, s'il gémit des malheurs qu'il annonce.

"Le cri de notre papillon est assés fort et aigu; il a
quelque ressemblance avec celui des souris, mais il est
plus plaintif; il a quelque chose de plus lamentable.
C'est surtout lorsque le papillon marche, ou qu'il se

---

* "Die Ton and Stimm Apparate der Inseckten," *Zeit. für Wiss.
Zool.*, 1866.

trouve mal à son aise, qu'il crie ; il crie dans les poudries, dans les boistes où on le tient renfermé ; ses cris redoublent lorsqu'on le prend, et il ne cesse de crier tant qu'on le tient entre les doigts. En général il fait grand usage de la faculté de crier, que la nature lui à accordée." *

There has been much doubt how the sound arises, but it appears to be ascertained that the moth produces it by rubbing the palpi against the base of the proboscis.†

Huber thought, and subsequent writers—as, for instance, Kirby and Spence, and Bevan—have concurred in the opinion, that the sound "operates on the bees like the voice of their queen, and thus enables the moth to commit the greatest ravages in the hives with perfect immunity." ‡ On the other hand, Huber ascertained by experiment that it exercises no such charm over humble bees.

Several other species of the genus Sphinx also produce a sound, and a few other moths, for instance, *Noctua fovea.* Darwin also mentions § a Brazilian butterfly, *Ageronia feronia*, as making " a noise like that produced by a toothed wheel passing under a spring catch, which could be heard at the distance of several yards."

The peacock butterfly (*Vanessa io*) ‖ is also said to possess the same power.

For further details with reference to the sounds produced by insects, and, indeed, by animals generally,

---

* " Mém. p. servir à l'Histoire des Insectes."

† Landois, " Die Ton und Stimm Apparate der Insekten," *Zeit. für Wiss. Zool.*, vol. xvii.

‡ Bevan, " On the Honey Bee."   § " Descent of Man," vol. i.

‖ " Die Ton and Stimm Apparate der Insekten," *Zeit. für Wiss. Zool.*, 1867.

I may refer to Landois's interesting work, "Thier-stimmen."

From the fact that the power of producing sounds audible to us is scattered among so many groups, and that the sounds themselves are often so shrill, I am disposed to suspect that many insects usually regarded as dumb really produce sounds, which, however, are beyond our range of hearing.

Among centipedes Gerstäcker has described* a sound-producing organ in *Eucorybar crotylus*. The posterior legs have the fourth segment much enlarged and leaf-like, with the edges raised and formed of very hard chitine. The legs are rubbed against one another, and thus produce a rasping sound. Bourne also has recently described† a stridulating organ in another genus (Sphærotherium). It is situated just behind the twenty-first pair of legs, and consists of a hood-like process bearing a number of parallel ridges.

There is a very general impression that spiders hear well, and even enjoy music! There seems, however, very little evidence of any value on the subject. No doubt they are extremely sensitive to vibrations. The presence of even a very small insect on their web is at once perceived. Mr. Boys has shown that the vibrations of a tuning-fork affect them strongly.‡ This sensitiveness to vibrations is, however, not necessarily the same as a true sense of hearing. Kraepelin says § that he knows only one observation which seems to him to possess sufficient exactness to justify the conclusion that spiders possess any sense of hearing—namely, that of Lehmann.

* Gerstäcker, "*Stettin Ent. Zeit.*, 1854.
† Bourne, *Linnean Journal*, 1885.   ‡ *Nature*, vol. xxiii.
§ " Ueber die Geruchsorgane der Gliederthiere."

It would be, on the other hand, most unsafe to conclude that spiders are incapable of hearing. Dahl * has given reasons for believing that some of their hairs serve as auditory organs. Westring has discovered, in certain species of Theridium (*T. serratipes, oculatum, castaneum*, etc.), a stridulating organ, consisting of a sort of raised bow attached to the upper part of the abdomen, which rubs against the under and hinder part of the cephalothorax, producing a whirring sound. Lebert † naturally observes that this appears to indicate a power of hearing on their part.

As regards insects, it would be easy to multiply such evidence almost indefinitely; I have given more illustrations than I should probably have otherwise thought necessary, because so excellent an observer as Forel, whose opinion I should value on such a point as much as that of any authority, expresses doubt whether insects really hear at all. "Ce qu'on semble," he says, in his last memoir on the subject, "considérer comme preuve de l'ouïe me paraît comme à Dugès reposer à peu d'exceptions près sur des ébranlements mécaniques de l'air ou du sol qui sont simplement perçus comme tels par les organes tactiles des insectes. Cela correspond à peu près à la dernière opinion de Graber sur" l'ouïe "de la Periplaneta. Mais on n'a pas le droit de nommer ouïe de pareilles sensations." ‡

Graber, however, has endeavoured to meet this objection by an ingenious experiment.§ He placed some water-boatmen (Corixa) in a deep jar full of

---

* "Das Gehör-und Geruchsorgane der Spinnen," *Arch. für Mic. Anat.*, 1885.

† "Die Spinnen der Schweiz."

‡ A. Forel, "Sensations des Insectes," *Recueil Zool. Suisse*, t. iv. 1887.

§ *Arch. für Mic. Anat.*, 1882.

water, at the bottom of which was a layer of mud. He dropped a stone on the mud, but the beetles, which were reposing quietly on some weeds, took no notice. He then put a piece of glass on the mud, and dropped the stone on to it, thus making a noise, though the disturbance of the water was the same. The water-boatmen, however, then at once took flight.

In face of all the evidence, then, I do not think there can reasonably be any doubt on the subject, and it seems to be clearly established that insects do possess the sense of hearing.

CHAPTER V.

THAT many of the lower animals have special organs for the production of sound, and possess the sense of hearing, has been shown in the preceding chapter.

I now proceed to consider the mechanism by which sounds are perceived. In our own ear we have, first of all, the external ear, much less important in man than in many other animals, as in the horse, for instance, where it may be seen moving continually, and almost automatically assuming the position most favourable for conveying the waves of sound down the outer passage (Fig. 46, D) to the tympanum, or drum. This is a membrane stretched between the outer air on the one hand, and the drum on the other, which also contains air, transmitted through the mouth by means of the Eustachian tube (Fig. 46, E). The drum is separated from the brain by a hard, bony partition in which are two orifices, one oval and the other round. Across the drum stretches a chain of little bones (Fig. 47); first the "hammer," secondly the "anvil," and lastly the "stirrup." The flat plate of the stirrup, again, lies against the oval orifice, or fenestra ovalis, as it is technically called, of the drum. Thus the sounds are intensified by being conveyed from the tympanic membrane to one which is twenty times smaller. Behind the

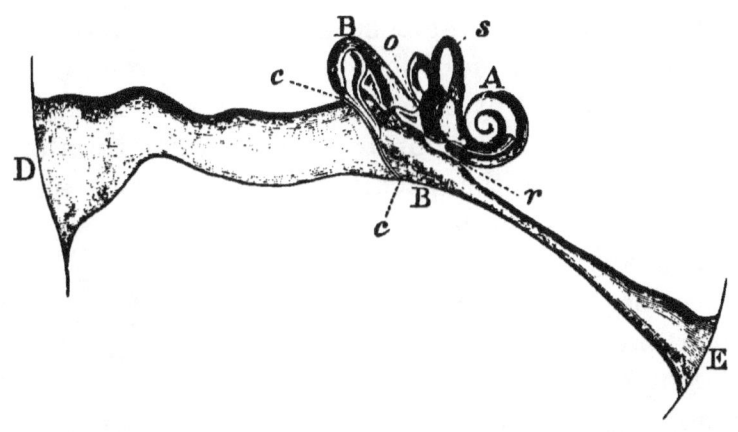

Fig. 46.—Diagram of human ear (after Bernstein). D, Auditory canal; E, mouth of Eustachian tube; cc, tympanic membrane; B, tympanic cavity; o, fenestra ovalis; r, fenestra rotunda; s, semicircular canals; A, cochlea.

fenestra ovalis is the labyrinth, which is filled with fluid, and on which the final filaments of the auditory nerve are distributed. This fluid is thrown into vibrations by those of the stirrup, but as it is enclosed in a bony case, the vibrations would be greatly curtailed if it were not for the second membrane, or fenestra rotunda. This round membrane, therefore, acts as a counter opening, for if the fluid is compressed in one place, it must claim more room in another. The labyrinth consists mainly of two parts,

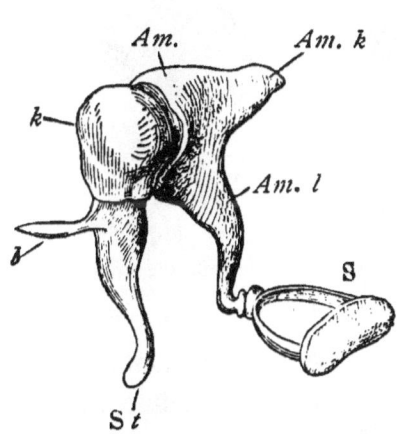

Fig. 47.—Ossicles of the ear. H, Hammer; Am, anvil; Am. k, shorter process of the anvil; Am. l, longer process of the anvil; S, stirrup; St, long process of the hammer.

the cochlea and the semicircular canals. The semi-circular canals are three in number, and stand at right angles to one another. No satisfactory explanation of their function has yet been given; but there is some evidence that, in addition to, or apart from, hearing, they are affected by the position of the head, and thus serve as organs for maintaining the equilibrium of the body. Each of the canals commences with an oval dilatation, or ampulla. In the ampulla is a projecting ridge, on which are long, stiff, delicate, hair-like processes, the vibrations of which probably give certain sound-sensations. In the canals certain parts bear shorter hairs, over which are minute ear-stones, or otolithes, consisting of carbonate of lime, embedded in a gelatinous substance. The cochlea contains, moreover, a compli-

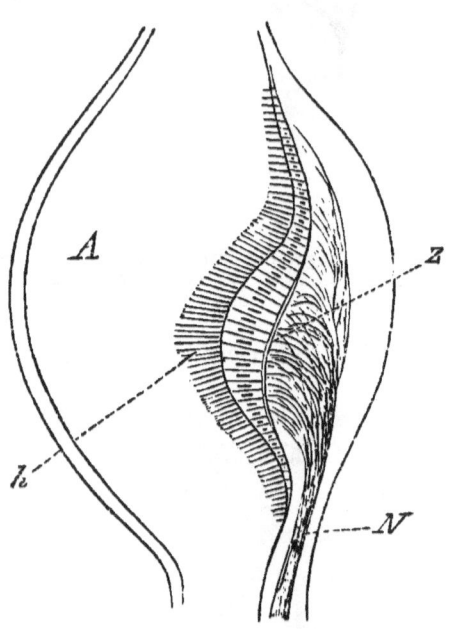

Fig. 48.—Section through the ampulla (after Bernstein). *N*, Nerve; *z*, terminal cells; *h*, auditory hairs.

cated and wonderful organ, discovered by Count Corti. This appears to be, in fact, a microscopic musical instrument, composed of some four thousand complex arches, increasing regularly in length and diminishing in height from the base to the summit of the cochlea. The waves of sound have been supposed to play on this organ, almost like the fingers of a performer on the keys of a musical instrument.

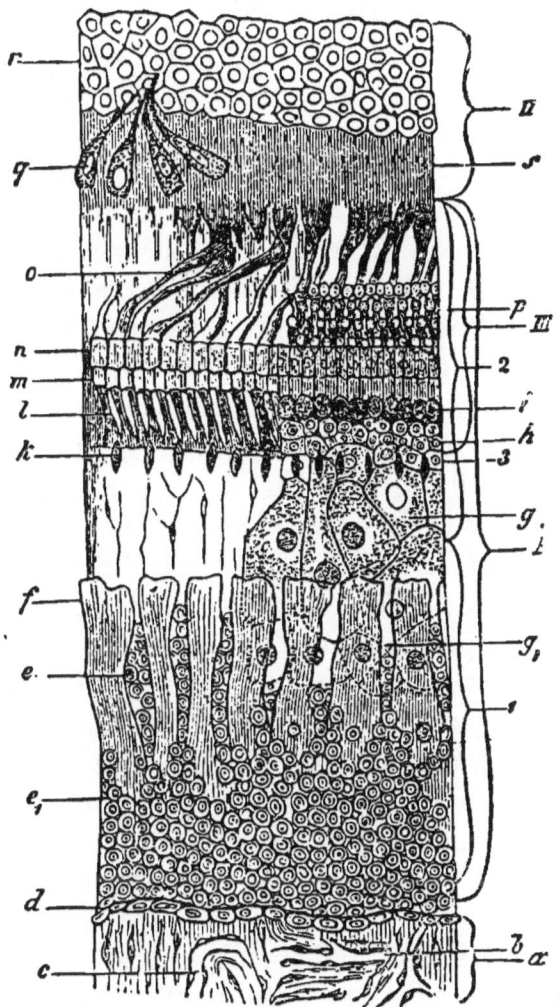

Fig. 49.—Tympanal wall of the ductus cochlearis, from the dog. Surface view from the side of the scala vestibuli, after the removal of Reissner's membrane, ³⁹⁰. **I.** Zona denticulata Corti. **II.** Zona pectinata Todd-Bowman: 1, Habenula sulcata Corti ; 2, Habenula denticulata Corti ; 3, Habenula perforata Kölliker. **III.** Organ of Corti: *a*, portion of the lamina spiralis ossea (the epithelium is wanting); *b* and *c*, periosteal blood-vessels ; *d*, line of attachment of Reissner's membrane ; *e* and *e₁*, epithelium of the crista spiralis ; *f*, auditory teeth, with the interdental furrows; *g*, *g₁*, large-celled (swollen) epithelium of the sulcus spiralis internus, over a certain extent shining through the auditory teeth ; from the left side of the preparation they have been removed ; *h*, smaller epithelial cells near the inner slope of the organ of Corti ; *k*, openings through which the nerves pass ; *i*, inner hair cells ; *l*, inner pillars ; *m*, their heads ; *o*, outer pillars ; *n*, their heads; *p*, lamina reticularis ; *q*, a few mutilated outer hair cells ; *r*, outer epithelium of the ductus cochlearis (Claudius's cells of the author's); removed at *s* in order to show the points of attachment of the outer hair cells. After Waldeyer, in Stricker's " Manual of Histology."

The fibres of Corti, according to Helmholtz, may be distributed among the seven octaves which are in general use, so that there will be $33\frac{1}{3}$ fibres to every semitone, and 400 to each octave. Weber has estimated that a skilful ear can perceive a difference even of the $\frac{1}{64}$ of a tone, or nearly four thousand sounds, and this would agree fairly well with the number of fibres.

But why, it may be asked, should a given musical sound act more on one of these " keys " than another ? If several tuning-forks which sound different notes are placed on a table, and another in vibration be brought near them, the one sounding the same note is thrown into vibration, while the others are unaffected. A second tuning-fork would affect its own fellow, but no other, and so on.* A very slight change in the tuning-fork, such, for instance, as would be made by fastening a piece of wax to one of the prongs, is sufficient to destroy the sympathetic vibrations. The sound of the human voice has been known to break a bell-shaped glass by the agitation thus caused. The difficulty is to hit the pitch with sufficient precision, and retain the tone long enough. It is probable, therefore, that each of Corti's arches is set for a particular sound, and sensitive to it alone. This suggestion derives additional probability from the observations of Hensen (see p. 93) on the auditory hairs of Crustacea.

We thus obtain a glimpse, though but a glimpse, of the manner in which the arches of Corti may possibly act. There are many problems still to be solved, but it is at least easy to see that so complex an organ may be capable of conveying very complex sensations.

* Helmholtz, " Sensations of Tone."

ON THE ORGANS OF HEARING IN THE LOWER
ANIMALS.

The semicircular canals in the human ear (see p. 79)
have been supposed by some, in addition to, or apart
from, their functions as organs of hearing, to assist in
maintaining the equilibrium of the body; at all events,
when they are injured, the movements frequently become disorderly, and the otolithic organs of the lower
animals appear, at any rate in certain cases, to perform
a similar function.*

Otolithes, as we have seen, are present in our own
ears, but they play a much more important part in
those of the lower animals. In the lowest, the sound-
waves may be considered to produce a certain effect
upon the general tissues. The soft parts of the body
are, however, not well calculated to receive such
impressions. Their effect would be heightened by the
presence of any solid structures, whether spicules, as
in sponges, etc., or solid hairs projecting from the
general surface, as in a great many of the lower
animals.

The Medusæ (jelly-fishes, Fig. 50) present round the
edge of the umbrella certain "marginal bodies," with
reference to which there have been great differences of
opinion. O. F. Müller, by whom they were discovered,
regarded them as orifices for the exclusion of digested
food, Rosenthal and Escholtz considered them to be
glands, Milne Edwards as ovaries; but it seems now
clearly established that some are organs of hearing,

---

* Delage, "Sur une fonction nouvelle des Otocystes," *Arch. d. Zool.
Exp.*, 1887. Engelmann, "Ueber d. Function der Otolithen," *Zool.
Anz.*, 1887.

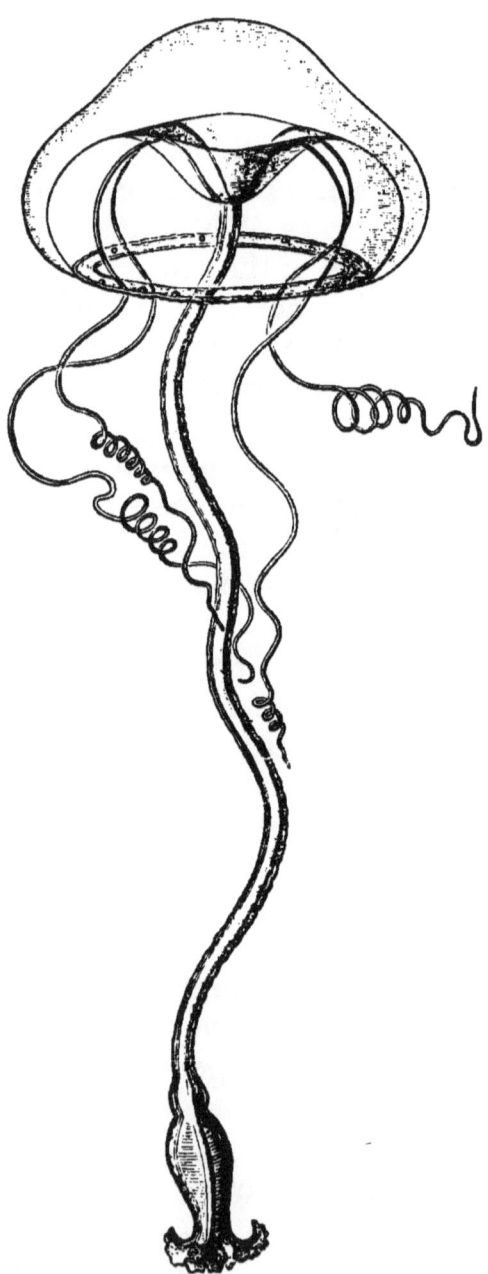

Fig. 50.—*Eutima gigas* (after Haeckel).

and others of sight. Some species possess both, but, as a general rule, among Medusæ, where organs of hearing are present, those of sight are wanting, and *vice versâ*. It may seem extraordinary that there should be such differences of opinion as to these organs. The earlier naturalists, however, had but imperfect microscopes, and probably often examined specimens in a bad state of preparation. As regards the alternative between the view that they served as eyes and that which regarded them as ears, it must, moreover, be remembered that as long as we merely know that there was a capsule containing a transparent body, the function might well be doubtful.

The auditory organs of the jelly-fishes were first recognized as such by Kölliker.* They are ranged round the umbrella, and vary considerably in number, ranging up to sixty in Cunina, eighty in Mitrocoma, and as many as six hundred in Œquorea.

There are three types. In the first, the auditory organ is an open pit, lined with cells. The majority of those on the outer side contain an otolithe, while a row on the opposite side are strap-shaped, their free ends terminating in auditory hairs, which reach to the cells containing the otolithes, while their inner ends are continuous with fibres from the inner nerve-ring.

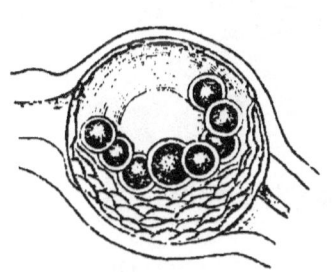

Fig. 51.—Auditory organ of *Ontorchis Gegenbauri.*

In such an auditory organ as that of Ontorchis (Fig. 51), the otolithes present a very deceptive resemblance to the lenses of an eye.

* "Ueber die Randkörper der Quallen," *Frorieps Neue Not.*, 1843.

Fig. 52 represents the somewhat more complex auditory organ of Phialidium.

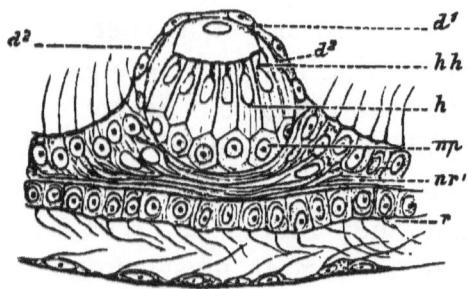

Fig. 52.—Auditory organ of Phialidium (after Hertwig). d^1, Epithelium of the upper surface of the velum; d^2, epithelium of the under surface of the velum; hh, auditory hairs; h auditory cells; np, nervous cushion; nr', nerve-ring; r, circular canal at the edge of the velum.

The second type is more advanced, the vesicle being closed, and the otolithes fewer in number, the Eucopidæ, indeed, having only one.*

In the third type, that of the Trachymedusæ, the

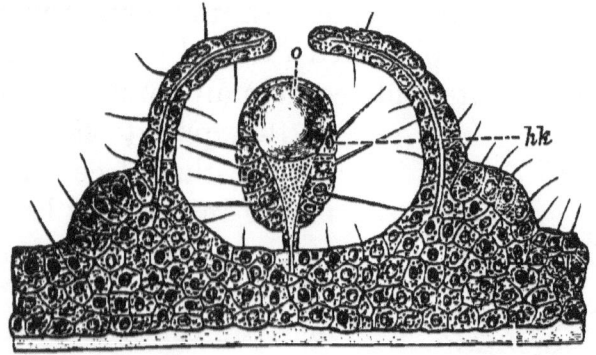

Fig. 53.—Auditory organ of Rhopalonema, still showing a small orifice (after Hertwig). hk, Modified tentacle; o, auditory organ.

auditory organs are modified tentacles. They form a club-shaped body, with a central endodermal axis, and

* Hertwig considers that the supposed hairs shown by Hensen in his figure of the ear of Eucope are really the edges of auditory canals.

bearing at the apex one or more sometimes spherical, sometimes prismatic, otolithes. In some cases the organ becomes enclosed in a cup, which in Geryonia closes at the top.

In another family of the Hydromedusæ, the Oceanidæ, these organs are absent, and appear to be replaced by certain pigment spots at the base of the tentacles, which, however, from their structure are considered to be rudimentary organs of vision, and will be described in the chapter on eyes.

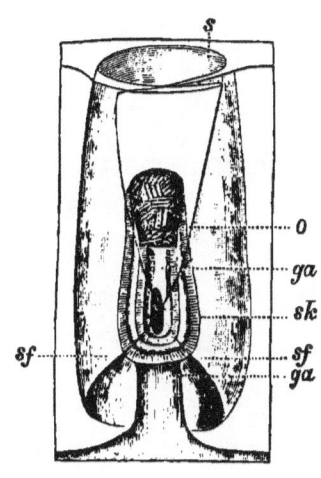

Fig. 54.—Sense-organ of Pelagia (after Hertwig). *o*, Group of crystals; *sk*, sense-organ; *sf*, fold of the skin; *ga*, gastro-vascular channel.

Some species have, in addition, other organs, obviously of sense, but the function of which is still far from clear. Fig. 54 represents one of these curious sense-organs in Pelagia, after Hertwig. It is in the form of a somewhat bent finger, is situated in a deep fold of the umbrella, contains a branch of the gastrovascular canal, and is filled at the tip with a group of solid, shining, rod-like crystals.

The auditory organ in worms and molluscs consists of a closed vesicle, containing one or more otolithes, and lined with nerve-cells, which are, in the higher groups, connected at their base with the auditory nerve, and bear setæ at the other end. De Quatrefages was the first who established clearly the existence of auditory organs in worms.

In the Mollusca, the existence of an organ of hearing in some Gasteropods was justly inferred by Grant from the fact that one species, *Tritonia arborescens*, emits certain sounds, doubtless intended to be heard by its fellows.

The ciliæ contained in the auditory vesicle are sometimes short, and scattered over the general surface, as in Unio (Fig. 55); sometimes long and borne on papillary projections, as in Carinaria and Pterotrachea* (Fig. 56), where also there are certain special cells, supposed to act as buffers or dampers. The otolithe is sometimes single, and nearly spherical, as in Acephala and Heteropoda, and consists of calcareous matter with an organic base; in the Gasteropods, Pteropods, and

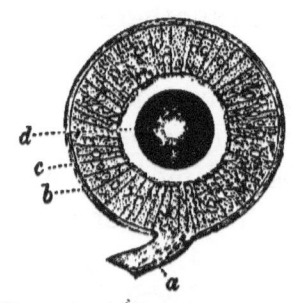

Fig. 55.—Auditory organ of Unio (after Leydig). *a*, Nerve; *b*, cells; *c*, ciliæ; *d*, otolithe.

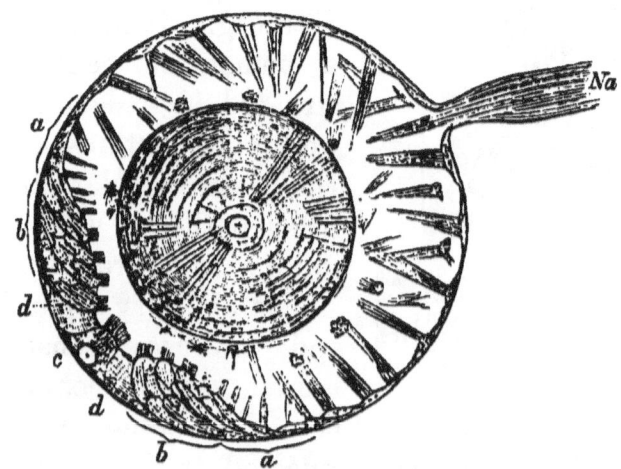

Fig. 56.—Auditory organ of *Pterotrachea Friderici* (after Claus). *Na*, Auditory nerve; *c*, central cells; *d*, supporting plate; *b*, outer circle of auditory cells; *a*, ciliated cells.

some Annelides (Arenicola, Amphicora) they are

* Claus., "Ueber den Acoust. App. im Gehörorgane der Heteropoden," *Arch. für Mic. Anat.*, 1878.

numerous, and sometimes, as in Cymbulia, collected
into a mulberry-like group.

In many cases the auditory sac rests directly on the
ganglion.

The actual mode of termination of the nerves is still
uncertain. I have already mentioned that vibrations, if
fewer than thirty in a second, do not produce on us the
effect of sound. But it is possible that these organs in
the lower animals are intended quite as much to record
movements in the water as for hearing properly so called.

The Organs of Hearing in Crustacea.

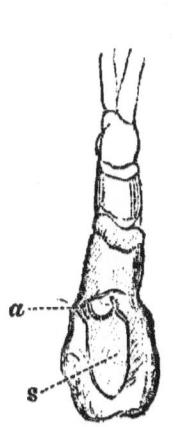

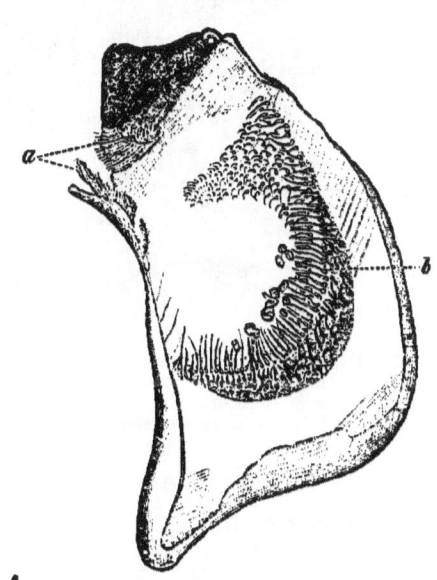

Fig. 57. — Base of
right antennule of
lobster (*Astacus
marinus*), after
Farre. *a*, Orifice ;
s, sac.

Fig. 58.—Interior of auditory sac of lobster (after
Farre). *a*, Orifice , *b*, auditory hairs.

It was long supposed that the auditory organ of the
Crustacea was situated in the basal segment of the
outer antenna. The true auditory organ was, indeed,
discovered by Rosenthal in 1811,[*] who, however, re-

* Reil's *Arch. für Phys.*, 1811.

garded it as an olfactory organ, as did also Treviranus, Fabricius, Scarpa, Brandt, Milne Edwards, and, in fact, the older naturalists generally. The discovery of its true nature is due to Farre,* was confirmed by Huxley †️ and Leuckart, and is now generally admitted. It is a sac situated in the base, or first segment, of the lesser pair of antennæ, which is slightly dilated. In some species the sac communicates freely with the

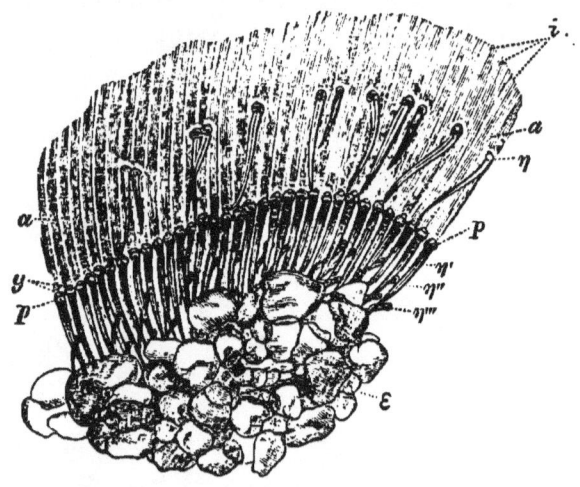

Fig. 59.—Part of wall of auditory sac of lobster (*Astacus marinus*); after Hensen. *a*, Thickened bars in the membrane of the sac ; *η*. first row of auditory hairs ; *η'*, second row of auditory hairs ; *η''*, third row of auditory hairs ; *η'''*, fourth row of auditory hairs ; *ε*, grains of sand, serving as otolithes.

water by means of an orifice situated towards the inner and anterior margin, and guarded by rows of fine hairs. In others the orifice is closed, but its position is always marked, as the auditory sac is at this point connected with the skin.

Both contain otolithes. Those of the closed sacs are generally rounded; while, on the contrary, those of

* *Philosophical Transactions,* 1843.
† *Ann. and Mag. of Natural History,* 1851.

the open sacs are simply grains of sand, and are so numerous as sometimes to occupy one-fourth, or even one-third, of the sac.

Farre stated that the otolithes in the auditory sacs of Crustacea were simply grains of sand, selected by the Crustacea, and put into their own sacs to serve as otolithes. It seemed, however, so improbable that Crustacea should pick up suitable particles of sand and place them in their ears, that the statement was not unnaturally received with incredulity. The observation of Hensen appears, however, to leave no doubt on the subject. The sac, whether open or closed, is an extension of the outer skin, and is cast with it at each moult. Hensen examined them shortly after moulting, and found that the sacs contained no stones; he saw the shrimps carefully selecting particles of sand, but could never detect one in the very act of placing one in the auditory sac. He therefore placed some shrimps in a vessel of filtered sea-water, and strewed over the bottom some crystals of uric acid. Soon afterwards one of the shrimps moulted, and the auditory sac was found on examination to contain a few grains of sand, but no crystals of uric acid. Three hours later, however, Hensen found that the new sac contained numerous crystals of uric acid, but none resembling common sand. Evidently, therefore, the Crustacea pick up grains of sand, and actually introduce them into their own ears to serve as otolithes.

Otolithes are not, however, universally present. In the true crabs (Brachyura) they appear to be always wanting, so that the auditory hairs (which present very nearly the same character as those of the lobsters, etc.) are capable of being thrown into vibrations without the mediation of otolithes.

The interior of the sac is thus described by Farre: "Along the lower surface of the vestibular sac is seen running a semicircular line, broader at its upper than its lower extremity (Fig. 58, b). This part is more easily examined after the sand has been washed away by agitation under water. It is then seen, with a power of 18-linear, to consist of several rows of ciliated processes, of which one row is more regular and prominent than the rest, and crests the entire margin of the ridge. The processes diminish in size and number on either side, and are in some places seen in groups, but always assume the general form represented in" Fig. 58.

In Astacus there are four rows of hairs. The first are somewhat scattered, and above the otolithes; the second consists of larger hairs, arranged close together; the third and fourth are smaller again, and more scattered. These three rows of hairs are covered by the otolithes. They stand in connection with the terminal fibrils of the acoustic nerve, and through their vibrations the sense of sound is supposed to be conveyed. In the lobster Hensen counted 548 auditory hairs. He divides auditory hairs of Crustacea into three classes: otolithe hairs; free hairs, enclosed in the auditory sac; and auditory hairs on the outer body surface.

These latter auditory hairs (Fig. 59) are situated over an orifice in the chitinous integument, and stand in direct communication with a fibril from the nerve; the stem of the hair does not rest directly on the chitinous integument, but is supported by a delicate membrane, which is sometimes dilated at the base; the edge of the chitine at one side of the hair is raised into a tooth; lastly, according to Hensen, each auditory hair possesses a sort of appendage, or languette, to which the nerve is attached.

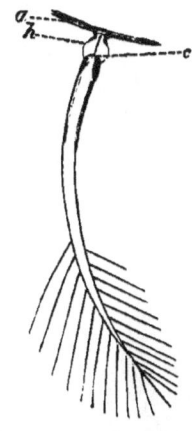

Fig. 60. — Auditory hair of the crab (*Carcinus mænus*), × 500. *a*, Skin; *c*, nerve; *h*, delicate intermediary membrane or hinge (after Hensen).

As far as details are concerned—the form of the sac, the number, form, and arrangement of the hairs, etc.—the auditory organs of the Crustacea offer endless variations in the different species, while very constant in each.

In the higher groups the auditory sac is always at the base of the small antennæ. In one of the lower forms, however—the curious genus Mysis—the ear is situated in the tail.

The genus Mysis (Fig. 61) is a group of Crustaceans, in outward appearance very like shrimps, but differing in the absence of external gills, and in the structure of the legs and other particulars, so that it is placed in a different family. Frey and Leuckart, moreover, made the interesting discovery that it possesses two ears *in its tail*.

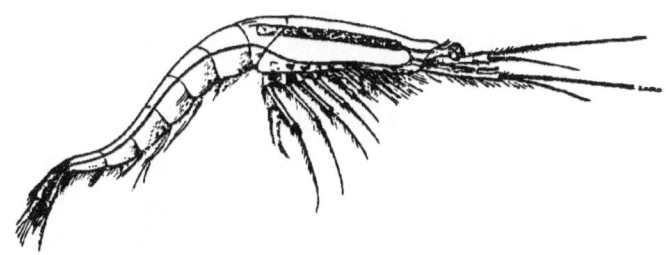

Fig. 61.—Mysis (after Frey and Leuckart).

The tail, like that of a lobster, consists of five flaps. In each of the two smaller flaps is an oval sac (Fig. 62) containing a single, lens-shaped otolithe, consisting of a calcareous matter embedded in an organic substance. That Crustacea do, as a matter of fact, possess the power of perceiving sounds, there can be no doubt. Hensen himself has made various experiments on the subject. Moreover, strychnine possesses the peculiar property of augmenting the reflex power of the nervous centres. Taking advantage of this, Hensen placed some shrimps in sea-water containing strychnine. He then found that they became extremely sensitive to even very slight noises. Further than this, Hensen availed himself of Helmholtz's researches on the perception of sound, and, suspecting that the different hairs might be affected by different notes, found that was actually the case.

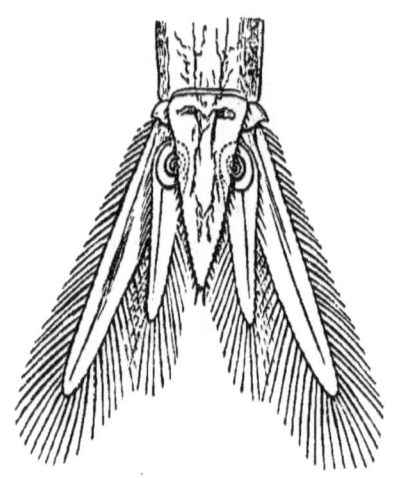

Fig. 62.—Tail of *Mysis vulgaris*, showing the auditory organ.

The vibration of the hairs is mechanical, not depending on the life of the animal. Hensen took a Mysis, and fixed it in such a position that he could watch particular hairs with a microscope. He then sounded a scale; to most of the notes the hair remained entirely passive, but to some one it responded so violently and vibrated so rapidly as to become invisible. When the note ceased, the hair became quiet; as soon as it was resounded, the hair at once began to vibrate again. Other hairs in the same way responded to other notes. The relation of the hairs to particular notes is probably determined by various conditions; for instance, by its length, thickness, etc.

That these plumose hairs, then, really serve for hearing may be inferred, not only from their structure and position, but also from the observed fact that they respond to sound-vibrations.

Hensen's observations * have been repeated and verified by Helmholtz.

THE ORGANS OF HEARING IN INSECTS.

I now pass on to insects. There has been great difference of opinion as to the seat of the organ of hearing in this group.

The antennæ have, as already mentioned, been regarded as ears by many distinguished authorities, including Sulzer, Scarpa, Schneider, Bolk-Hausen, Bonsdorff, Carus, Strauss-Dürkheim, Oken, Burmeister, Kirby and Spence, Newport, Landois, Hicks, Wolff and Graber, who have supported their opinion by numerous observations.

Kirby states that once "a little moth was reposing upon my window; I made a quiet, not loud, but distinct noise: the antennæ nearest to me immediately moved towards me. I repeated the noise at least a dozen times, and it was followed every time by the same motion of that organ, till at length the insect, being alarmed, became more agitated and violent in its motions." And again: "I was once observing the motions of an Apion (a small weevil) under a pocket microscope; on seeing me it receded. Upon my making a slight but distinct noise, its antennæ started. I repeated the noise several times, and invariably with the same effect." †

* "Sensations of Tone."
† Introduction to "Entomology," Kirby and Spence, vol. iv.

Among beetles, the genus Copris, "particularly," says Newport, "*Copris molossus*, in which I first remarked it, have the antennæ composed of ten joints, the last three of which form the knob or club with which it is surmounted.

" When the insect is in motion, these plates or auditory organs, if we may be allowed so to call them, are extended as wide as possible, as if to direct the insect in its course; but upon the occurrence of any loud but sudden noise are instantly closed, and the antennæ retracted as if injured by the percussion, while the insect itself stops and assumes the appearance of death. A similar use of the antennæ is made by another family, Geotrupidæ, which also act in the same manner under like circumstances.

*   *   *   *   *

"These facts, connected with the previous experiments, have convinced me," he says, "that the antennæ in all insects are the auditory organs, whatever may be their particular structure; and that, however this is varied, it is appropriated to the perception and transmission of sound." †

Will has made some interesting observations on some of the Longicorn beetles (Cerambyx), which tend to confirm this view. These insects produce a low shrill sound by rubbing together the prothorax and the mesothorax. The posterior edge of the prothorax bears a toothed ridge, and the anterior end of the mesothorax a roughened surface, and when these are rubbed together, a sound is produced something like that made by rubbing a quill on a fine file.

* Newport, "On the Antennæ of Insects," *Transactions of the Entomological Society*, 1836-40, vol. ii.

Will took a pair of Cerambyx (beetles), put the female in a box, and the male on a table at a distance of about fifteen centimetres (four inches). They were at first a little restless, but are naturally calm insects, and soon became quiet, resting as usual with the antennæ half extended. The male evidently was not conscious of the presence of the female. Will then touched the female with a long needle, and she began to stridulate. At the first sound the male became restless, extended his antennæ, moving them round and round as if to determine from which direction the sound came, and then marched straight towards the female. Will repeated this experiment many times, and with different individuals, but always with the same result. As the male took no notice of the female until she began to stridulate, it is evident that he was not guided by smell. From the manner in which the Cerambyx was obviously made aware of the presence of the female by the sound, Will considered it clearly proved that in this case he was guided by the sense of hearing.

Will has also repeated with these insects the experiments I made with ants, bees, and wasps, and found that they took no notice whatever of ordinary noises; but when he imitated their own sounds with a quill and a fine file, their attention was excited—they extended their antennæ as before, but evidently perceived the difference, for they appeared alarmed, and endeavoured to escape.[*]

Hicks in 1859 justly observed that, "Whoever has observed a tranquilly proceeding Capricorn beetle which is suddenly surprised by a loud sound, will have seen

[*] Will, "Das Geschmacksorgan der Insekten," *Zeit. für. Wiss. Zool.*, 1885.

how immovably outward it spread its antennæ, and holds them porrect, as it were with great attention, as long as it listens, and how carefully the insect proceeds in its course when it conceives that no danger threatens it from the unusual noise." *

Other similar observations might be quoted, but these sufficiently indicate that in some insects, at any rate, the organs of hearing are situated in the antennæ.

On the other hand, Lehmann long ago observed that the house cricket (*Acheta domestica*), when deprived of its antennæ, remained as sensitive to sounds as previously. This is quite correct; and yet, if a cricket be decapitated, and a shrill noise be made near the head, the antennæ are thrown into vibration by each sound.

In fact, not only do the highest authorities differ, but the observations themselves appear at first sight to be contradictory. The explanation seems to be that the sense of hearing is not confined to one spot. That the antennæ do serve as ears, at least in some insects, the evidence leaves, I think, no room for doubt. But there is no reason, in the nature of things, why the sense of hearing should be confined to one part of the body. Taste, indeed, would be useless except in or near the mouth, and almost the same may be said of smell. But the sense of touch is spread, in greater or less perfection, over the whole skin. Indeed, there is among the lower animals a great tendency to repetition, and not least so amongst insects. The body consists normally of a number of segments, each with a pair of appendages and a ganglion. There are three pairs of legs; two pairs of jaws, opening, not vertically,

* *Transactions of the Linnean Society*, vol. xxii.

as ours do, but laterally; several pairs of breathing-holes arranged along the sides of the body; and two kinds of eyes. Moreover, unquestionable organs of sense occur in very different parts of the body. The Crustacean genus Mysis, as already mentioned, has ears in its tail; one group of sea-worms (the Polyophthalmata) have a pair of eyes on each segment of the body.

Of Amphicorine, a small worm of our coasts, M. de Quatrefages says that often,* "C'est la queue qui marche la première, explorant évidemment le terrain avec une grande activité et donnant autant de signes d'intelligence et de spontanéité que pourrait le faire la partie antérieure du corps. . . . Cette queue porte à son extremité un disque élargi sur lequel sont placés deux points rouges. . . . Je ne mets nullement en doute que ces points ne soient en effet des organes de vision." He was not able, indeed, to make out their finer structure. On the other hand, the lateral eyes of the Polyophthalmata possess a well-formed lens.

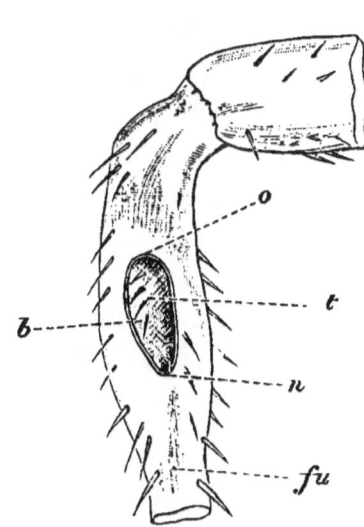

Fig. 63.—Part of leg of Grasshopper (Gryllus); after Graber. o, t, n, b, Tympanum.

We need not, then, assume that the organs of hearing in insects must necessarily be in the head, or, indeed, that they need be concentrated in one part of the body.

It had long been known that grasshoppers and

* *Ann. des Sci. Nat.*, 1850.

crickets have on their anterior legs two peculiar, glassy, generally more or less oval, drumlike structures; but these were supposed by the older entomologists to serve as resonators, and to reinforce or intensify the well-known chirping sounds which they produce.

. Johannes Müller was the first who suggested that these drums, or tympana, act like the tympanum of our own ears, and that they are really the external parts of a true auditory apparatus. That any animal should have its ears in its legs sounds, no doubt, *à priori* very unlikely, and hence probably the true function of this organ was so long unsuspected. That it is, however, a true ear the following particulars, taken especially from the memoirs of Müller,* Siebold,† Leydig,‡ Hensen,§ Graber,‖ and Schmidt,¶ conclusively prove.

The Leaping Orthoptera fall into three well-marked groups: the locusts (Locustidæ), which have short antennæ; the crickets (Achetidæ), which have long antennæ, and the wings flat on the back; and, thirdly, the Gryllidæ, or grasshoppers (as I may perhaps call them), which have also long antennæ, but in which the wings are sloping. This is the nomenclature adopted by English authorities, such as Westwood; but unfortunately many foreign entomologists call the

* "Zur vergleichenden Physiologie des Gesichtsinnes." 1826.

† "Ueber die Stimm und Gehörorgane der Orthopteren," *Arch. für Natur geschichte*, 1844.

‡ "Ueber Geruchs-und Gehörorgane der Krebse und Insekten," *Reicherts' Arch. für Anat.*, 1860.

§ "Ueber das Gehörorgan von Locusta," *Zeit. für Wiss. Zool.*, 1866.

‖ "Die Tympanalen Sinnesapparate der Orthopteren," *Arch. für Mic. Anat.*, vol. xx., 1875.

¶ "Die Gehörorgane der Heuschrecken," *Arch. für Mic. Anat.*, vol. xi.

crickets Gryllidæ, the grasshoppers Locustidæ, and the locusts Acridiidæ.*

In grasshoppers (Gryllidæ) and crickets (Achetidæ) the auditory organ lies in the tibia of the anterior leg, on both sides of which there is a disc (Fig. 63), generally more or less oval in form, and differing from the rest of the surface in consisting of a thin, tense, shining membrane, surrounded wholly or partially by a sort of frame or ridge. In some species the two tympana are similar in form; in others they differ. For instance, in the field cricket, the hinder tympanum is elliptic, the front one nearly circular in outline.

In many of the Gryllidæ, the tympana are protected by a fold of the skin, which projects more or less over them. The corresponding spiracle is also specially modified in the stridulating locusts, while in those which are dumb it is formed in the same manner as the others.

The tympana are not always present, and it is an additional reason for regarding them as auditory organs, that both among the Achetidæ and the Gryllidæ, in those species which possess no stridulating organs, the tympana are also wanting.†

* The destructive "locust" of the East, which is so numerous that in one year our Government[1] in Cyprus destroyed no less than 150,000,000,000 of eggs, and whose ravages are used in Eastern poetry as types of destructiveness, has short antennæ, and belongs to the first division; to which, therefore, English entomologists apply the name Locusta, while our foreign friends, on the contrary, apply the name to a totally different insect. However, I merely refer to this now, to explain why the terms I have used do not in all cases agree with those adopted by the observers to whom I am referring.

† This rule seems, however, not to be entirely without exceptions. At least, Aspidonotus and Hetrodes are said to possess tympana, but

_____

[1] Report on the Locust Campaign, Parl. Paper, 5250 of 1888.

Graber regards the covered tympana as a development from the open ones, and suggests that in time to come the species in which the tympana are now exposed may develop a covering fold.

If now we examine the interior of the leg, the trachea or air-tube will be found to be remarkably modified. Upon entering the tibia it immediately enlarges and divides into two branches, which reunite lower down. To supply air to this wide trachea the corresponding spiracle, or breathing-hole, is considerably enlarged, while in the dumb species it is only of the usual size. An idea of the form of the trachea will be given by Fig. 69, which, however, represents the anterior tibia of an ant, where these tracheæ are less considerably enlarged, and where one of the branches is much smaller than the other, while in locusts they are nearly equal in width, and one lies against each tympanum. The enlarged trachea occupies a considerable part of the tibia, and its wall is closely applied to the tympanum, which thus has air on both sides of it; the open air on the outer, the air of the trachea on its inner surface. In fact, the trachea acts like the Eustachian tube in our own ear; it maintains an equilibrium of pressure

no stridulating apparatus. For instance, in the following forms, both the stridulating apparatus and the tympana are absent, viz.:—

Among the Œcanthidæ: Phalangopsis and Gryllomorpha (both are wingless).

    „   Platydactylidæ: Metrypa and Parametrypa (both wingless).

    „   Tettigonidæ: Trigonidium.

    „   Gryllidæ: *Gryllus apterus, Parabrachytrupes Australis,* and Apiotarsus (all wingless).

    „   Gryllotalpidæ: *Tridactylus apicalis.*

    „   Mogoplistidæ: Mogoplistes, Myrmecophila, Physoblemma (all wingless), and Cacoplistes.

on each side of the tympanum, and enables it freely
to transmit the atmospheric vibrations.

These tracheæ, though formed on a similar plan,
present many variations, corresponding to those of
the tympana, and showing that the tympana and
the tracheæ stand in intimate connection with one
another. For instance, in those species where the
tympana are equal, the tracheæ are so likewise; in
Gryllotalpa, where the front tympanum only is developed, though both tracheal branches are present, the
front one is much larger than the other; and where
there is no tympanum, the trachea remains comparatively small, and even in some cases, according to
Graber, undivided.

The tibia is thus divided into three parts, as shown
in the diagram (Fig. 64), the central
portion being occupied by the two
tracheæ (Fig. 64, *tr, tr*).

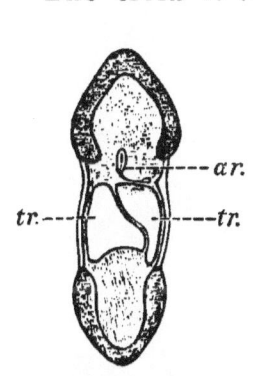

Of the other two spaces, one (the
lower one in the figure) is occupied
by the muscles, nerves, etc., while
the other is mostly filled with blood,
which thus surrounds and bathes the
auditory vesicles and rods (*ar*).

The acoustic nerve—which, next
to the optic, is the thickest in the
body—divides soon after entering
the tibia into two branches; the one
forming almost immediately a ganglion, the supra-
tympanal ganglion, to which I shall refer again presently; the other passing down to the tympanum,
where it expands into an elongated flat ganglion, known
after its discoverer as the organ of Siebold (Fig. 65),
and closely applied to the anterior tracheæ.

It is well shown in Fig. 65, taken from Graber. At the upper part of the ganglion is a group terminating below in a single row of vesicles, the first few of which

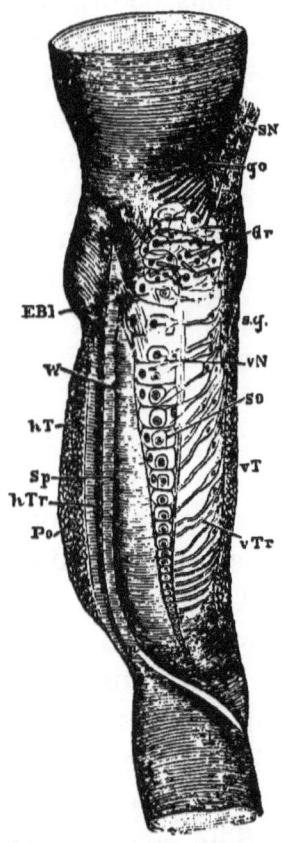

Fig. 65.—The tracheæ and nerve-end organs from the tibia (leg) of a grasshopper (*Ephippigera vitium*); after Graber. *EBl*, Terminal vesicles of Siebold's organ; *hT*, hinder tympanum; *Sp*, space between the tracheæ; *hTr*, hinder branch of the trachea; *SN*, nerves of the organ of Siebold; *go*, supra-tympanal ganglion; *Gr*, group of vesicles of the organ of Siebold; *vN*, connecting nerve-fibrils between the ganglionic cells and the terminal vesicles; *So*, nerve terminations of the organ of Siebold; *vT*, front tympanum; *vTr*, front branch of the trachea.

are approximately equal, but which subsequently diminish regularly in size. Each of these vesicles is connected with the nerve by a fibril (Fig. 65, *vN*), and contains an auditory rod (Fig. 66).

One of these auditory rods is shown in Fig. 66, and the general arrangement is shown in the subjoined diagrammatic figure (Fig. 67). The rods were first described by Siebold, who considered them to be auditory from their association with the stridulating organs. They have since been discovered in many other insects, and may be regarded as specially characteristic of the acoustic organs of insects. They are brightly refractive, more or less elongated, slightly club-shaped, hollow (in which they differ from the retinal rods), and terminate, in Graber's opinion,* in a separate end-piece (Fig. 66, *ko*). In different insects, besides being in some cases more elongated than in others, they present various minor modifications in form, but are nearly uniform in size—about ·016 mm.; being as large, for instance, in the young larva of a Tabanus (2 mm. long) as in much larger insects. They are, as we shall see, widely distributed in insects, but as yet unknown in other animals.

Fig. 66.—Auditory rod of a grasshopper, *Gryllus viridissimus* (after Graber, Fig. 90). *fd'*, Auditory rod; *ko*, terminal piece.

At the upper part of the tibial organ of Ephippigera there is, as already mentioned, a group of cells, and below them a single row (Fig. 65) of cells gradually diminishing in size from above downwards. One cannot but ask one's self whether the gradually diminishing size of the cells in the organ of Siebold (Fig. 66) may not have reference to the perception of different

* Graber, "Die chordotonalen Sinnesorgane und das Gehor der Insekten," *Arch. für Mic. Anat.*, 1882.

notes, as is the case with the series of diminishing arches in the organ of Corti (*ante*, p. 80) of our own ears.

I have already alluded to the supra-tympanal ganglion; this also terminates in a number of vesicles

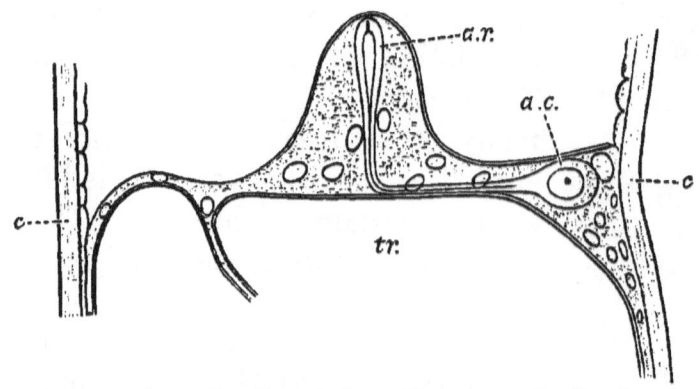

Fig, 67.—Diagram of a section through the auditory organ of a Grasshopper (Meco-nema). *c*, cuticle; *a.r*, auditory rod; *a.c*, auditory cell; *tr*, tracheæ.

containing auditory rods, which are said to be somewhat more elongated than those in the organ of Siebold.

The arrangement of the organ is very curious, and will best be understood by reference to Fig. 68.

The great auditory nerve, as already mentioned, bifurcates almost immediately after entering the tibia, and one of the branches swell into a ganglion: from this ganglion proceed fibres which enlarge into vesicles (Fig. 68), each containing an auditory rod; and then again contract, approximate into a close bundle, and coalesce with the hypoderm (inner skin) of the wall of the tibia. The supra-tympanal organ of the crickets closely resembles that of the grasshoppers, while, on the other hand, they appear entirely to want the organ of Siebold (Fig. 65). This is a very remarkable difference to exist in two organs otherwise so similar.

There appear to be two ways in which the atmospheric

vibrations may be communicated to the nerve: either the vibrations of the tympanum may act upon the air in the tracheæ, and so upon the auditory rods, or the air in the tracheæ may remain passive, and the vibrations may act upon the auditory rods through the fluid in the anterior chamber of the leg. The fact that the auditory rod is turned away from the tracheæ would seem to favour this hypothesis.

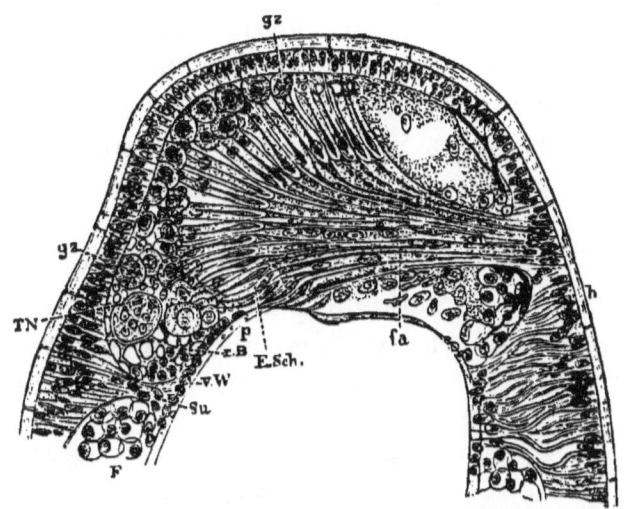

Fig. 68.—Outer part of a section through the tibia of a *Gryllus viridissimus* (after Graber). *h*, Hind surface of leg; *p*, wall of trachea; *F*, fat bodies; *Su*, suspensor of the trachea; *vW*, tracheal wall; *TN*, nerve; *gz*, ganglionic cells; *rR*, tissue connecting the ganglionic cells; *E.Sch.*, end tubes of the ganglionic cells, each containing an auditory rod; *fa*, terminal threads of ditto.

In the true Locustidæ (Acridiodeæ of Graber) the organ of hearing is situated, not in the anterior tibiæ, but in the first segment of the abdomen; externally it is marked by a glistening appearance, and it is oval, or in some cases nearly ear-shaped. It was first noticed by Degeer. Behind the tympanum is a large tracheal sac, as in the families already described, and the tension of the tympanum is regulated by one, or in some cases by two muscles. The tympanum also presents two chitinous or horny thickenings, a small triangular knob, and a larger, somewhat complicated piece, consisting of two processes—a shorter upper, and a longer lower one, making a broad angle with one another.

As in the preceding families, so also in the Locustidæ, the acoustic nerve is in close connection with the tracheæ; it swells into a ganglion, which contains in some species as many as 150 auditory rods, and then, as in the supra-tympanal organ (see p. 105), contracts into a tapering end, which is attached to the small chitinous knob. The auditory rods differ in no respect, as yet ascertained, from those already described.

For many years no structure corresponding to the tibial auditory organ of the Orthoptera was known in any other insect.

In 1877, however, I discovered * in ants a structure which in some remarkable points resembles that of the Orthoptera, and which I described as follows:—"The large trachea of the leg (Fig. 69) is considerably

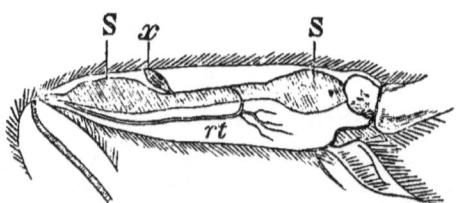

Fig. 69.—Tibia of yellow ant (*Lasius flavus*), × 75. *S, S,* Swellings of large trachea; *rt,* small branch of trachea; *x,* chordotonal organ.

swollen in the tibia, and sends off, shortly after entering the tibia, a branch which, after running for some time parallel to the principal trunk, joins it again.

"Now, I observed that in many other insects the

* Lubbock, "On the Anatomy of Ants," *Microscopical Journal,* 1877.

tracheæ of the tibia are dilated, sometimes with a recurrent branch. The same is the case even in some mites. I will, however, reserve what I have to say on this subject, with reference to other insects, for another occasion, and will at present confine myself to the ants. If we examine the tibia, say of *Lasius flavus*, we shall see that the trachea presents a remarkable arrangement (Fig. 69), which at once reminds us of that which occurs in Gryllus and other Orthoptera. In the femur it has a diameter of about $\frac{1}{3000}$ of an inch; as soon, however, as it enters the tibia, it swells to a diameter of about $\frac{1}{500}$ of an inch, then contracts again to $\frac{1}{800}$, and then again, at the apical extremity of the tibia, once more expands to $\frac{1}{500}$. Moreover, as in Gryllus, so also in Formica, a small branch rises from the upper sac, runs almost straight down the tibia, and falls again into the main trachea just above the lower sac.

"The remarkable sacs (Fig. 69, *S, S*) at the two extremities of the trachea in the tibia may also be well seen in other transparent species, such, for instance, as *Myrmica ruginodis* and *Pheidole megacephala*.

"At the place where the upper tracheal sac contracts (Fig. 69) there is, moreover, a conical striated organ (*x*), which is situated at the back of the leg, just at the apical end of the upper tracheal sac. The broad base lies against the external wall of the leg, and the fibres converge inwards. Indications of bright rods may also be perceived, but I was never able to make them out very clearly."

This closely resembles both in structure and position the supra-tympanal auditory organ of the Orthoptera.

Graber has entirely confirmed this account and discovered some insects in which the structure is more clearly visible than in any which I had examined. Fig. 70 represents part of the tibia of *Isopteryx apicalis*.

These organs do not, however, appear to be universally present. In some very transparent species no trace of them can be found.

But though so similar in structure, and probably in

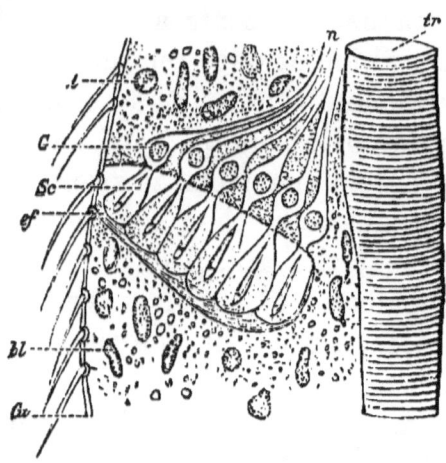

Fig. 70.*—Part of the tibia of *Isopteryx apicalis* (after Graber). *Sc*, Auditory organ; *ef*, terminal filament; *Cu*, cuticle; *G*, ganglion cells; *ef*, terminal filaments; *tr*, trachea; *n*, nerve.

function, it may be doubted whether this tibial organ in the ants can be traced to a common origin with that of the Orthoptera. According to Graber, the direction of the rods is reversed in the two cases, which he regards as clear proofs that they have arisen independently. He is even of opinion that the tympana themselves have originated independently in the different groups of Orthoptera. Moreover, Graber has found this organ in certain insects not only in the anterior, but also in the two other pairs of legs. Indeed, rods of the same character have been found in other regions of the body.

* In this, as in one or two of the other figures, the explanation of some of the lettering appears to be omitted in the original. At least, I have been unable to find it.

As long ago as 1764 Keller * observed that the base
of the curious club-like "halteres," or rudimentary
hind-wings of flies, "est garnie de poils très courts,
où la tige a le plus d'epaisseur près du corps; elle est

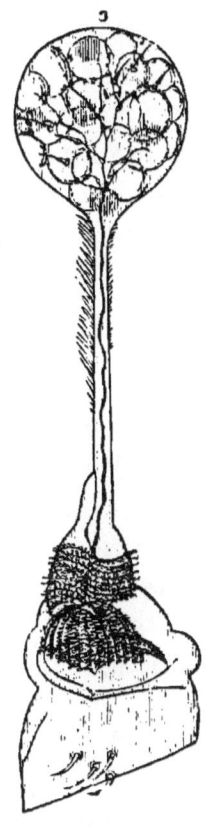

inflexible, et presque garrotté par en
haut de plusieurs nerfs; en un mot, elle
est faite de manière que l'on peut juger
par sa force par les dehors." This
observation remained unnoticed, and no
further description appears to have been
given of the organ until it was redis-
covered by Hicks in 1856, and more
fully described in 1857.†

He found that though in the Diptera
(flies and gnats) the hind wings are
reduced to two minute, club-shaped
organs, they still receive a nerve which
is the largest in the insect, except that
which goes to the eyes. This proves
that they must serve some important
function, and renders it almost certain
that they are the seats of some sense.
He also found at the base of the halteres
a number of "vesicles," arranged in four
groups, and to each of which the nerve
sends a branch, though the mode of preparation which he adopted did not
permit him to see the finer structure of the nerves,
which he figures as mere fine, hard lines. He describes
the "vesicles" as "thin, transparent, hemispherical, or

---

* "Geschichte der gemeinen Stubenfliege," 1764. I have not seen
the original, and quote from Hicks's paper.
† *Transactions of the Linnean Society*, vol. xvii.

more nearly spherical projections from the cuticular surface," and as placed in rows. The number and arrangement differ in different species: the blowfly (*Sarcophaga carnaria*) has ten rows, *Syrphus luniger* as many as twenty.

These organs have recently been again examined by Bolles Lee.* The vesicles are, according to him, undoubtedly perforated, contain a minute hair, and those of the upper groups are protected by hoods of chitine. He inclines to correlate them with the similar antennal organs, which he regards as olfactory. His view of the minute structure of these rods differs from that of previous authors, and the subject requires further study.

He finds, moreover, that the sense-organ containing the rods has nothing to do with the vesicular plates, but that they are attached to the cuticle in a different place, and where it presents no special modification.

The numerous small membranes in the halteres of insects seem to bear somewhat the same relation to the single tympanum of, say, the locust, as the many-faceted eyes do to those with a single cornea. The head of the halteres is divided into two separate spaces by a membrane composed of elongated hypodermal cells. The upper part contains a number of large vesicular cells, like those which are in connection with the ends of the tracheæ. It does not appear to contain any special sense-organ, and, in fact, the large nerve is almost entirely devoted to the sense-organs at the base. M. Bolles Lee suggests that it perhaps serves principally to regulate the pressure on these delicate structures.

* "Les Balanciers des Diptères," *Recueil Zool. Suisse*, 1885.

7

Special sense-organs occur also on the wings of other insects. Hicks found them "most perfect in the Diptera, next so in the Coleoptera, rather less so in the Lepidoptera, but slightly developed in the Neuroptera, scarcely at all in the Orthoptera (though this assertion may be hereafter modified), and that only a trace of them exists in the Hemiptera." They are similarly constituted and equally developed in both sexes. Hicks regarded them as organs of smell. Leydig,* on the contrary, considered them as auditory organs. His mode of preparation displayed better the structure of the nerves, and he found that they end in peculiar, club-shaped rods (*Stäbchen oder Stafle*), closely resembling those in the ears of Orthoptera. He observes that, as in the case of the tibial auditory rods of Orthoptera these rods are of two sorts, which are arranged separately, those in one part of the organs being shorter and blunter, those in another more pointed and elongated. Bolles Lee, on the contrary, considers that the supposed existence of two forms, pointed and rounded, is merely due to an optical deception, and that in reality they are all similar. Leydig also observed in some cases that the rods were thrown into fine ridges. He found also somewhat similar papillæ on the front wings of certain insects, but could not detect in them the characteristic nerve-cnds. It must be confessed that the base of the wing would not seem a convenient place for an organ of hearing. The movements of the wing, it might well be supposed, would interfere with any delicate sensations. Still, this objection would apply to almost any sense being thus placed.

"Auditory rods" are now, moreover, known to occur

* *Müller's Archiv.*, 1860.

in other parts of the body; for instance, they have been discovered in the antennæ of a water-beetle (Dytiscus) and of Telephorus by Hicks, Leydig, and Graber, and in the body segments of several larvæ by Leydig, Weissmann, Graber, Grobben, and Bolles Lee. In the larva of Dytiscus, indeed, they have been observed in the body, antennæ, palpi, under lip, and legs. Moreover, while, as we have seen, in the tibiæ of Orthoptera and the halteres of flies they are numerous, in some of these cases they are few, sometimes, indeed, only a single rod being present, as discovered by Grobben in Ptychoptera.* Nevertheless the evidence that they are really acoustic organs is, in the case of the Orthoptera, so strong, their structure is so peculiar, and the gradation of these organs from the most complex to the most simple is so complete, that it seems reasonable to attribute to them the same function.

Moreover, as regards the very simplest forms there is another consideration pointing to this conclusion. We have seen that in the Orthoptera the terminal filaments close up, and are attached to the skin. Now, it seems to be a very general rule, in reference to these organs, that they are attached to the skin at two points, between which is situated the attachment of the nerve. These points, moreover, are so selected as to be maintained at the same distance from one another, thus preserving an equable tension in the connecting filament.

Fig. 72, for instance, represents part of one segment of the body of the larva of a gnat (Corethra). This larva is as transparent as glass, and very common in ponds, a most beautiful and instructive microscopic object. EG is the ganglion; a is the nerve in question, which

---

* *Sitz. der K. Akad. der Wiss. Wien*, 1876.

swells into a little triangular ganglion at g; from g the auditory organ runs straight to the skin at e, and contains two or three auditory rods (not, however, shown in the figure) at the point Chs; in the opposite direction, a fine ligament passes from g to the

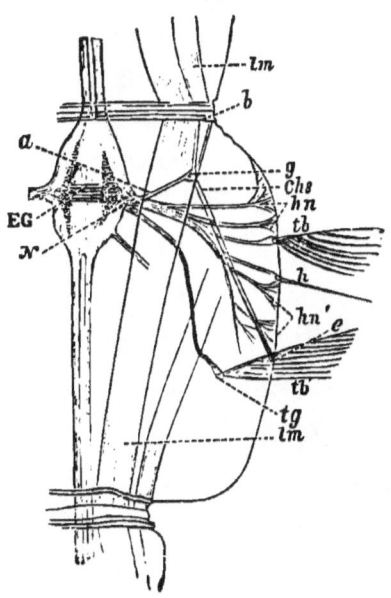

Fig. 72.—Right half of eighth segment of the body of the larva of a gnat (*Corethra plumicornis*); after Graber. *EG*. Ganglia; *N*, nerve; *g*, auditory ganglion; *gb* auditory ligament; *Chs*, auditory rods; *a*, auditory nerve; *e*, attachment of auditory organ to the skin; *b*, attachment of auditory ligament to the skin; *hn*, *hn'*, termination of skin-nerve; *tb*, plumose tactile hair; *h*, simple hair; *tg*, ganglion of tactile hair; *lm*, longitudinal muscle.

skin at b. Hence the organ ge is suspended in a certain state of tension, and is favourably situated to receive even very fine vibrations.*

There are, as we have seen, a large number of observations which point to the antennæ as organs of hearing, and many more might have been given. When we come to consider, however, the anatomical provision which renders the perception of sound

* Similar organs occur in other insects, as, for instance, in Ptychoptera.

possible, we are met by great difficulties. The evidence is, I think, conclusive that the antennæ are olfactory as well as tactile organs, and I believe that they serve also as organs of hearing. There are, moreover, as shown in the last chapter, various remarkable structures in the antennæ, and I have given reasons for thinking some of them to be the seat of the sense of smell. Which, if any, of the remainder convey the sense of sound, it is not easy to determine. I have suggested that Hicks's bottles (Fig. 43) may act as microscopic stethoscopes; * but they occur, so far as we at present know, only in ants and certain bees.

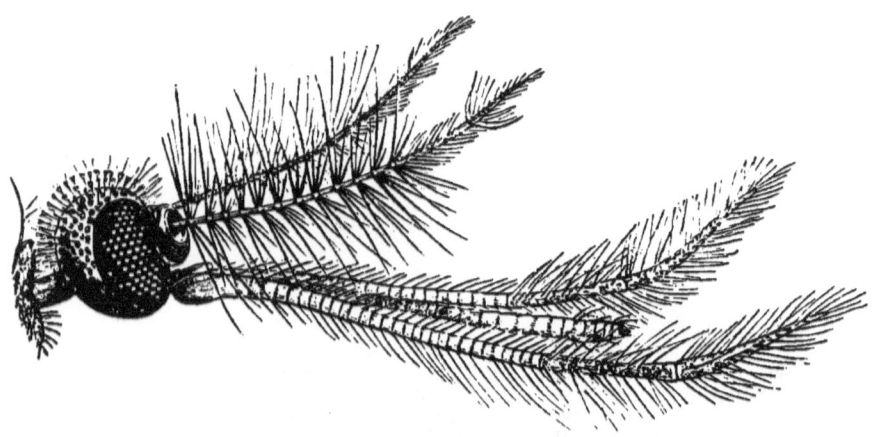

Fig. 73.—Head of gnat.

That some of the antennal hairs are auditory can, I think, no longer be doubted. Johnson, whose figure I give (Fig. 73), suggested† in 1855 that the hairs on the antennæ of gnats serve for hearing. Mayer also,‡

* I am glad to see that Leydig, who, however, does not appear to have read either Hicks's paper or mine, also regards these as chordotonal organs (*Zool. Anz.*, 1886).

† *Quarterly Journal of Microscopical Science*, 1855.

‡ *American Journal of Science and Arts*, 1874.

led by the observations of Hensen, has made similar experiments with the mosquito, the male of which has beautifully feathered antennæ. He fastened one down on a glass slide, and then sounded a series of tuning-forks. With an Ut$_4$ fork of 512 vibrations per second he found that some of the hairs were thrown into vigorous movement, while others remained nearly stationary. The lower (Ut$_3$) and higher (Ut$_5$) harmonics of Ut$_4$ also caused more vibration than any intermediate notes. These hairs, then, are specially tuned so as to respond to vibrations numbering 512 per second. Other hairs vibrated to other notes, extending through the middle and next higher octave of the piano. Mayer then made large wooden models of these hairs, and, on counting the number of vibrations they made when they were clamped at one end and then drawn on one side, he found that it " coincided with the ratio existing between the numbers of vibrations of the forks to which co-vibrated the fibrils." It is interesting that the hum of the female gnat corresponds nearly to this note, and would consequently set the hairs in vibration.

Moreover, those auditory hairs are most affected which are at right angles to the direction from which the sound comes. Hence, from the position of the antennæ and the hairs, a sound will act most intensely if it is directly in front of the head. Suppose, then, a male gnat hears the hum of a female at some little distance. Perhaps the sound affects one antenna more than the other. He turns his head until the two antennæ are equally affected, and is thus able to direct his flight straight towards the female.

The auditory organs of insects, then, are situated in

different insects in different parts of the body, and there is strong reason to believe that even in the same animal the sensitiveness to sounds is not necessarily confined to one part. In the cricket, for instance, the sense of hearing appears to be seated partly in the antennæ, and partly in the anterior legs. In other cases, as in Corethra, the division appears to be carried still further, and a "chordotonal" organ occurs in each of several segments.

No doubt the multiplication of complex organs, like our ears, arranged as they are to appreciate a great variety of sounds, would be so great a waste that any theory implying such a state of things would be quite untenable; but with simple organs, such, for instance, as that of Corethra * (gnat; Fig. 72), the case is different, and there would seem to be an obvious advantage in such organs occurring in different parts of the body, ready to receive sound-waves coming from different directions. Moreover, the different organs exist; they do not appear to be organs of touch, yet they are clearly organs of sense, and that sense, whatever it be, whether hearing or any other, and though it may well be simple, and even perhaps confused, must be seated in various parts of the body. The fact of their being so distributed does not make it more improbable that they should be organs of hearing, than of any other sense.

At the same time, it is an interesting result of recent investigations that the auditory organs of insects are not only situated in various parts of the body, but are constructed on such different principles.

* Where, however, the number does not approach to that in certain Medusæ (see *ante*, p. 84).

CHAPTER VI.

IT might at first sight seem easy enough to answer the question whether an animal can see or not. In reality, however, the problem is by no means so simple. We find, in fact, every gradation from the mere power of distinguishing a difference between light and darkness up to the perception of form and colour which we ourselves enjoy.

The undifferentiated tissues of the lower animals, and even of plants, are, as we all know, affected in a marked manner by the action of light.

But to see, in the sense of perceiving the forms of objects, an animal must possess some apparatus by means of which—firstly, the light coming from different points, a, b, c, d, e, etc., is caused to act on separate parts of the retina in the same relative positions; and secondly, by means of which these points of the retina can be protected from the light coming in other directions.

There are three modes in which it is theoretically possible that this might be effected.

Firstly, let S S' be an opaque screen, with a small orifice at o. Let a b c d e be a body in front of the screen. In this case the rays from the point c can pass straight through the orifice o, and fall on the retina of an eye, or on a flat surface at c'. There is no other direction in which the rays from c could pass through o. In the same way, the light from a would fall on the point a', that from b on b', from d on d', and e on e'.

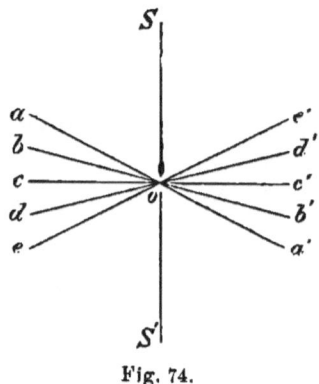

Fig. 74.

The results which would be given in this way would be, however, very imperfect, and, as a matter of fact, no eye constructed on this system is known to exist.

Secondly, let a number of transparent tubes or cones with opaque walls be ranged side by side in front of the retina, and separated from one another by black pigment. In this case the only light which can reach the optic nerve will be that which falls on any given tube in the direction of its axis.

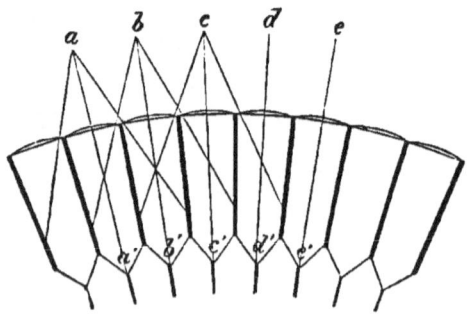

Fig. 75.

For instance, in Fig. 75 the light from a will pass to a', that from b to b', that from c to c', and so on. The light from c, which falls on the other tubes, will not reach the nerve, but will impinge on the sides and be absorbed by the pigment. Thus, though the light from *c* will illuminate the whole surface of the eye, it will only affect the nerve at *c'*.

In this mode of vision, which was first clearly explained by Johannes Müller, the distinctness of the image will be greater in proportion to the number of separate cones. "An image," he says.* "formed by several thousand separate points, of which each corresponds to a distinct field of vision in the external world, will resemble a piece of mosaic work, and a better idea cannot be conceived of the image of external objects which will be depicted on the retina of beings endowed with such organs of vision, than by comparing it with perfect work of that kind."

There is, it will presently be seen, reason to suppose that the compound eyes of insects, crustacea, and some molluscs, are constructed on this plan.

Thirdly, let *L* (Fig. 76) be a lens of such a form

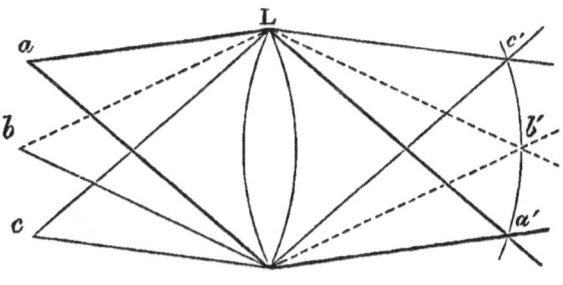

F.g. 76.

that all the light which falls upon its surface from the point *a* is re-collected at the point *a'*, that from *b* at *b'*, from *c* at *c'*, and so on. If now other light be excluded,

* "Phys. of the Senses," by Johannes Müller, translated by Dr. Baly.

an image of *a b c* will be thrown on a screen or on a retina at *a′ b′ c′*. The image, it will be observed, is necessarily reversed. This is the form of eye which we possess ourselves: it is, in fact, a camera obscura. It is that of all the higher animals, of most molluscs, the ocelli of insects, etc.

Fig. 77, taken from Helmholtz, will give an idea of the manner in which we see.

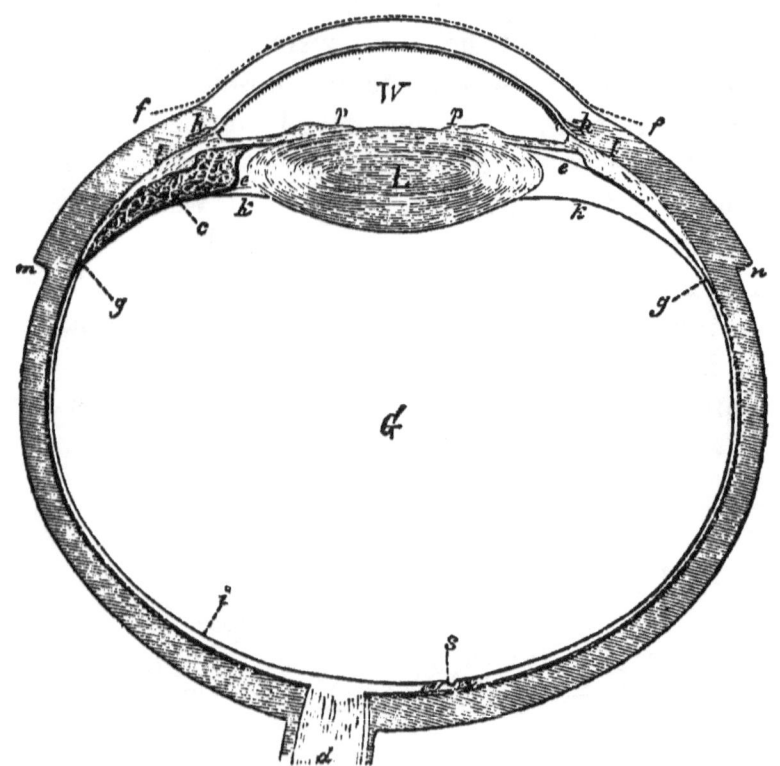

Fig. 77.—*G*, Vitreous humor; *L*, lens; *W*, aqueous humor; *c*, ciliary process; *d*, optic nerve; *e e*, suspensory ligament; *k k*, hyaloid membrane; *f f*, *h h*, cornea; *g g*, choroid; *i*, retina; *l l*, ciliary muscle; *m f*, *n f*, sclerotic coat; *p p*, iris; *s*, the yellow spot.

The eyeball is surrounded by a dense fibrous membrane, the sclerotic coat, or *white of the eye, m f, n f,* which passes in front into the glassy, transparent cornea, $f\,f$, $h\,h$; the greater part of the centre of the eye is occupied by a clear gelatinous mass, the vitreous humor, G, in front of which is the lens, L; while between the lens and the cornea is the aqueous humor, W. The sclerotic coat is lined at the back of the eye by a delicate, vascular, and pigmented membrane—the choroid, $g\,g$, so called from the great number of blood-vessels which it contains; in front this membrane joins the iris, $p\,p$, which leaves a central opening, the pupil, so called from the little image of ourselves, which we see reflected from an eye when we look into it. The iris gives its colour to the eye, its posterior membrane containing pigment-cells; if these are few in number, it appears blue, from the layer behind shining through, and the greater the number of these cells the deeper the colour. $e\,e$, is a peculiar membrane, which serves to retain the lens in its place. The optic nerve, d, enters at the back of the eye, and, spreading out on all sides, forms the retina, i, of which one spot, s, *the yellow spot*, is pre-eminently sensitive. The action of the eye resembles that of a camera obscura, and, as shown in Fig. 76, the rays which fall upon it are refracted so as to form a reversed picture on the back of the eye.

The retina (Fig. 78) is very complicated, and, though no thicker than a sheet of thin paper, consists of no less than nine separate layers, the innermost (Figs. 78, 79) being the rods and cones, which are the immediate recipients of the undulations of light. Fig. 79 represents the rods and cones isolated and somewhat more enlarged.

The number of rods and cones in the human eye is enormous. At a moderate computation the cones may be estimated at over 3,000,000; and the rods at 30,000,000.*

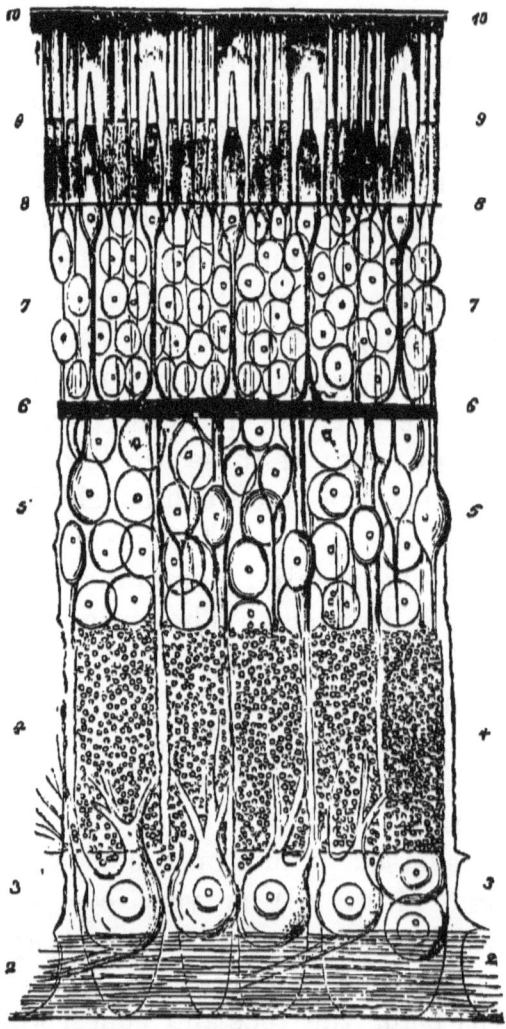

Fig. 78.—Section through the retina (after Max Schultze). Beginning from the outside, 1, limitary membrane; 2, layer of nerve-fibres; 3, layer of nerve-cells; 4, nuclear layer; 5, inner nuclear layer; 6, intermediate nuclear layer; 7, outer nuclear layer; 8, posterior membrane; 9, layer of small rods and cones; 10, choroid.

* Sulzer estimates the cones at 3,360,000; Krause places the cones at 7,000,000, the rods at 130,000,000; but Professor M. Foster tells me that he thinks the latter figure is too high.

It will be observed that the nerve does not, as one might naturally have expected, enter the eye and then spread itself out at the back of the retina; but, on the contrary, pierces the retina and spreads itself out on the front, so that the cones and rods look inwards, and not outwards—towards the back of the eye, and not at the object itself. In fact, we do not look outwards at the actual object, but we see the object as reflected from the base of our own eye.

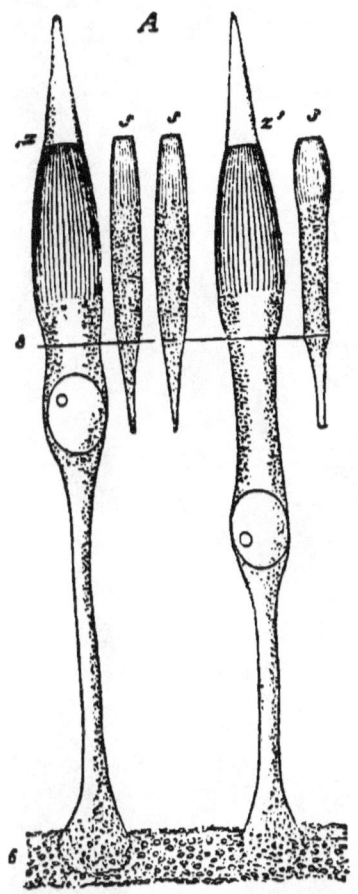

Fig. 79.—*A*, Inner segments of rods (*s, s, s*) and cones (*z, z'*) from man, the latter in connection with the cone-granules and fibres as far as the external molecular layer, 6. In the interior of the inner segment of both rod and cone fibrillar structure is visible. × 800.

From the arrangement of the rods in the eyes of vertebrata, then, the light has necessarily to pass through the retina, and is then reflected back on it. This involves some loss of light; on the other hand, it perhaps secures the advantage that the sensitive terminations of the rods and cones can be more readily supplied with blood.

I do not propose to enter into the reason for this peculiar arrangement, which is connected with the development of the eye. But it is so different from what might have been expected, is in itself so interesting, and makes so important a contrast with the form which is general, though not universal among the lower animals, that I think it will not be out of place to mention a very simple and beautiful experiment by which every one can satisfy himself that it is so.

One result is that we have in each eye a blind spot, that at which the nerve enters. Turn the present page, so that the white circle is in front of the left eye and the small cross in front of the right. Then close the right eye, look steadily across at the cross with the left, and move the book slowly backwards and forwards. At one particular distance, about ten inches, the white circle will come opposite the blind spot and will instantaneously disappear. Across an ordinary room, if a man stands in front of a screen, his head may in the same way be made entirely to vanish.

The ordinary vertebrate eye consists of two main divisions: the refractive

Fig. 80.

part, which is a modified portion of the skin; and the

receptive part, which arises from the central nervous system; and the inverted arrangement of the rods is, we can hardly doubt, connected with the development of the eye, though it is not yet, I think, satisfactorily explained.

There is, however, another eye in vertebrates, with reference to which I must say something, and which, though now rudimentary, is most interesting. Our brain contains a small organ, about as large as a hazel-nut, known, from its being shaped somewhat like a cone of a pine, as the pineal gland. Its function has long been a puzzle to physiologists. Descartes suggested that it was perhaps the seat of the soul; and though this idea, of course, could not be entertained, no suggestion even plausible had been made.

So matters stood until quite recently, when a most unexpected light has been thrown upon the question. As long ago as 1829, Brandt, describing the skull of a lizard (*Lacerta agilis*), pointed out that in the centre of the top of the head was a peculiar spot, one of the scales being quite unlike the rest. Leydig[*] subsequently observed that on the head of the slow-worm (*Anguis fragilis*) there is a dark spot surrounding a small unpigmented body immediately over the pineal gland. Rabl-Rückhard,[†] in 1884, again called attention to this structure, and suggested that it might serve for the perception of warmth. Ahlborn,[‡] in the same year, was the first to suggest that it was a rudimentary eye. De Graaf [§] has the merit of dis-

---

[*] "Die Arten der Saurier."

[†] "Entw. des Knochenfischgehirn," *Bericht der Sitz. naturf. Freunde.* Berlin: 1882.

[‡] "Ueber d. Bedeutung der Zirbeldrüse," *Zeit. für Wiss. Zool.,* 1884.

[§] "Zur. Anat. und Ent. der Epi. b. Amphibien und Reptilien," *Zool. Anz.,* 1886.

covering that in the slow-worm the pineal gland is actually modified into a structure resembling an invertebrate eye. This remarkable structure has since been examined in various Reptilia by Mr. Spencer.* It appears to be more highly organized in Hatteria than in any other form yet studied; but the retrogression of the different structures has not proceeded *pari passu*, in some cases the lens, in some the retina, in others the nerve, having been most modified, or having disappeared. In Hatteria and Varanus the eye is very distinct; the interior parts being more perfect in the former; while in the latter it is externally most conspicuous, standing out prominently from its creamy whiteness. The lens is cellular in structure, and thins away rapidly at the sides. The "rods" are well developed, and embedded in pigment.

Spencer describes the various modifications of the organ in the iguanas, chameleons, flying lizards, geckos, etc.

Fig. 81 represents the external aspects of the eye-scale in a small lizard (Calotis), with the transparent cornea in the middle, through which the eye is seen; and the diagram Fig. 82 a section through the eye-scale of a small lizard (Lacerta).

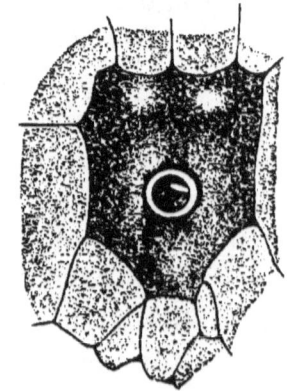

Fig. 81.—Pineal eye-scale on the head of a small lizard (Calotis); after Spencer.

A very interesting point in connection with the pineal eye consists in the fact that the optic nerve does not penetrate the retina, and then spread out on its outer

---

* *Quarterly Journal of Microscopical Science*, October, 1886.

surface, as in the lateral eyes of all vertebrates, but, on the contrary, is distributed over its exterior surface. It is, therefore, as De Graaf pointed out, formed in this respect on the type of the usual invertebrate eye; so that we have the remarkable fact that in the same

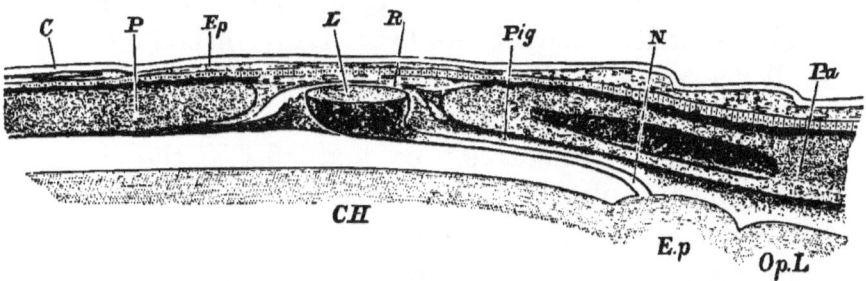

Fig. 82.—Diagram of a section through the skull and pineal eye of *Lacerta viridis*. *C*, Cuticle; *Pa*, parietal bone; *Ep*, epidermis; *L*, lens; *Pig*, Pigment; *R*, rete muscosum; *CH*, cerebral hemisphere; *N*, nerve; *E.p*, epiphysis; *OpL*, optic lobe of brain.

vertebrate animal we find eyes formed on two different types. Not only so, but the development is dissimilar, the lens of the pineal eye being formed out of the walls of the neural canal. So that the lens of the pineal eye is a totally different structure from that of the lateral eyes.

Spencer observed no effect whatever when he threw a strong light on the pineal eye. In fact, he does not believe that in any of the species examined by him the organ is at present in a functional condition. Indeed, in some cases the cornea is quite opaque, and in others the nerve to the brain is not continuous; so that there can be no vision. At the same time, it seems to be established that this organ is the degraded relic of what was once a true eye.

From the size of the pineal orifice in the skull of

the huge extinct reptiles, such as Ichthyosaurus and Plesiosaurus, it has been, I think, fairly inferred that the pineal eye was much more developed than in any known living form.

In living fish and Amphibia, so far as they have been yet examined, the organ is even more rudimentary than in reptiles. But in the fossil Labyrinthodonts the skull possesses a large and well-marked orifice for the passage of the pineal nerve. This orifice is, in fact, so large that it can scarcely be doubted that the eye in these remarkable amphibia was also well developed, and served as a third organ of vision.

In birds the organ is present, but retains no resemblance to an eye. It is solid and highly vascular. In mammals it is still more degenerate, though a trace is still present even in man himself.

The larval Ascidians, which present so many points of resemblance to the lowest vertebrates, and especially to the Lancelet (Amphioxus), have hitherto been regarded as differing from them in the possession of a central eye. It now, however, appears that the vertebrate type did originally possess a central eye, of which the so-called pineal gland is the last trace.

It seems, then, very tempting to regard the pineal eye as representing the central eye of Amphioxus; but Spencer points out that the two organs differ greatly in structure, and he himself doubts whether the pineal eye is really the direct representative of the central eye in the Tunicata.

Béraneck* also regards the pineal as entirely different from the central eye of the Tunicata. Indeed, he considers its differentiation as an eye to be a

* "Ueber d. Parietal Auge der Reptilien," *Jenaische Zeit.*, 1887.

secondary modification, and considers that it had previously served some other function.

However this may be, it cannot be doubted that the pineal gland in Mammalia is the representative of the cerebral lobe which supplies the rudimentary pineal eye of Reptilia, and this itself is probably the degenerate descendant of an organ which in former ages performed the functions of a true organ of vision.

THE ORGANS OF VISION IN THE LOWER ANIMALS.

Mere sensibility to light is possible without any optical apparatus. Even plants, as we know, can well distinguish between light and darkness; and though it seems that in our own case the general surface of the skin has lost its sensitiveness to light, still, in many of the lower animals, light seems to act generally and directly on the tissues.

Some microscopic vegetable forms even, as, for instance, Englena (Fig. 83), possess a red spot,* which appears to be specially sensitive to light.

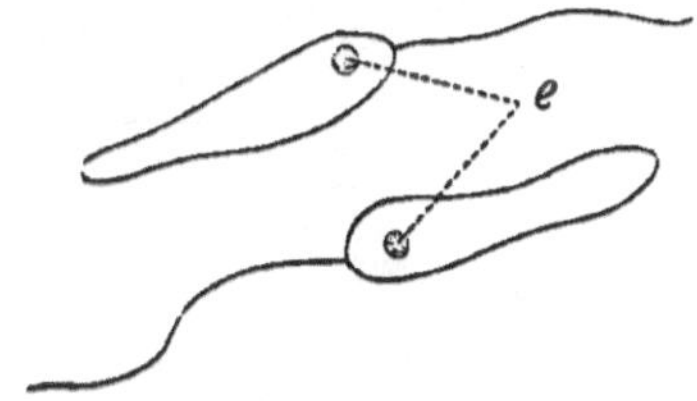

Fig. 83.—*Englena viridis.*
e, Eye-spot.

The lower animals are, in a great many cases, very transparent. Light passes easily through them, and, except in so far as it is absorbed, can hardly be supposed to produce any effect. The most rudimentary form of a light-organ, then, may be considered to be a coloured spot.

In the first chapter I have endeavoured to show how

---

* The moving zoospores of certain algæ also possess a red spot, which may perhaps have special reference to light.

it may be possible to trace an almost complete series from such a mere spot of colour in the skin up to a complex organ of vision, such, for instance, as that of a snail; indeed, in the development of the eye in the individual animal may be traced some of the same stages as have probably been passed through by the ancestral forms of the animal itself in long bygone ages.

We must not, however, suppose that all eyes can be traced back to one and the same origin, or have been developed in the same manner. There are even cases in which an organ fulfilling a different function appears to have been modified into an eye.

Look, for instance, at the organ of touch of Onchidium * (Fig. 16). The cuticle (see p. 14) is thickened into a biconvex, almost lens-like body; the epithelial cells are elongated, and below is a mass of cells, to which runs a nerve. A very little change would make this an organ capable of distinguishing light from darkness, and some of the eyes of On-chidium appear, indeed, to have thus originated.

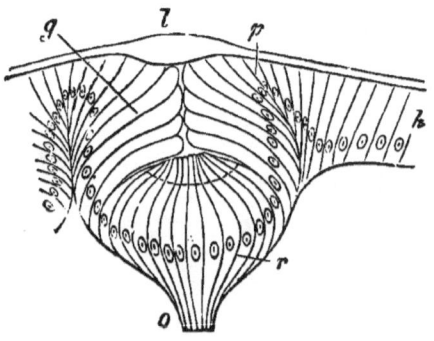

Compare with this, for instance, the ocellus of the young larva of a water-beetle (Fig. 84), as figured by Grenacher.

Fig. 84.—Section through the simple eye of a young Dytiscus larva (after Grenacher). *l*, Corneal lens; *g*, cells forming the vitreous humor; *r*, retina; *o*, optic nerve; *h*, hypoderm.

The eye-spots of Medusæ were first noticed by Ehrenberg in 1836, and the lens was discovered many years afterwards by de Quatrefages. It is, in fact, by no means universally

* A slug-like genus of molluscs.

present; the eye, if so it can be called, in many species consisting merely of a coloured spot, while in others it is entirely absent.*

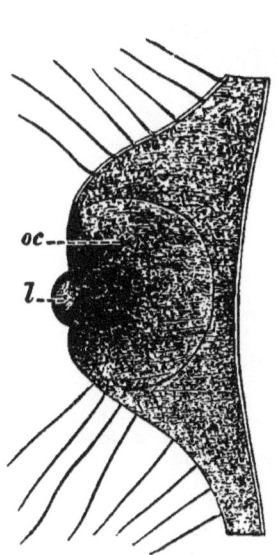

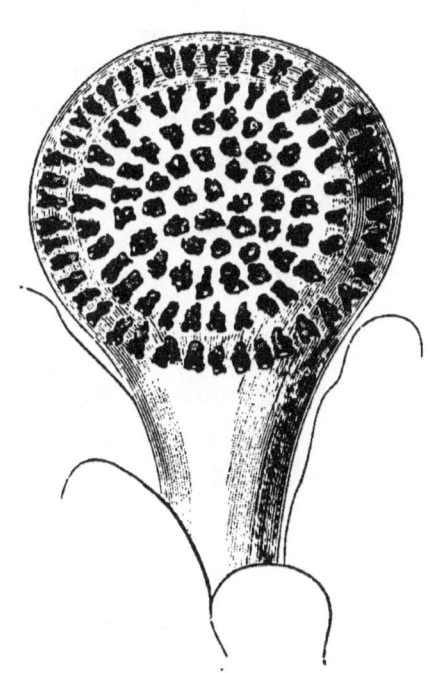

Fig. 85.—Eye-spot of Lizzia (after Hertwig). *oc*, Ocellus; *l*, lens.

Fig. 86.—Eye-bulb of Astropecten (after Haeckel).

In the Echinoderms, the eyes, which were discovered by Ehrenberg, have been described by Haeckel,† Wilson,‡ Lange, and others.§ They are in some cases situated, as in Astropecten, on a pear-shaped bulb (Fig. 86).

They consist of a lens (Fig. 87), supplied with a nerve, and lying in a mass of pigment. In Solaster or

* Allman, "Mon. of the Hydroids," *Ray Society*, 1871.

† "Ueber die Augen und Nerven der Seesterne," *Zeit. für Wiss.*, vol. x.

‡ *Transactions of the Linnean Society.*

§ Lange, "Beit. z. Anat. und Hist. der Asterien und Ophiuren," *Morph. Jahrbuch*, 1876.

Asteracanthion the lenses look like brilliant eggs, "each in its own scarlet nest."

In some species there are as many as two hundred eyes; but there appears to be no retina, so that they can do little more than distinguish between light and darkness.

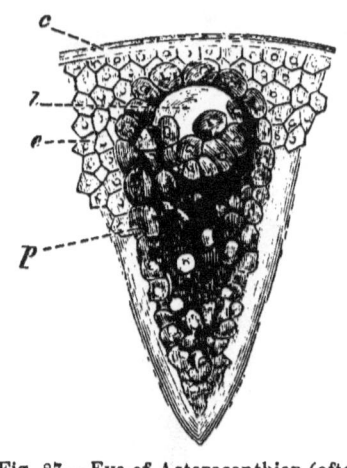

It is quite possible that in some of the lower animals, where the eye-spot is supposed to consist merely of a layer of pigment at the end of a nerve, a lens may hereafter be discovered.

In the Turbellaria * the eyes, which were first noticed

Fig. 87.—Eye of Asteracanthion (after Haeckel). c, Cuticle ; e, epithelium ; l, lens ; p, pigment.

by de Quatrefages, are numerous, and lie immediately under the epithelium (skin). They consist of a certain number of crystalline rods and corresponding retinal cells, resting on a cup-shaped bed of pigment, and connected with a nerve. There is often a group on each side of the head, immediately over the brain. In species which possess tentacles the eyes are generally combined with them ; in others they are scattered over the whole periphery of the body, and look in all directions. They differ greatly in size, and in the number of rods and retinal cells—the larger tentacular eyes having several; the small, scattered ones, which are generally more deeply situated, even as few as two or three.

* " Die Polycladen," Fauna und Flora des Golfes von Neapel, 1884. Carrière, " Die Augen von Planaria," *Arch. für Mic. Anat.*, 1882.

In most of the Annulata (worms), the eyes, so far as they have yet been described, are very simple, and probably in most cases not capable of giving more than a mere impression of light. In some species the eye-spot is merely a group of pigmented epithelial cells. In many (Fig. 87) there is, besides the pigment, a well-marked lens. At the same time, it is probable that in some cases this supposed simplicity is more apparent than real. The dioptric part is often cellular, consisting sometimes of one cell, sometimes of several. They are generally, but not always, situated on the head. The Polyophthalmians (Fig. 90), as already mentioned, have a series along the sides of the body, in pairs from the seventh to the eighteenth segments. I agree with Carrière that there is no sufficient reason for considering the supposed "eyes" of the leech as organs for the perception of light, but other species of the same group (Clepsine) possess well-marked, though rudimentary eyes.[*]

Certain leeches—for instance, *Piscicola respirans*—in addition to the pigmented spots on the head, have also some on the posterior sucking disc. These somewhat resemble the supposed organs of touch, but are larger, and surrounded by pigment. There is no lens, but the large cells are very transparent. It is not supposed that they give any distinct image, or can do more than distinguish light from darkness—as Leydig says, "feel" the light. Still, I must confess that the determination of these curious organs as eyes seems to me very doubtful.

Fig. 88 represents the anterior extremity of a small freshwater worm (Bohemilla).

---

[*] Graber, "Morph. Unt. über die Augen der frei-lebenden Borsten-würmer," *Arch. für Mic. Anat.*, 1880.

Fig. 89 represents an eye-dot of Nereis. In this genus there are two pairs of eyes, which differ some-

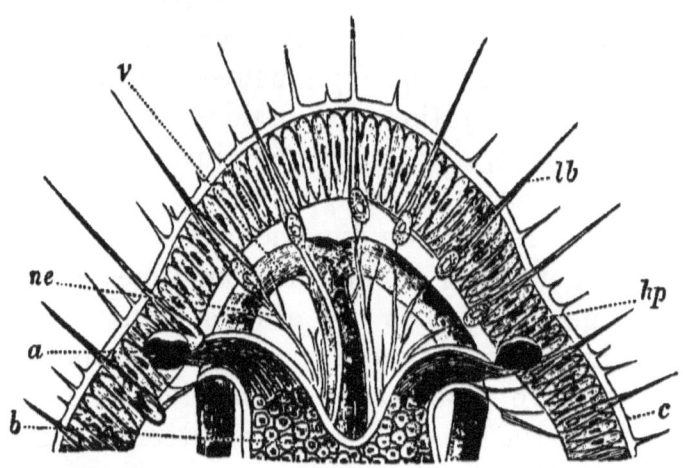

Fig. 88.—Anterior extremity of a freshwater worm (*Bohemilla comata*); after Vejdóvsky).* *a*, Eye; *b*, brain; *c*, cuticle; *hp*, hypoderm; *lb*, tactile hair; *ne*, nerve, *v*. blood-vessel.

what in structure, the lens in the anterior pair being flatter, that in the posterior more conical. In Hesione the difference is even more marked.† In Polyophthalmus, besides the eyes in the head, there is, as already mentioned, a series along the sides of the body, which differ some-what in structure from those in the head.

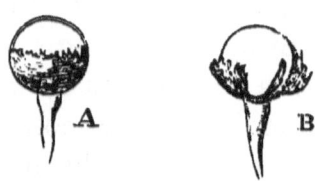

Fig. 89.—Eye-dot of Nereis (after Müller). In B the pigment is partly removed so as to show the lens.

As a general rule, in the Annelids each eye contains a single lens, but the cephalic eyes of Polyophthalmus, according to Mayer, contain three.

* "Sys. und Morph. der Oligochæten."

† Graber, "Morph. Unt. über die Augen der frei-lebenden Borsten-würmer," *Arch für Mic. Anat.*, 1880.

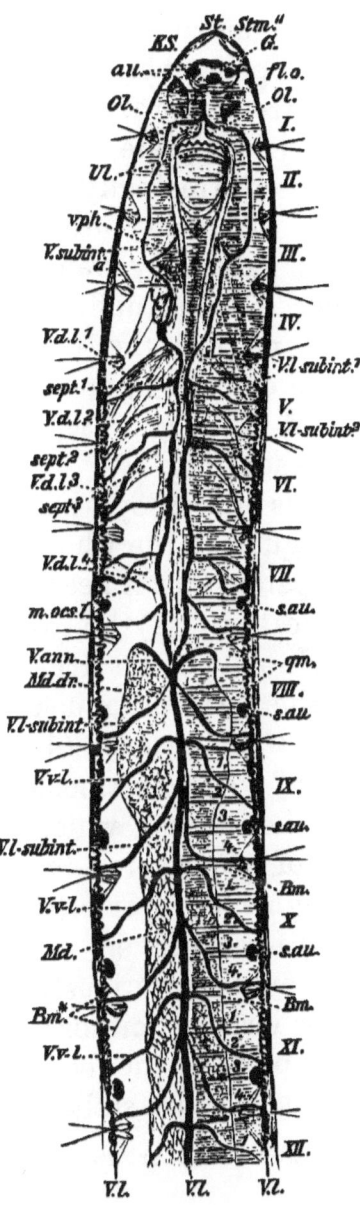

Fig. 90.—The first twelve segments of *Polyophthalmus pictus*, seen from below (after Mayer). The Roman numerals indicate the segments. *St*, Papillæ on the head; *KS*, head; *au*, head eye; *s.au*, side eyes; *Ol*, upper lip; *Ul*, under lip; *v.ph* pharyngeal vein; *V.subinta*, anterior ventral vein; *V.d.l¹⁻⁴*, veins connecting the superior lateral and vessels; *sept¹⁻³*, intersegmentary membranes; *m.ocs.l*, lateral muscle of the œsophagus; *V.ann*, pulsating circular vessel; *Md.dr*, stomach-glands; *V.v-l*, vein connecting the inferior and lateral blood-vessels; *Md*, stomach; *Bm*, muscles of the hairs; *G*, brain; *fl.o*, ciliated organ; *qm*, transverse muscle.

The most highly organized eyes in Annelids appear to be those of the Alciopidæ, which have been described by Krohn,[*] de Quatrefages,[†] and especially by Greef[‡] and Graber.[§] The Alciopidæ are small sea-worms; they live principally in the open sea, and, like many other pelagic animals, are extremely transparent. It is, indeed, often difficult to see more of them than the two very large eyes, red or orange, and a pair of dark violet dots (the segmental organs) on each ring.

The principal parts of their eyes are —(1) the outer integument, the whole of which is so transparent that it needs scarcely any modification; (2) the so-called "eye-skin," as to the true nature of which there is still much difference of opinion; (3) the lens; (4) the "corpus ciliare;" (5) the vitreous humor; and (6) the retina, which again is composed of four layers—(a) the rods; (b) pigment layer; (c) granular layer; (d) fibrous layer.

Fig. 91.—Alciope (after de Quatrefages).

In Mollusca the eyes are variously situated; being, for instance, either placed on the posterior tentacles; or between the feelers, as in the freshwater species; or on a short stalk at the side of the

* "Zool. und Anat. Bemerk. über die Alciopeden," *Wiegmann's Arch.*, 1845.

† "Etudes s. l. typ. Inf. de l'emb. des Annelés," *Ann. Sci. Nat.*, 1850.

‡ "Unt. über die Alciopiden," *Nova Acta Acad. Leop. Carol.*, vol. xxxix. 11, 1876.

§ *Arch. für Mic. Anat.*, 1880.

feelers, as in the Prosobranchiata; or on the back. In some cases they are deeply sunk, even into the brain.

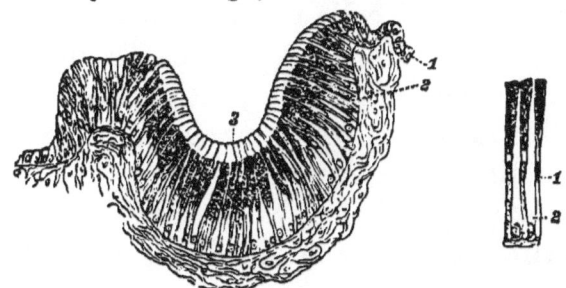

Fig. 92.—Perpendicular section through the eye-pit of a limpet (Patella); after Carrière. 1, Epithelial cells; 2, retina cells; 3, vitreous body.

The mussels are generally deficient in eyes; and some which are, as larvæ, provided with an eye, lose their eyes when mature.

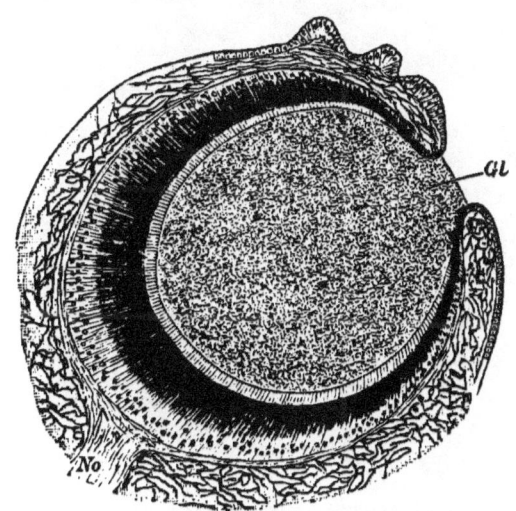

Fig. 93.—Eye of *Trochus magus* (after Hilger).* *Gl*, Vitreous body; *No*, nerve.

In the limpet (Patella),* on the outer side of the tentacles, where the eyes are situated in more highly organized species, are certain spots, which may be

* "Fraisse. Ueber Molluskenaugen," *Zeit. für Wiss. Zool.*, 1881.

† "Beit. zur Kennt. der Gastropodenaugen," Gegenbaur's *Morph. Jahrbuch*, 1885.

regarded as a very rudimentary organ for the perception of light. The skin is thrown into a pit, within which the epithelial cells are elongated and pigmented.

In the sea-ear (Haliotis), and in Trochus (Fig. 93), the arrangement is similar, but the depression is deeper, the mouth is very much restricted, and the interior is filled by a vitreous body.

In Murex (Fig. 94) the eye is still further developed, and is entirely closed in, a lens being present.

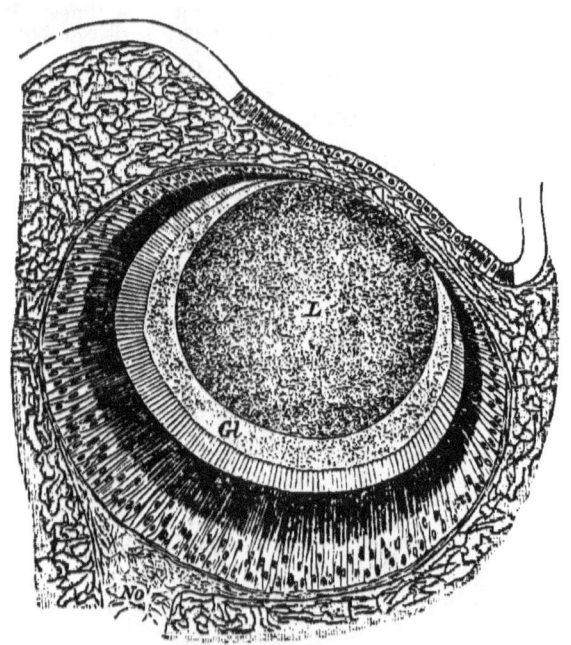

Fig. 94.—Eye of *Murex brandaris* (after Hilger). *L*, Lens; *Gl*, vitreous body; *No*, nerve.

In the snail (Helix) the eye is still more highly organized. It consists of a cornea, which lies immediately below the skin; a lens, behind which is the retina, consisting of three layers, (1) the rods, (2) a cellular layer, (3) a fibrous layer. This, indeed, appears to be a very general arrangement in the Mollusca. The power of sight given by such an eye can be but small. Indeed, it is probable that it does little more

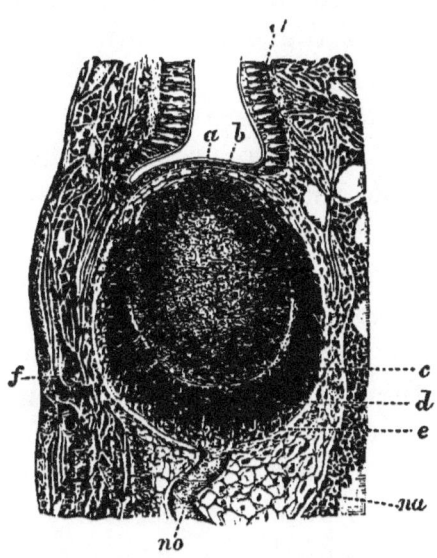

Fig. 95.—Eye of *Helix pomatia* (after Simroth).* *ct*, Cuticle; *a*, epithelium; *b*, cornea; *c*, envelope of the eye; *d*, cellular layer; *e*, fibrils of the optic nerve; *f*, feeler cell; *na*, nerve of the tentacle; *no*, optic nerve.

than distinguish degrees of light. According to Lespès, a Cyclostoma only perceives the shadow of a hand at a distance of five inches, and a Paludina of eight.

It is interesting that, as Lankester first showed,† the eye of Mollusca, in its gradual development, passes through the stages which we find are the permanent conditions in Patella and Haliotis, commencing as a depression, which grows deeper and deeper, and gradually closes over.

Even in the Nautilus the cornea leaves an opening,

* Simroth, "Ueber die Sinneswerkzeuge uns. einh. Weichthiere," *Zeit. für Wiss. Zool.*, 1876.

† "Obs. on the Dev. of Cephalopoda," *Quarterly Journal of Microscopical Science*, 1875.

through which the water has free access to the interior of the eye.

In the higher cuttle-fishes (Cephalopoda) the eye is very complex, and the optic ganglion is in some cases the largest part of the brain; but, while we find the same parts, as, for instance, in Helix, though in a higher state of development, there does not seem sufficient reason to regard the two organs as homologous, but it appears possible that the eye of the cuttle-fish had an independent origin.

Certain bivalves (Lamellibranchiata) possess bright spots round the edge of the mantle, or on the siphon, which some naturalists maintain to be eyes, while others deny them this character, leaving their true function, however, undecided.

But though there is much doubt in some cases, there are other eye-spots which are certainly true eyes. Of these there are two distinct types—those of Spondylus, Pecten, etc., on the one hand; of Arca, Pectunculus, etc., on the other. The latter present several features of the compound insect's eye. This was first noticed by Will,[*] and they have since been more fully described by Carrière[†] and Patten.[‡] They are composed (Fig. 96) of large conical cells with the points turned inwards. Pigment is deposited in the periphery of the cells. The outer surface is arched, and forms a biconvex lens. These cells pass gradually into those of the ordinary epithelium.

It will be most convenient to consider the mode in which these compound eyes act when we come to

---

[*] "Ueber die Augen der Bivalven," *Frorieps Notizen*, 1844.

[†] "Die Sehorgane der Thiere," 1885.

[‡] "Eyes of Molluscs and Arthropods," *Mitt. Zool. Stat. Neapel*, 1886.

consider those of insects, where they are more highly
developed.

The eyes of Pecten and Spondylus are, again, formed
on a totally different plan.

It has been already observed that there is an

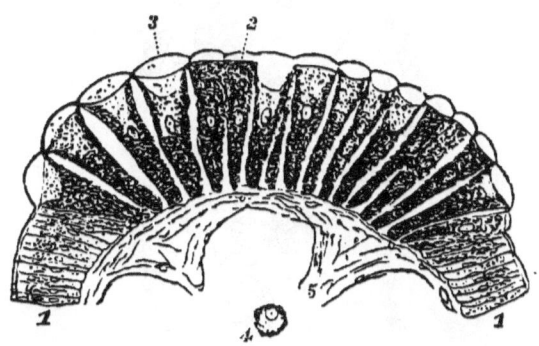

Fig. 96.—Perpendicular section through an eye of *Arca Noœ* (after Carrière). 1,
Epithelium of the edge of the mantle ; 2, cells of vision ; 3, lens ; 4, 5, connective
tissue ; 6, section of one of the cells.

essential difference between the typical vertebrate and
the typical invertebrate eye ; in that while in the
former, the optic nerve (Fig. 77) penetrates the retina
and then spreads out on the anterior surface, so that
the "rods" point away from the light ; in the normal
invertebrate eye, on the contrary, the nerve spreads
out on the back of the retina, so that the rods point
towards the light. Krohn,* however, made the remarkable discovery that in the genus Pecten the rods, like
those of the vertebrates, are turned away from the light.
In this case, however, the optic nerve does not enter
the retina directly from behind, but runs round it and
passes, so to say, over the lip of the cup.

Here, then, we get a remarkable approach to the
vertebrate eye ; but the similarity is still greater in

* *Müller's Arch.*, 1840. See also Hensen, "Ueber das Auge einiger
Lamellibranchiaten." *Zeit. für Wiss. Zool.*, 1865.

Onchidium (a genus of slugs, widely spread over the Southern Hemisphere), in which Semper has shown * that the nerve actually pierces the retina as in verte-

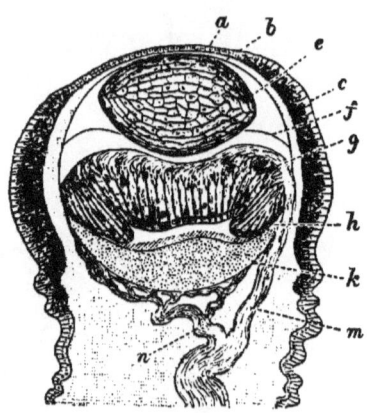

Fig. 97.—Diagram of eye of Pecten (after Hickson). *a*, Cornea; *b*, transparent basement membrane supporting the epithelial cells of cornea; *c*, the pigmented epithelium; *d*, the lining epithelium of the mantle; *e*, the lens; *f*, the ligament supporting the lens; *g*, the retina; *h*, the tapetum; *k*, the pigment; *m*, the retinal nerve; *n*, complementary nerve.

brates. That this distinctive character should thus reappear in so distant a group is very interesting, and it is also remarkable that Onchidium possesses two kinds of eyes: some on the head, which are constructed on the same type as those of other molluscs; while the peculiar eyes just mentioned are scattered over the back, and their nerves arise, not from the cephalic, but from the visceral ganglion. Moreover, they differ in number, not only in the different species, some having one hundred, some as few as twelve, and others none at all, but even in different individuals of the same species. Indeed, they are continually growing and being reabsorbed. But while thus resembling a simple vertebrate eye, the dorsal eyes of Onchidium have a totally

* " Ueber Schnecken Augen am Wirbelthier typus," *Arch. für Mic. Anat.*, 1877.

different development, arising, except the nerve, entirely from the integument; on the contrary, in the vertebrate eye, while the cornea and lens are formed from the skin, the retina is an outgrowth from the brain.

Semper does not suppose that the Onchidia perceive any actual image with their dorsal eyes, and thinks that they are merely able to distinguish differences in the amount of light.

They are shore-living molluscs, and are preyed on by small fishes belonging to the genus Perophthalmus, which has the curious habit of leaving the water and walking about on the sand in search of food. The back of the Onchidium contains a number of glands, each opening by a minute pore; and Semper suggests that, when warned by the shadow of the fish, the little slugs eject a shower of spray, drive off their enemy, and save themselves. This is not quite so far-fetched as might at first sight appear, for we know that there are many other animals, the sepia, many ants, the bombardier and other beetles, etc., which defend themselves in a similar manner.

It seems difficult to understand why the Onchidia should be endowed with so many eyes. The irrelative repetition of organs meets us, however, continually in the lower animals. Moreover, in the present case Semper has thrown out a plausible suggestion. The organs of touch (see *ante*, p. 14) curiously resemble eyes in structure, and a very slight change might make them capable of perceiving light. It is possible, then, that some of them may undergo a change of function, and that this may throw some light on the variability in number.

In the Chitonidæ, where dorsal eyes have recently

been discovered by Moseley,* they are even more numerous. Chiton itself, indeed, has none; but in Schizochiton there are 300, and in Corephium more

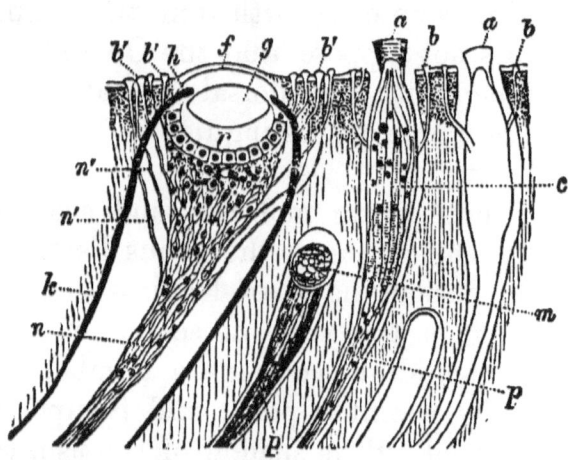

Fig. 98. Schematic representation of the soft and some of the hard parts in a shell of a Chiton (Acanthopleura), as seen in a section vertical to the surface, and with the margin of the shell lying in the direction of the left side of the drawing. *a*, Conical termination of sense-organ; *b*, *b'*, ends of nerve; *c*, nerve; *f*, calcareous cornea; *g*, lens; *h*, iris; *k*, pigmented capsule of eye; *m*, body of sense-organ cut across; *n*, nerve of eye; *p*, nerve of sense-organ; *r*, rods of retina.

than ten thousand. As in Onchidium, they probably arose as modifications of the organs of touch, and are supplied by the same nerves. They possess (1) a cornea, (2) a perfectly transparent and strongly biconvex lens, and (3) the retina, which presents a layer of short but well-defined rods. It is interesting that they point towards the light, and not, as in Onchidium, away from it.

* "On the Presence of Eyes in Shells of certain Chitonidæ," *Quarterly Journal of Microscopal Science*, 1885.

CHAPTER VII.

I NOW pass on to the eyes of insects. In most species of this group there are two distinct kinds: the large compound eyes, which are situated one on each side of the head; and the ocelli, or small eyes, of which there are generally three, arranged in a triangle, between the other two.

Speaking roughly, the ocelli of insects may be said to see as our eyes do; that is to say, the lens throws on the retina an image, which is perceived by the fine terminations of the optic nerve. One type of such an eye in a young water-beetle (Dytiscus) is shown in Fig. 84, p. 131. This illustrates the mode of development of an ocellus, which has been already referred to (*ante*, p. 131).

The structure of fully formed ocelli is shown by Fig. 99. In details, indeed, they present many differences, and it is remarkable that in some species this is the case even with those of the same individual; for instance, in those of one of our large spiders, *Epeira diadema* (Fig. 99).

In this case the eye *B* would receive more light, and the image, therefore, would be brighter; but, on the other hand, the image would be pictured in greater detail by the eye *A*.

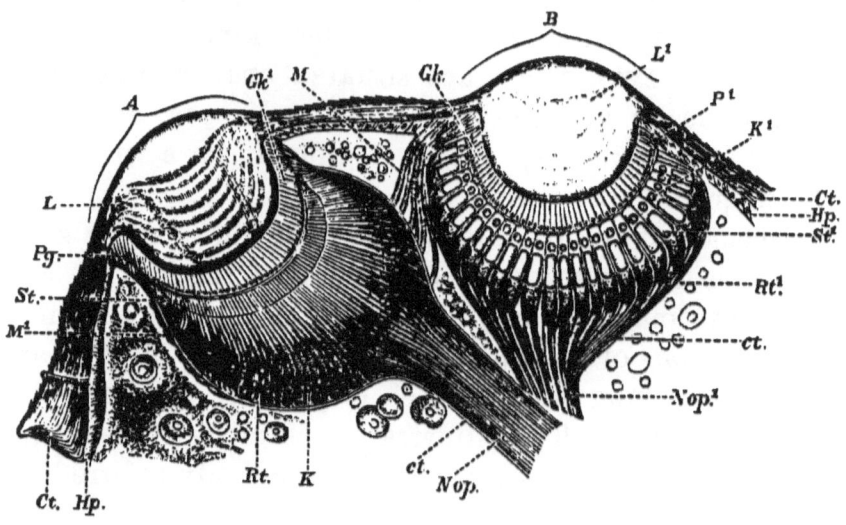

Fig. 99.—Long section through the front (*A*) and hinder (*B*) dorsal eyes of *Epeira diadema* (after Grenacher). *A*, Anterior eye; *B*, posterior eye; *Hp*, hypoderm; *Ct*. cuticle; *ct*, boundary membrane; *K*, nuclei of the cells of the retina; *M*, muscular fibres; *M*, *M'*, cross sections of ditto; *St*, rods; *Pg*, *P'*, pigment cells; *L*, lens; *Gk'*, vitreous body; *Kt*, crystalline cones; *Rt*, retina; *Nop*, optic nerve.

Speaking generally, an ocellus may be regarded as consisting of—

1. A lens, forming part of the general body covering.

2. A layer of transparent cells.

3. A retina, or second layer of deeper lying cells, each of which bears a rod in front, while their inner ends pass into the filaments of the optic nerve.

4. The pigment.

From the convexity of the lens it would have a short focus, and the comparatively small number of rods would give but a very imperfect image, except of very near objects.

But though these eyes agree so far with ours, there is an essential difference between them. It will be at once seen that the pigment is differently placed, being in front of the rods, while in the vertebrate eye it is behind them. Again, the position of the rods themselves is reversed in the two cases.

Passing on to the compound eye, Fig. 100 gives a section of the eye of a cockchafer (Melolontha), after Strauss-Dürckheim. The separate facets of such an

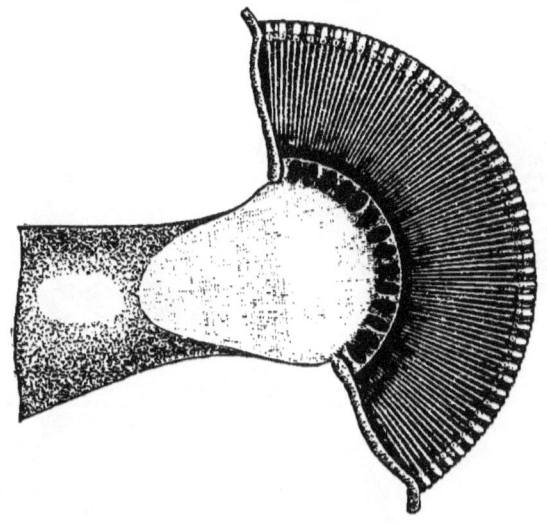

Fig. 100.—Section through the eye of a cockchafer (Melolontha); after Strauss-Dürckheim.

eye act themselves as lenses, and give a very perfect image.

As regards the number of facets, Leeuwenhoek calculated that there were 3180 facets in the compound eye of a beetle which, however, he does not name. In the house-fly (Musca) there are about 4,000; in the gadfly (Œstrus), 7,000; in the goat moth (Cossus), 11,000; in the death's-head moth (*Sphinx atropos*), 12,000; in a butterfly (Papilio), 17,000; in a dragon-fly (Æschna), 20,000; in a small beetle (Mordella), as many as 25,000.

The size of the facets seems to bear some relation to the size of the insect, but even in the smallest species none have been observed less than $\frac{1}{2000}$ of an inch in diameter. Butterflies, which fly in the day, have the facets smaller than those of moths, which are generally evening insects.

The facets are in most cases similar, six-sided, and

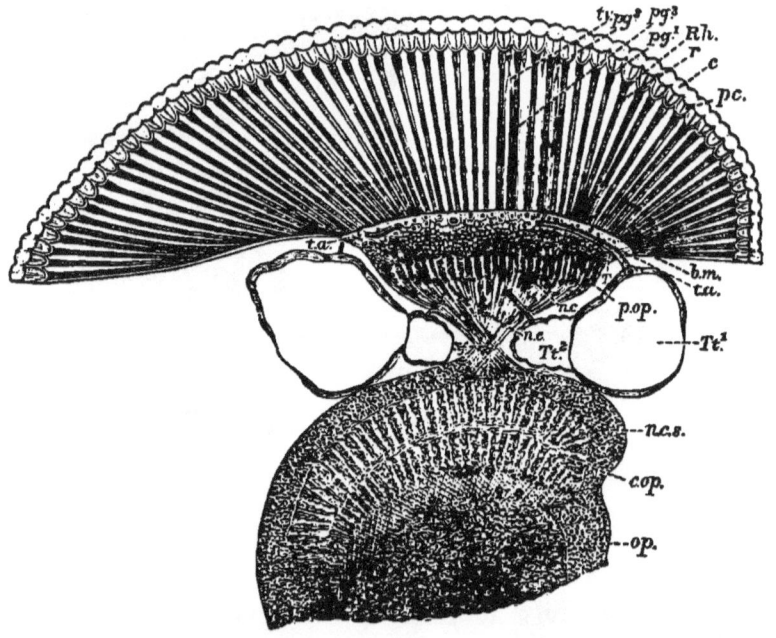

Fig. 101.—Section through the eye of a fly (after Hickson). *b.m*, Basilar membrane; *c*, cuticle; *c.op*, epioptic ganglion; *n.c.*, nuclei; *n.c.s.*, nerve-cell sheath; *N.f*, decussating nerve-fibres; *op*, optic ganglion; *pc.*, pseudocone; *pg*, pigment cells; *p.op*, perioptic ganglion; *r*, retinula; *Rh.*, rhabdom; *T*, trachea; *t.a.*, terminal anastomosis; *Tt*, trachea; *ti*, tracheal vesicle.

very regular. In locusts, however, they vary a good deal both in form and size. In some flies (Diptera) and dragon-flies (Libellulidæ) those in the upper part of the eye are larger than the lower ones, and the junction of the two often forms a well-marked, curved line.

The wonderful complexity is well shown in the preceding figure, which represents a section through the eye of a fly, after Hickson.[*]

In illustration of the finer structure, I may take the eye of the bee (Apis) (Fig. 102), as described and figured by Grenacher in his beautiful work.[†] Fig. 102, the general accuracy of which has been confirmed recently by Dr. Hickson, represents two of the elements of the faceted eye.

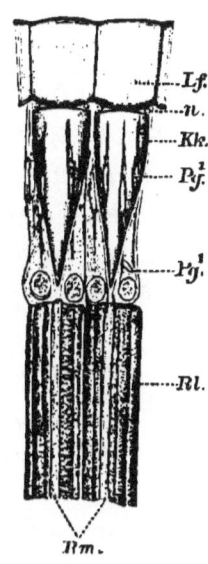

Fig. 102.—Two separate elements of the faceted eye of a bee (after Grenacher). *Lf.* Cornea; *n,* nucleus of Semper; *Kk,* crystalline cone; *Pg, Pg'*, pigment cells, *Rl,* retinula; *Rm,* rhabdom.

The structure of the eyes varies considerably in different groups. They may be said to consist of the following principal parts :—

1. The cornea (*Lf,* Fig. 102).

2. The crystalline cones (*Kk*), of which there is one immediately behind each facet. The development of the crystalline cone has been carefully studied by Claparède. It consists of from four to sixteen original, but completely combined segments, secreted by cells which lie immediately behind each facet, but of which, when the eye is completely developed, only the nuclei, known as Semper's nuclei (*n*), finally remain.

3. Next comes the retinula (*rl*), which stands in more or less intimate connection with the pointed inner end of the crystalline cone. It is generally composed of seven, but sometimes of as few as four, or as many

---

[*] " The Eye and Optic Tract of Insects," *Quarterly Journal of Microscopical Science,* 1885.

[†] " Untersuchungen über das Sehorgan der Arthropoden." 1879.

as eight, originally separate, but closely combined cells. They converge on the optic lobe, and form an outer nucleated sheath, enclosing a strongly refractive, generally quadrangular, rod (the rhabdom, Rm), the relation of which to the filaments of the optic nerve is not yet well understood.

4. The pigment (Pg).

Between each separate eyelet (ommateum, or ommatidium, as it is termed by Hickson), is—at least, in some insects—a long, tubular, thin-walled trachea. These are difficult to see in prepared specimens, but have been mentioned by several observers. They were first, I think, figured by Leydig,* and more recently by Hickson.

Finally, the eye is bounded by a basilar membrane, which is perforated by two sets of apertures, a series of larger ones for the passage of the tracheal vessels, and of smaller ones for the nerve-fibrils.

The crystalline cone is not, however, always present, and Grenacher divides the compound eyes of insects into three types: acone eyes, in which the crystalline cone is not present, but is represented throughout life by distinct cells ; pseudocone eyes, in which there is a special conical and transparent medium ; and, lastly, eucone eyes, with true crystalline cones." †

---

* "Zum feineren Bau der Insekten," *Müller's Arch. für Anat. u. Phys.*, 1855.

† *Acone* eyes occur in Nematocera (gnats), Hemiptera (bugs), Forficula (earwigs), and those Coleoptera (beetles), which have less than five tarsal joints. *Pseudocone* eyes occur in the true flies (Muscidæ). *Eucone* eyes prevail among other insects: Lepidoptera, Hymenoptera, Neuroptera, Orthoptera, Cicadidæ, the Coleoptera with five tarsal segments, and among Diptera the single genus Corethra, which, moreover, is remarkable as possessing compound eyes, even in the larva and pupa.

The last form differs principally from the two first in that the elements which constitute the crystalline cone and the retinula have become completely coalesced and solidified. The differences are, no doubt, important, but I need not enter into them at length here.

Even the eucone eyes differ considerably, as may be seen from the following figures, representing (Fig. 103) an eyelet from the eye of a cockroach (Periplaneta), and (Fig. 104) one from that of a cockchafer (Melolontha), both taken from Grenacher.

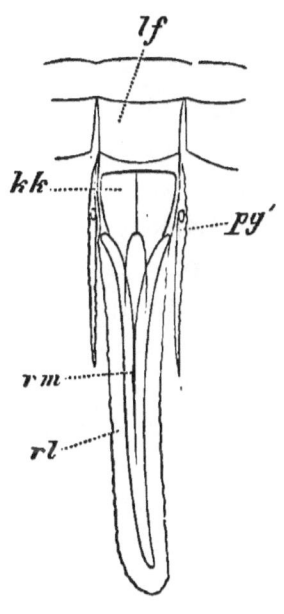

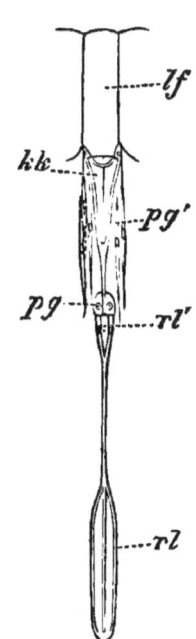

Fig. 103.—Eyelet of cockroach (after Grenacher). *lf*, Cornea; *kk*, crystalline cone; *pg'*, pigment cell; *rl*, retinula; *rm*, rhabdom.

Fig. 104.—Eyelet of cockchafer (after Grenacher). *lf*, Cornea; *kk*, crystalline cone; *pg. pg'*, pigment cells; *rl*, retinula; *rl'*, rhabdom.

With some few exceptions (Corethra, Libellula, etc.), the larvæ of insects do not possess faceted eyes; indeed, as a general rule their powers of vision are very limited, or they are altogether blind. Most caterpillars have

on each side of the head five or six eye-spots, containing each a crystalline body, but, as we shall presently
see, they can probably do little more than distinguish
between light and darkness.

I do not propose to attempt to give here any detailed
account of the structure of the insect brain, but I must
say a few words on the subject.   Between the brain
proper and the eye itself there are, in, for instance, the
blow-fly (*Musca vomitoria*), three distinct ganglionic
swellings, which Hickson, a copy of whose beautiful
figure I have given (Fig. 101), terms the "opticon"
(*op*), epiopticon (*c.op*), and periopticon (*p.op*).   It will
be seen that the nerve-fibrils do not pass in a direct
course, but actually decussate, or cross from one side to
the other, three times, once between each two ganglionic
swellings.   The optic lobes of the two sides are also connected by a fibrous bundle.   The structure of the three
nervous swellings is also very complex.   It consists of a
fine granular matrix, traversed by a meshwork of very
minute fibrillæ, and, at least in the periopticon, is collected into a series of cylindrical masses.   It is entirely
beyond our present range of knowledge to explain the
origin or purpose of these complex arrangements,
though we cannot doubt that they do serve important
functions.   It is remarkable that these arrangements,
though apparently very constant in individual species
and genera, differ greatly in different groups of insects;
for instance, Hickson asserts that in the water-scorpion
(Nepa), there is no decussation, and Carrière makes the
same statement as regards Libellula; but it seems
very extraordinary that this arrangement should be
present in some insect eyes, and absent in others
formed apparently on so nearly the same plan.

ON THE RELATION OF THE EYE TO THE OCELLUS.

In considering the relation of the eye to the ocellus, it is obvious that we cannot regard either as derived from the other. They are, as Grenacher says, " sisters," and derived from a common origin.

The ocellus consists of a single lens in front of a larger or smaller number of visual rods. The compound eye consists of a number of facets, each in front of a single rod; which is produced by from four to sixteen cells: in some cases each cell at first produces a separate rod, and these then subsequently coalesce more or less completely. Starting, then, from a simple form of eye consisting of a lens and a nerve-fibre, which would be capable of perceiving light, but would give no picture of the external world, we should arrive at the compound eye by bringing together a number of such eye-spots, and increasing the number of lenses, while the separate cells beneath each combined to form a single cone and rod; while, on the other hand, by increasing the size of the lens, and multiplying the nervous elements behind it, we should obtain the ocellus of an insect, or the typical eyes of a vertebrate animal.

There is, indeed, no need to suppose that these two eyes are derived from a common origin. We know that, while very similar eyes occur in distant groups of animals, on the other hand nearly allied species often differ greatly in the structure of their eyes; that, indeed, eyes of very different types often occur even in the same animal, so that we have strong reasons for assuming that they had an independent and separate origin.

The spiders have simple ocelli only, the higher Crustacea compound eyes only, while many of the lower Crustacea and of the great class of the insects possess both eyes and ocelli. It would seem probable, therefore, that the ancestral stock must have possessed both, though not perhaps in so perfect a form as that which has now been attained, and that the spiders have lost the compound eyes, while, on the contrary, in the higher Crustacea the ocelli have disappeared.

Moreover, though the ocellus of a spider at first sight closely resembles the eye of a Scolopendra, the internal structure is, according to Grenacher, altogether different. In the ocellus of a spider or an insect we find, at a greater or less distance behind the lens, a retina consisting of a receptive surface, extended concentrically with that of the lens, and consisting of a number of more or less rod-like perceptive elements so arranged that the light falls on their ends.

On the contrary, in the eyes of Myriapods there is, he says, either a single element behind the cornea, or where there are many such elements, they are arranged with their longer axes perpendicular to the direction of light; so that any separate perception of the rays of light coming from different points seems to be an impossibility. In the eye of Lithobius, behind the biconvex lens, he states that the cells lining what I may call the tube of each separate eye, terminate in filaments, between the free ends of which is left a narrow passage, down which the light must pass to reach the end of the optic nerve. Such a structure is certainly very remarkable, and seems entirely to preclude the possibility of the formation of a true image. Altogether the account given by Grenacher, both as to the mode of action of the eyes of the Myriapods and as to their internal structure, differs entirely from that of Graber.

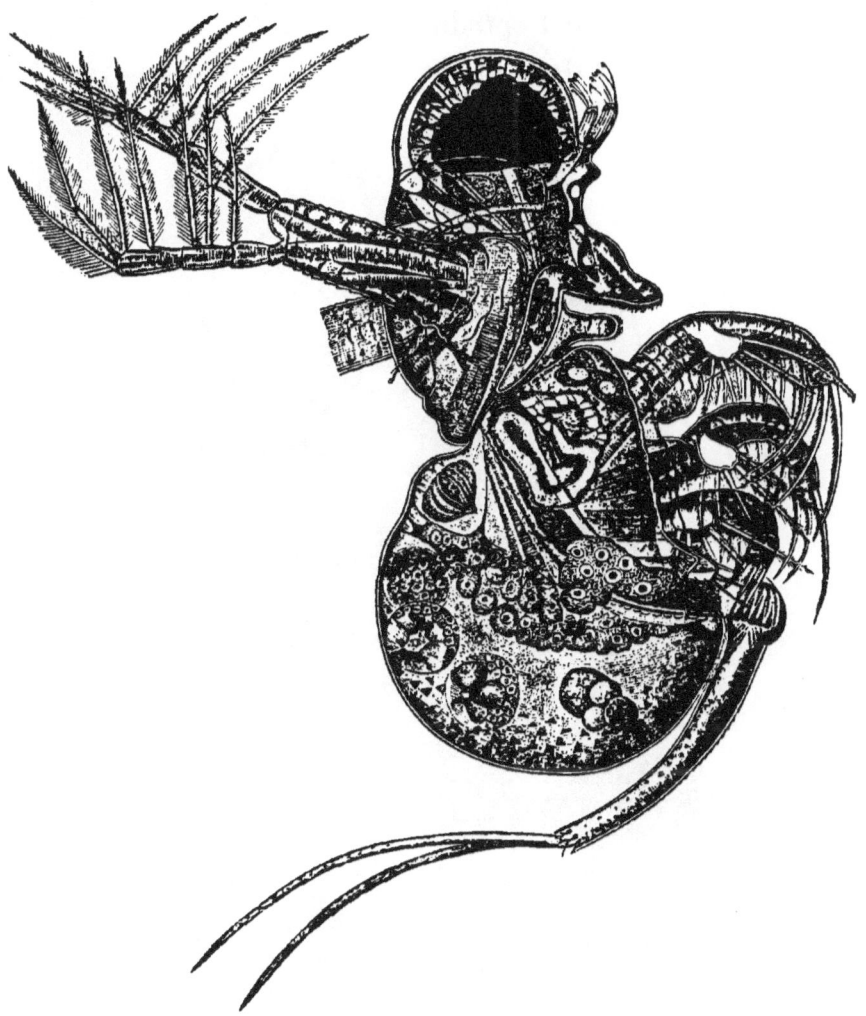

Fig. 105.—Leptodora hyalina.

THE EYES OF CRUSTACEA.

The eyes of many Crustacea are highly developed. In the higher families (thence named Podophthalmata, or stalk-eyed) they are situated on more or less elongated pedestals. In some of the lower forms, though less complex, they are very large, occupying, as in the curious Leptodora (Fig. 105) of our deep lakes, the whole front of the head; while in Corycæus

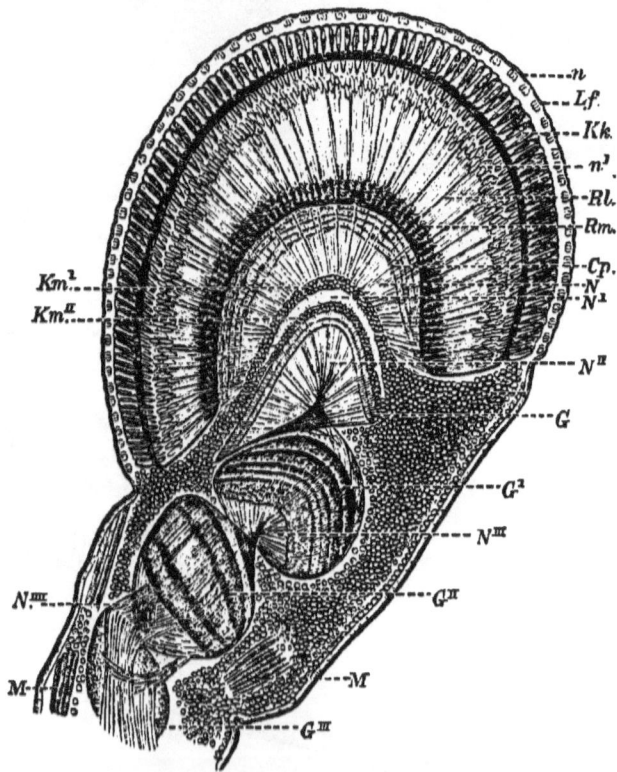

Fig. 106.—Eye of Mysis (after Grenacher). *n*, Nuclei; *Lf*, facets; *Kk*, crystalline cones; *n'*, cells of the retinula; *Rl*, retinula; *Rm*, rhabdom; *Cp*, blood-vessels; *N*, fibres of the optic nerve; *N'*, *N''*, *N'''*, *N''''*, decussations of the fibres of the optic nerve; *G*, *G'*, *G''*, *G'''*, ganglia; *M*, muscles for the movement of the eye-stalk; *Km'*, *Km''*, nuclei.

(Fig. 107) they extend to more than one-half of the whole length of the body.

The higher Crustacea possess no ocelli. In the lower species, on the contrary, a central ocellus is often present, especially in the young state.

In illustration of the compound eyes of Crustacea, I give a figure of an eye of Mysis (Fig. 106).

In the higher Crustacea the nervous elements of the eye are, moreover, very complex. There are no less than four optic ganglia (Fig. 106), and there is a chiasma, or decussation of fibres (N^1, N^{11}, N^{111}, N^{1111}), between each.

The eyes of lobsters and of crabs offer a curious difference. In the former, the crystalline cones are very long, and the retinulæ comparatively short; while in the crabs, on the contrary, the crystalline cone is short, and the retinulæ long.

The eye of Corycæus (Fig. 107) is very interesting. It is extremely large in proportion to the size of the

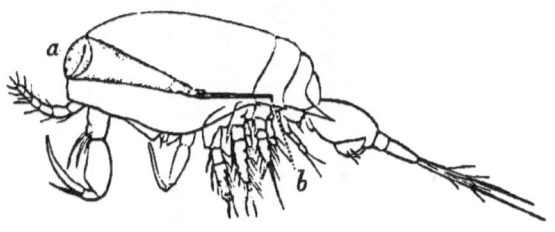

Fig. 107.—Corycæus (after Leuckart).　a, b, The eye.

animal, extending from the front of the head to the beginning of the abdomen. The perceptive part of the eye (b) is, therefore, far removed from the lens (a). The eye of Corycæus appears to represent, in fact, a single element of a compound eye.

The eye of Copilia is also very remarkable, the retinula being, at about the end of the first third of its length, bent at a right angle. Here also the eye is about one-third as long as the body.

The ocelli of Crustacea have not been much studied with reference to their microscopic structure. Those of Calanella are very remarkable, and, indeed, but for their position and the presence of pigment, would hardly be recognized as eyes. They are three in number, and together form an X-shaped body (Fig. 108), supplied by a large nerve (*N.op.*), and consisting of three groups of large nerve-cells, embedded in pigment. There are eight in each of the two side groups, and ten in the central. In form they are pear-shaped, with the narrow end turned towards the nerve. The organ contains no lens nor rods.

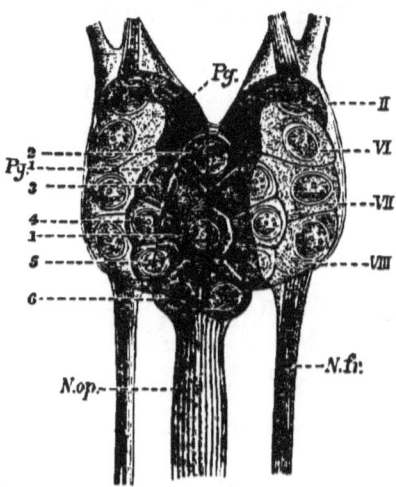

Fig. 108.—Eyes of *Calanella Mediterranea* (after Gerstarker) *Pg.*, pigment cells; *N.fr.*, frontal nerves; *N op.*, nervus opticus. The numbers show the numbers of the cells.

The eyes of the king crab (Limulus) have been described by Grenacher and by Lankester and Bourne.* The two lateral eyes form a polished, kidney-shaped protuberance on each side of the great shield. The outer side is smooth, but on the inner surface it is produced into a number of conical processes (Fig. 109),

* "On the Eyes of Scorpio and Limulus," *Quarterly Journal of Microscopical Science*, 1883.

each of which forms a special lens.   Underneath each
of these secondary lenses is a group of large, elongated
pigmented cells, arranged round a central space, and
touching the lens with their outer ends, while the

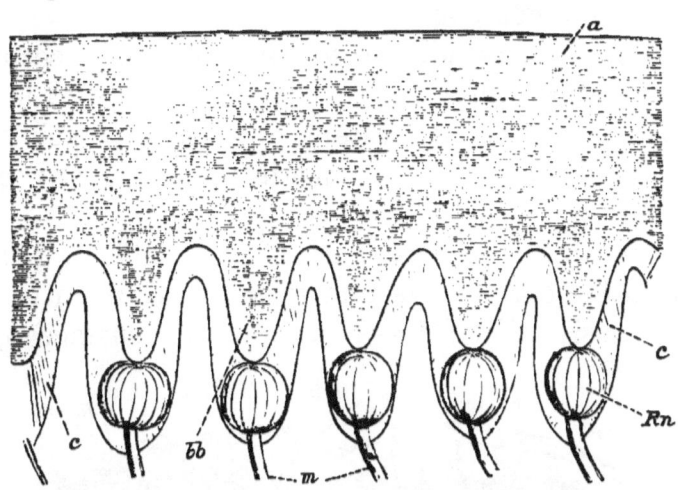

Fig. 109.—Diagram of a vertical section through a portion of the lateral eye of *Limulus
polyphemus*, showing some of the conical lenses, and corresponding retinulæ (after
Lankester and Bourne). *a*, Cuticle; *bb*, cuticular lens ; *cc*, hypoderm ; *Rn*,
retinula; *m*, nerves.

inner ones are continued into the optic nerve.   These
nerve-end cells form the "retinula," while their sides,
which face one another, are thickened, and coalesce
into a rod, the rhabdom, which is hollow at the end
nearest the lens, but solid towards the nerve.   The
central eye is very different.   It possesses a single
lens, like that of an ordinary ocellus, underneath
which is a layer of cells not differing much in appearance from those of the hypoderm, and below which
again is another layer of large nerve-cells, which, however, are so irregular as to suggest the idea that the
central eye of the king crab may have partially lost its
function.   The king crab, then, so remarkable in other
ways, is also very interesting in reference to the peculiar

structure of its eyes. These can hardly be regarded as homologous with the compound eyes of insects and Crustacea, but appear to have originated independently. They have, indeed, hardly anything in common, except that of being compound eyes.

Lastly, I may allude to the eyes of scorpions, which, though very different from those of Limulus in appearance, in Lankester's opinion approach them more nearly in essential constitution than any other known eyes.

Before quitting this part of my subject, 1 must mention the curious eye-like organs of Euphausia.

Euphausia (Fig. 110)—a shrimp-like crustacean, be-

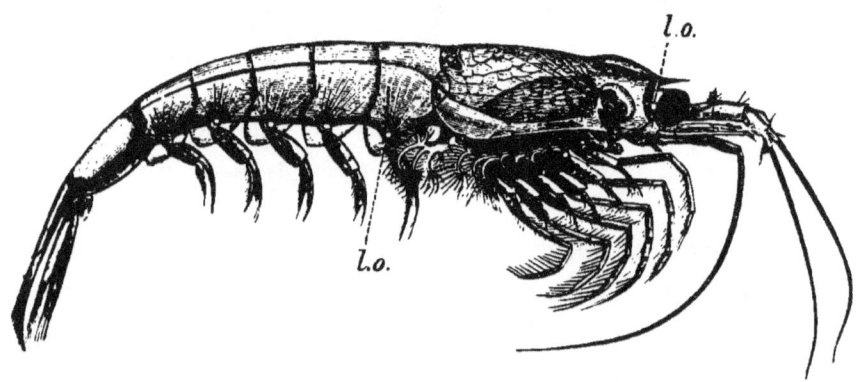

Fig. 110.—*Euphausia pellucida* (after Sars). *l.o.,* Luminous organ.

longing to the same group as Mysis—and some of its allies, are remarkable for possessing at the base of some of the thoracic legs, and on the four anterior abdominal segments, luminous eye-like organs. They form small bulbs, each containing a vitreous body, some pigment, a lens, and a fan-shaped bundle of delicate fibres, and are very conspicuous from their beautiful red color and glistening lustre.

Claus * regards them as true accessory eyes. Sars,†
on the contrary, considers that they have no power of
sight, but are highly differentiated luminous organs.
He admits that they present a deceptive resemblance
to true eyes, but has convinced himself by observations
of the living animal that they have no power of
vision.

The fibrous fascicle (Fig. 111, *f*) he finds to be the
chief light-producing part,‡ and the lens-like body in
front serves, as he supposes, for a condenser, producing
a bright flash of light, the direction of which the
animal, by means of its muscles, is able to control.
The anterior pair (Fig. 112, *lo*), which differ somewhat in structure from the rest, are situated on the

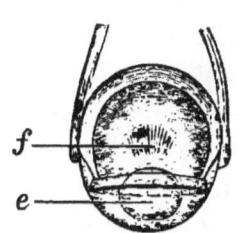

Fig. 111.—Luminous organ of
Euphausia (after Sars). *f*,
Fibres ; *e*, lens.

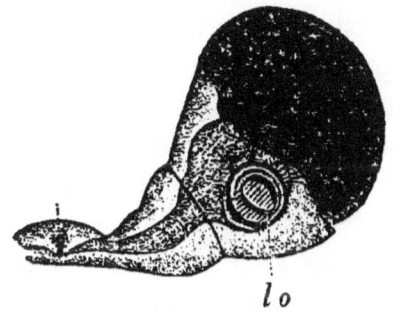

l o

Fig. 112.—Eye-stalk of *Euphausia* (after
Sars). *lo*, Luminous organ ; *a*, lower
eye.

eye-stalks, and appear to serve as " bull's-eyes " to
the true organs of vision. Sars considers that the
luminous organs do not serve as eyes, on the grounds

* " Ueber einige Schizopoden und niedere Malacostraceen," *Zeit.
für Wiss. Zool.*, 1863.

† " On the Schizopoda," " Challenger Reports," vol. xiii.

‡ Valentine and Cunningham, in a memoir just published
(*Quarterly Journal of Microscopical Science*, vol. xxviii.) deny this, and
attribute it to the inner surface of the reflector.

that the nerve which supplies them is but small; that the structure is not really analogous to that of a true eye, and that the position would be very unsuitable, one of them being actually situated on the stalk of the compound eye.

The question does not, however, seem to be by any means clearly solved, and it must, I think, be admitted that, with the exception of the anterior pair, if the position does not seem suitable for true eyes, neither is it that which one would expect in light-organs.

On the Mode of Vision by Means of Compound Eyes.

Johannes Müller, in his great work on the Physiology of Vision,* was the first to give an intelligible explanation of the manner in which insects see with their compound eyes. According to his view (see Fig. 75), those rays of light only which pass directly through the crystalline cones, or are reflected from their sides, can reach the corresponding nerve-fibre. The others fall on and are absorbed by the pigment which separates the different facets. Hence each cone receives light only from a very small portion of the field of vision, and the rays so received are collected into one spot of light. The larger and more convex, therefore, is the eye, the wider will be its field of vision; while the smaller and more numerous are the facets, the more distinct will the vision be. In fact, the picture perceived by the insect will be a mosaic, in which the number of points will correspond with the number of facets.

* "Zur vergleichenden Physiologie des Gesichtsinnes."

This theory was at first received with much favour. In 1852, however, Gottsche * attacked Müller's view, pointing out that each separate cornea of a compound eye can, and in fact does, give a separate and distinct image. This had, indeed, long previously been observed by Leeuwenhoek, who said, "When I removed the tunica cornea a little from the focus of the microscope, and placed a lighted candle at a short distance, so that the light of it must pass through the tunica cornea, I then saw through it the flame of the candle inverted, and not a single one, but some hundreds of flames appeared to me, and these so distinctly (though wonderfully minute) that I could discern the motion of trembling in each of them." †

Of this, indeed, it is easy to satisfy one's self. It is only necessary to look at a candle through the cornea of an insect, and then slightly draw back the microscope, when a thousand small images of the candle, each formed by one of the lenses, will be plainly seen. If, then, in such cases there was a retina placed at the proper distance, a true image would be formed, as on the retina in our own eyes. This paper of Gottsche's threw great doubt on Müller's explanation, which, indeed, was, in Dors's words, " abandonnée par tout le monde." ‡

It is one thing, however, to see that the lenses throw distinct pictures, but quite another to understand how such pictures could be received on the retina, or combined into one distinct image.

* " Beit. zur Anat. und Phys. der Fliegen und Krebse," *Müller's Arch.*, 1852.

† A. Van Leeuwenhoek, " Select Works," translated by S. Hoole.

‡ " De la vision chez les Arthropodes," *Ar. des Sci. Phys. et Nat.* Geneva : 1861.

It must, moreover, be remembered that in our eyes the whole field of vision is reversed, so that different objects remain in the same relative position. In the case of insects, however, it would be the image thrown by each facet which would be reversed, and hence the general effect would be altogether false.

We must not attach too much importance to the mere presence of an image. Any lens-like object, even a globule of fat, will give one. Moreover, as Müller and Helmholtz have shown, the lenses of the cornea would be an advantage on the theory of mosaic vision, by assisting to condense the rays of light on the termination of the nerve.

Gottsche's observation was made on the eye of the blow-fly (*Musca vomitoria*), and, as a matter of fact, the fly is one of those insects which do not possess a true crystalline cone. It is, therefore, probable that the image which he saw was that of the cornea. Moreover, as is shown by his figure, which I give below (Fig. 113), he states * that the image was formed at x, while the retina is far away at y. He suggested, indeed, that the so-called optic ganglion really corresponds with the retina of our own eye; but this would not remove

---

* His words are—"An der hintern Fläche der Crystallkörper im Fliegenauge kehrt sich sicher das Bild um, weil das Bild dem object in der Lage gleich ist, und da das Mikroskop das Object einmal umkehrt, so muss hier eine *doppelte* Umkehrung stattfinden, einmal durch das Mikroskop und vorher durch den parabolischen Crystall-körper. Entsteht nun bei x (Fig. 113) ein umgekehrtes Bild, so ist die Frage, wird das ganze Bild von x durch den Stiel zur Retina und zur Perception bei y hingeleitet oder wirkt dieser dünne Stiel gleichsam wie ein Diaphragma und giebt er nur einen Theil des Bildes bei x nach y" (Gottsche, "Beit. zur Anat. und Phys. des Auges der Krebse und Fliegen," *Arch. für Anat. Phys. und Wiss. Medicin.*, 1852).

the difficulty, because, if any definite picture is to be formed, the sensitive rods, cones, or other structures must lie in the plane of the image, and this is not, in fact, the case.

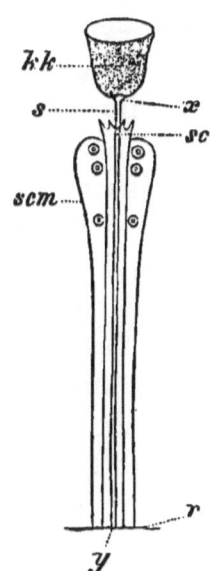

Dor suggested that the crystalline cones are nervous structures, and correspond to the rods of the vertebrate eye (Fig. 79). He admits, however, that, as a matter of fact, the image is not formed at the anterior surface of the crystalline cones.*

And yet in his final summary, having shown that the image is formed, not at the anterior surface, but deep down in the crystalline cones, he expresses quite a different view, compares the crystalline cone to the vitreous body, and considers that the true retina is to be found in an envelope which surrounds the cone.

Fig. 113.—One of the elements of the eye of a fly (after Gottsche). *kk*, Crystalline cone; *x*, position of the image; *s*, rod; *sc*, sheath; *scm*, outer sheath; *r*, retina; *y*, seat of vision.

Plateau † regards the mosaic theory of Müller as definitively abandoned, but rather seems to have had in his mind that of Gottsche. At least, he states that, according to Müller, the mosaic is formed by a number of partial images, each occupying the base of one of the elements composing the compound eye. This, however, is not Müller's theory.

* " La cornée avec sa convexité postérieure correspond à la cornée et au cristallin des vertébrés, le corps cristallin (avec le soi-disant corps vitré) et la fibre nerveuse qui s'y attache à la couche des bâtonnets, enfin le ganglion optique à celles des couches de la rétine, qui sont composées des granulations, des cellules, et des fibres nerveuses."

† " Rech. Exp. sur la Vision des Arthropodes." Bruxelles: 1887.

On the other hand, Boll,[*] Exner,[†] and Grenacher seem to me to have proved that the compound eyes of insects cannot act as ours do; that the theory which assumes that each facet acts as a separate eye and projects an image on a retina, is physically untenable.

In the first place, there are cases—for instance, Forficula, Dytiscus, and Stratiomys among insects; Ligia and many others among Crustacea—where the corneæ are not sufficiently arched to give any distinct image. But even where an image is thrown by the cornea, it would be destroyed by the crystalline cone.

In certain Crustacea the crystalline cones are elongated and curved; this, which Oscar Schmidt [‡] regarded as fatal to Müller's theory, is, on the contrary, as Exner has pointed out, quite compatible with it, but, on the contrary, cannot be reconciled with the theory of an image.

There are few beetles in which the cornea give better images than in the firefly (*Lampyris splendidula*). On the other hand, the crystalline cones entirely destroy these images. If the eye is looked at through a microscope, and the crystalline cones are left *in situ*, the field of view appears perfectly black, with a bright spot of light at the end of each cone. No trace of an image can be any longer perceived. In fact, the images seen by Leeuwenhoek and Gottsche are thrown by the cornea only.

In most cases, then, it would appear that the image formed by the cornea is destroyed by the crystalline

* "Beit. zur Phys. Optik," *Arch. für Anat. Phys. und Wiss. Medicin.*, 1871.

† "Ueber das Sehen von Bewegungen und der Theorie des zusammengesetzten Auges," *Sitz. K. Akad. d. Wiss. Wien.*, 1875.

‡ Ibid., 1876.

cone. This does not, indeed, always occur; but even in such cases the image does not coincide with the posterior end of the cone. Grenacher repeated the experiment of Gottsche with moths. Here the crystalline cones are firm, and are attached to the cornea. Thus he was able to remove the soft parts, and to look through the cones and the cornea. When the microscope was focussed at the inner end of the cone, a spot of light was visible, but no image. As the object-glass was moved forward, the image gradually came into view, and then disappeared again. Here, then, the image is formed in the interior of the cone itself. Exner had endeavoured to make this experiment with the eye of Hydrophilus (the great black water-beetle), but the crystalline cones always came away from the cornea. He, however, calculated the focal length, refraction, etc., of the cornea, and concluded that, even if, in spite of the crystalline cone, an image could be formed, it would fall much behind the retinula. In these cases, then, an image is out of the question. Moreover, as the cone tapers to a point, there would, in fact, be no room for an image, which must be received on an appropriate surface. In many insect eyes, indeed, as in those of the cockchafer (Fig. 100), the crystalline cone is drawn out into a thread, which expands again before reaching the retinula. Such an arrangement seems fatal to any idea of an image.

Moreover, for definite vision by the formation of an image, it is necessary that the eye should possess some power of accommodation for different distances. It is obvious, from Fig. 76, that no distinct vision would be given unless the receptive surface follows the line a' b' c'. But the position of this surface will

depend upon the distance of *a b c* from the lens. As
a matter of fact, Leydig * and Leuckart † thought they
had discovered, between the cornea and the crystalline
cones, certain muscular fibres which might regulate
the distance between the two, and thus effect this
object. Subsequent observers, however, have failed to
detect these fibres.

Again, it will be seen, from a glance at Fig. 76,
that in an eye constituted like ours, on the principle
of a camera obscura, the retina must follow a regular
curve. If it is brought at all too far forward, or forced
the least too far back, the image is at once blurred.
Hence, in our own case the frequent need for spectacles,
and hence it would seem that a conical retina is a
physical impossibility.

Plateau, indeed, adopts ‡ a suggestion made by
Grenacher that the absence of any means of adaptation
may be rendered unnecessary by the length of the
cones, the rays coming from distant objects acting on
the anterior end, those from nearer ones at a greater or
less depth. This, I confess, seems to me inadmissible.
In the first place, the light must surely act immediately it impinges on the organ of perception ; and, in
the second, the cones are, as a general rule, absolutely transparent—the light passes unimpeded through
them.

Again, if insects see with their compound eyes as we
do with ours, they must, of course, possess a retina.
No such structure, however, has been as yet shown to

* "Zum feineren Bau der Arthropoden," *Müller's Arch. für Anat.
und Phys.*, 1855.

† "Carcinologisches," *Wiegmann's Arch.*, 1858.

‡ "Rech. Exp. sur la vision chez les Arthropodes," 1887.

exist. Wagner,* indeed, observed that in some cases the optic nerve embraces the end of the cone, and he supposed that it thus forms a sort of retina, for which, however, its form is little suited.

I ought also to mention that Max Schultze † considered that he had, in some few cases—for instance, in Syrphus—been able to observe that the termination of the nerve does divide into a number of fibres. Patten,‡ more recently, has also maintained the existence of numerous nerve-fibrils, which, however, subsequent observers—for instance, Kingsley § and Beddard ∥—have been unable to discover. Even, however, if we admit the perfect correctness of Schultze's observation, these cases are exceptional, and the fibres so few that they can hardly, I think, affect the general conclusion. To give anything like a distinct vision, a very large number would be required.

A last objection is the extreme difficulty which would exist of combining so many different images into one idea, though it must be admitted that at first sight this difficulty (though to a minor degree) exists even in the case of simple eyes, the number of which varies considerably. Spiders have six to eight; some aquatic larvæ twelve; while the Oniscoidæ (wood-lice), assuming that their eyes are aggregates of simple eyes, as Müller supposed, have as many as twenty to forty.

* Einige Bemerk. über den Bau der zus. Augen," *Arch. für Nat.,* 1835.

† "Unt. über die zus. Augen der Krebse und Insecten," 1868.

‡ "Eyes of Molluscs and Arthropods," *Mitth. Zool. St. Neapel,* 1886.

§ " On the Divisions of the Compound Eye," *Journal of Morphology,* 1887.

∥ "On the Structure of the Eye in Cymothoidæ," *Trans. Roy. Soc. Edin.,* 1887.

These, however, take in different parts of the field of vision.

The principal reasons, then, which seem to favour Müller's theory of mosaic vision are as follows:— (1) in certain cases—for instance, in Hyperia—there are no lenses, and consequently there can be no image; (2) the image would generally be destroyed by the crystalline cone; (3) in some cases it would seem that the image would be formed completely behind the eye, while in others, again, it would be too near the cornea; (4) a pointed retina seems incompatible with a clear image; (5) any true projection of an image would in certain species be precluded by the presence of impenetrable pigment, which only leaves a minute central passage for the light-rays; (6) even the clearest image would be useless, from the absence of a suitable receptive surface, since both the small number and mode of combination of the elements composing that surface seem to preclude it from receiving more than a single impression; (7) no system of accommodation has yet been discovered. Finally, (8) a combination of many thousand relatively complete eyes seems quite useless and incomprehensible.

On the Power of Vision in Insects, etc.

As regards the practical vision of insects, our knowledge is still very imperfect. No one, indeed, who has observed them can doubt that in some the sight is highly developed. It is impossible, for instance, to watch a dragon-fly hawking over a pond,—to see the rapidity and accuracy of its movements, and doubt that it can see well.

On the other hand, Claparède asserts that at a distance of twenty feet a hive bee would be unable to see any object which was less than eight or nine inches in diameter, and even at a distance of a foot he says that each facet would correspond to an inch and a third.

To determine how far a faceted eye could see, he takes the breadth of a facet, the radius of the eye-sphere, and the smallest angle of vision, and the distance in centimetres at which the facet would cover a centimetre, and finds for the bee, for instance, 6·7 centimetres.

He then proceeds to inquire at what distance from the faceted eye the image is as clear as in the human eye, and he thinks this would be about a millimetre, from which it would rapidly diminish, being only $\frac{1}{10}$ at a centimetre, and at a metre no distant vision being possible; so that at a very little distance such eyes would be as good as useless.

"In the human eye, for example, the distance between the centres of two adjacent cones is only $\frac{4}{1000}$ mm., but in Musca the distance between adjacent ommatidia is $\frac{1}{100}$ mm. In fact, the picture, as received by the nerve-end cells of the Vertebrate eye, is much more complete in itself than it can possibly be in any Arthropod eye, and consequently the latter possesses a much more elaborate and complete translating apparatus in its retina than the former possesses." [*]

Claparède arrives at this conclusion by taking the average curvature of the whole eye, as being true for each part. This, however, is not the case, and in the central region of the eye the adjacent facets

---

[*] S. J. Hickson, "The Eye and Optic Tract of Insects," *Quarterly Journal of Microscopical Science*, vol. xxv., new series, 1885, p. 242.

make but a small angle with one another.   Lowne has calculated that wasps, humble bees, dragon-flies, etc., would, at a distance of twenty feet, be able to distinguish objects from half an inch to an inch in diameter.   Thus a dragon-fly would see an object twenty feet from its eye in the same detail that a man would perceive it at a distance of a hundred and sixty feet.

Moreover, when Claparède * observes that bees will return from a considerable distance straight to the door of their nest, and that, under Müller's theory, the door would at such a distance be absolutely invisible, he forgets that the bee first probably guides itself by the known position of the door in relation to some tree or other large object, then with reference to the hive itself, and that it is quite unnecessary to assume that the door is actually seen from a distance.

With reference to the power which insects possess of determining form, Plateau † has recently made some ingenious experiments.   Suppose a room into which the light enters by two equal and similar orifices, and suppose an insect set free at the back of the room, it will at once fly to the light, but the two openings being alike it will go indifferently to either one or the other.   That such is the case Plateau's experiments clearly show, and, moreover, prove that a comparatively small increase in the amount of light will attract the insect to one orifice in preference to the other.   It occurred then to Plateau to utilize this by varying the form of the opening, so that the light admitted being

* "Zur Morph. der zus. Augen bei den Arthropoden," *Zeit. für Wiss. Zool.*, 1860.

† *Bull. de l'Acad. Roy. de Belgique*, t. x., 1885; *Comptes Rendus de la Soc. Ent. de Belg.*, 1887; "Rech. Exp. sur la Vision chez les Arthropodes," 1887.

equal, the opening on the one side should leave a clear passage, while that on the other should be divided by bars large enough to be easily visible, and sufficiently close to prevent the insect from passing.

His experiments were conducted in a room five metres square, lighted by two similar windows looking to the west. It was on the first floor, and looked out on to fields. Moreover, he had the glass of the windows slightly ground, so that, while the light penetrated, nothing outside could be seen. He then covered up the windows, leaving only two orifices, one of which was simple and square, while the other was divided by cross-bars. To secure equality of light, the latter was left somewhat larger than the other, and the equivalence of the two was determined by a Rumford's photometer. The insects were set free on a table at the back of the room, exactly between the two openings, and at a distance of four metres. He states that a very slight difference in the intensity of the light determined the flight of the insect to either one or the other opening; while, if the amount of light was as nearly as possible equal, they flew as often to the one as to the other.

Omitting the cases when the light was not equal, the numbers were as follows:—

	Clear opening.	Trellised opening.
Musca vomitoria (the bluebottle)	... 8	... 7

On the other hand, they were—for

	Clear opening.	Trellised opening.
Eristalis tenax (the bee fly)	... 4	... 8
Vanessa urticæ (tortoiseshell butterfly) ...	... 1	... 5
	13	20

In fact, then, the insects seem to have gone more

often to the trellised opening. M. Plateau concludes
that insects do not distinguish differences of form, or
can only do so very badly (" Ils ne distinguent pas la
forme des objects ou la distinguent fort mal ").

I confess, however, that these experiments, ingenious
as they are, do not seem to me to justify the conclusions which M. Plateau has deduced from them.
Unless the insects had some means of measuring
distance (of which we have no clear evidence), they
could not tell that even the smaller orifice might not
be quite large enough to afford them a free passage.
The bars, moreover, would probably appear to them
somewhat blurred. Again, they could not possibly
tell that the bars really crossed the orifice, and if they
were situated an inch or two further off they would
constitute no barrier.

I have tried some experiments, not yet enough to be
conclusive, but which lead me to a different conclusion
from that of M. Plateau. I trained wasps to come to
a drop of honey placed on paper, and, when the insects
had learned their lesson, changed the form of the paper,
as I had previously changed the color. It certainly
seemed to me that the insect recognized the change.
M. Forel has also tried similar experiments, and with
the same result.

We know, however, as yet very little with reference
to the actual power of vision possessed by insects.

On the Function of Ocelli.

Another interesting question remains. What is the
function of the ocelli ? Why do insects have two sorts
of eyes ?

Johannes Müller considered that the power of vision of ocelli "is probably confined to the perception of very near objects. This may be inferred partly from their existing principally in larvæ and apterous insects, and partly from several observations which I have made relative to the position of these simple eyes. In the genus Empusa the head is so prolonged over the middle inferior eye that, in the locomotion of the animal, the nearest objects can only come within the range. In the *Locusta cornuta*, also, the same eye lies beneath the prolongation of the head. . . . In the Orthoptera generally, also, the simple eyes are, in consequence of the depressed position of the head, directed downwards towards the surface upon which the insects are moving."

From these facts, he considers himself justified in concluding that the simple eyes of insects are intended principally for myopic vision. The simple eyes bear a similar relation to the compound eyes, as the palpi to the antennæ. Both the antennæ and compound eyes are absent in the larvæ of insects." *

Lowne observes † that "the great convexity of the lens in the ocellus of Eristalis must give it a very short focus, and it is manifestly but ill adapted for the formation of a picture. The comparatively small number of rods must further render the production of anything like a perfect picture, even of very near objects, useless for purposes of vision. I strongly suspect that the function of the ocelli is the perception of the intensity and the direction of light rather than of vision in the ordinary acceptation of the term."

* "Physiology of the Senses," translated by Baly.
† "On the Modification of the Eyes of Insects," *Phil. Trans.*, 1878.

Réaumur, Marcel de Serres, Dugès, and Forel also have shown that in insects which possess both ocelli and compound eyes, the ocelli may be covered over without materially affecting the movements of the animal; while, on the contrary, if the compound eyes are so treated, they behave just as if in the dark. For instance, Forel varnished over the compound eyes of some flies (*Musca vomitoria* and *Lucilia cæsar*), and found that, if placed on the ground, they made no attempt to rise; while, if thrown in the air, they flew first in one direction and then in another, striking against any object that came in their way, and being apparently quite unable to guide themselves. They flew repeatedly against a wall, falling to the ground, and unable to alight against it, as they do so cleverly when they have their eyes to guide them. Finally, they ended by flying straight up into the air, and quite out of sight. It seems, indeed, to be a very general rule that insects of which the eyes are covered, whether they are totally blinded, or whether the ocelli are left uncovered, fly straight up into the air—a very curious and significant fact of which I think no satisfactory explanation has yet been given.

Plateau * regards the simple eyes, or ocelli, as rudimentary organs of scarcely any use to the insect. Forel also states, as the result of his observations, that wasps, humble bees, ants, etc., find their way both in the air and on the ground, almost equally well without as with the aid of their ocelli.

I confess that I am not satisfied on this point. In such experiments great care is necessary. M. Forel's interesting experiments with ants, whose compound eyes

* *Bull. de l'Acad. Roy. de Belgique*, t. x., 1885.

he had covered with opaque varnish, might almost, for instance, be quoted to prove the same with reference to the compound eyes. "Mes Camponotus aux yeux vernis," he says, "attaquaient et tuaient aussitôt une *Formica fusca* mise au milieu d'eux, la saisissaient presque aussi adroitement que ceux qui avaient leurs yeux. Ils déménageaient un tas de larves d'un coin de leur récipient à l'autre avec autant de précision qu' avec leurs yeux." *

On the other hand, Forel goes so far as to say that if the compound eyes are covered with black varnish, insects cannot even perceive light ("Cela prouve qu'elles ne voyaient plus même la lueur"). In fact, the use of the ocelli seems a great enigma, at least when the compound eyes are present.

We must remember that some other Articulata—spiders, for instance—possess ocelli only, and they certainly see, though not probably very well.

Plateau has made some ingenious observations, from which it appears that spiders are very short-sighted, and have little power of appreciating form. He found they were easily deceived by artificial flies of most inartistic construction; and he concludes that even hunting spiders do not perceive their prey at a greater distance than ten centimetres (about four inches), and in most cases even less. Scorpions appeared scarcely to see beyond their own pincers.

I have also made some experiments on this point with spiders (*Lycosa saccata*). In this species, which is very common, the female, after laying her eggs, collects them into a ball, which she surrounds with a silken envelope and carries about with her. I captured a

* *Recueil Zool. Suisse,* 1887.

female, and, after taking the bag of eggs from her, put her on a table. She ran about awhile, looking for her eggs. When she became still, I placed the ball of eggs gently about two inches in front of her. She evidently did not see it. I pushed it gradually towards her, but she took no notice till it nearly touched her, when she eagerly seized it.

I then took it away a second time, and put it in the middle of the table, which was two feet four inches by one foot four, and had nothing else on it. The spider wandered about, and sometimes passed close to the bag of eggs, but took no notice of it. She wandered about for an hour and fifty minutes before she found it—apparently by accident. I then took it away again, and put it down as before, when she wandered about for an hour without finding it.

The same experiment was tried with other individuals, and with the same results. It certainly appeared as if they could not see more than half an inch before them —in fact, scarcely further than the tips of their feet.

I may also mention that they did not appear to recognize their own bags of eggs, but were equally happy if they were interchanged.

On the other hand, it must be remembered that the sac is spun from the spinnerets, and the Lycosa had perhaps actually never seen the bag of eggs. Hunting spiders certainly appear to perceive their prey at a distance of at least several inches.

Plateau has shown, in a recent memoir, that caterpillars, which possess ocelli, but no compound eyes, are very short-sighted, not seeing above one to two centimetres.*

* "Rech. Exp. sur la Vision chez les Arthropodes." *Bull. de 'Acad. Roy. de Belgique,* 1888.

Lebert has expressed the opinion * "that in spiders some of their eight eyes—those which are most convex and brightly coloured—serve to see during daylight; the others, flatter and colorless, during the dusk." Pavesi has observed † that in a cave-dwelling species (*Nesticus speluncarum*), which belongs to a genus in which the other species have eight eyes, the four middle eyes are atrophied. This suggests that they serve specially in daylight.

Returning for a moment to the ocelli of true insects, it seems almost incredible that such complex organs should be rudimentary or useless. Moreover, the evidence afforded by the genus Eciton seems difficult to reconcile with this theory. The species of this genus are hunting ants, which move about in large armies and attack almost all sorts of insects, whence they are known as driver ants, or army ants. They have no compound eyes, but in the place of them most species have a single large ocellus on each side of the head, while others, on the contrary, are blind. Now, while the former hunt in the open, and have all the appearance of seeing fairly well, the latter construct covered galleries, and seek their prey in hollow trees and other dark localities.

Insects with good sight generally have the crystalline lenses narrow and long, which involves a great loss of light. The ocelli are specially developed in insects, such as ants, bees, and wasps, which live partly in the open light and partly in the dark recesses of nests. Again, the night-flying moths all possess ocelli; while they are entirely absent in butterflies, with, accord-

* "Die Spinnen der Schweiz."
† "Sopra una nuova Specie di Ragui."

ing to Scudder, one exception, namely, the genus Pamphila.

On the whole, then, perhaps the most probable view is that, as regards insects, the ocelli are useful in dark places and for near vision.*

Whatever the special function of ocelli may be, it seems clear that they must see in the same manner as our eyes do—that is to say, the image must be reversed. On the other hand, in the case of compound eyes, it seems probable that the vision is direct, and the difficulty of accounting for the existence in the same animal of two such different kinds of eyes is certainly enhanced by the fact that, as it would seem, the image given by the medial eyes is reversed, while that of the lateral ones is direct.

Forel, in his last memoir, inclines to this opinion.

CHAPTER VIII.

ON PROBLEMATICAL ORGANS OF SENSE.

IN addition to the organs of which I have attempted in the preceding chapters to give some idea, and to those which from their structure we may suppose to perform analogous functions, there are others of considerable importance and complexity, which are evidently organs of some sense, but the use and purpose of which are still unknown.

"It is almost impossible," says Gegenbaur,* "to say what is the physiological duty of a number of organs, which are clearly sensory, and are connected with the integument. These enlargements are generally formed by ciliated regions to which a nerve passes, and at which it often forms enlargements. It is doubtful what part of the surrounding medium acts on these organs, and we have to make a somewhat farfetched analogy to be able to regard them as olfactory organs."

Among the structures of which the use is still quite uncertain are the muciferous canals of fishes. The skin of fishes, indeed, contains a whole series of organs of whose functions we know little. As regards the

* " Elements of Comparative Anatomy."

muciferous canal, Schultze has suggested * that it is a sense-organ adapted to receive vibrations of the water with wave-lengths too great to be perceived as ordinary sounds. Beard also leans to this same view. However this may be, it is remarkably developed in many deep-sea fish.

In some cases peculiar eye-like bodies are developed in connection (though not exclusively so) with the muciferous canal. Leuckart,† by whom they were discovered, at first considered them to be accessory eyes, but subsequent researches led him to modify this opinion, and to regard them as luminous organs. Ussow ‡ has more recently maintained that they are eyes, and Leydig considers them as organs which approach very nearly to true eyes ("welche wirblichen sehorganen sehr nahe stehen"). Whatever doubt there may be whether they have any power of sight, there is no longer any question but that they are luminous, and they are especially developed in the fishes of the deep sea.

These are very peculiar. The abysses of the ocean are quite still, and black darkness reigns. The pressure of the water is also very great.

Hence the deep seas have a peculiar fauna of their own. Surface species could not generally bear the enormous pressure, and do not descend to any great depth. The true deep-sea forms are, however, as yet little known. They are but seldom seen, and when

---

* "Ueber die Sinnesorgane der Seitenlinie bei Fischen und Amphibien," *Arch. für Mic. Anat.*, 1870.

† "Ueber muthmassliche Nebenaugen bei einem Fische." Bericht über die 39 Vers., *Deutscher Naturforscher, Giessen*, 1864.

‡ "Ueber den Bau der sog. augenähnlichen Flecken einiger Knochenfische," *Bull. Soc. Imp. Moscow*, 1879.

obtained are generally in a bad state of preservation. Their tissues seem to be unusually lax, and liable to destruction. Moreover, in every living organism, besides those usually present in the digestive organs, the blood and other fluids contain gases in solution. These, of course, expand when the pressure is diminished, and tend to rupture the tissues. The circumstances under which some deep-sea fish have occasionally been met with on the surface bears this out. They are generally found to have perished while endeavouring to swallow some prey not much smaller, or even in some cases larger, than themselves. What, then, has happened? During the struggle they were carried into an upper layer of water. Immediately the gases within them began to expand, and raised them higher; the process continued, and they were carried up more and more rapidly, until they reached the surface in a dying condition.*

It is, however, but rarely that deep-sea fish are found thus floating on the surface, and our knowledge of them is mainly derived from the dredge, and especially from the specimens thus obtained during the voyage of the *Challenger*.

In other respects, moreover, their conditions of life in the ocean depths are very peculiar. The light of the sun cannot penetrate beyond about two hundred fathoms; deeper than this, complete darkness prevails. Hence in many species the eyes have more or less completely disappeared. In others, on the contrary, they are well developed, and these may be said to be a light to themselves. In some species there are a number of luminous organs arranged within the area

* Günther. "Introduction to the Study of Fishes."

of, and in relation to, the muciferous system; while in others they are variously situated. These luminous organs were first mentioned by Cocco.* They have since been studied by Günther, Leuckart, Ussow, Leydig, and Emery. Lastly, they have been carefully described by Günther, Moseley, and von Lendenfeld in the work on "Deep-Sea Fishes," in vol. xxvii. of the "Challenger Reports." The deep-sea fish are either silvery, pink, or in many cases black, sometimes relieved with scarlet, and, when the luminous organs flash out, must present a very remarkable appearance.

We have still much to learn as to the structure and functions of these organs, but there are cases in which their use can be surmised with some probability. The light is evidently under the will of the fish. It is easy to imagine a Photichthys (Fig. 114), swimming

Fig. 114.—*Photichthys argenteus* ("Challenger Reports," vol. xxvii.).

in the black depths of the ocean, suddenly flashing out light from its luminous organs, and thus bringing into view any prey which may be near; while, if danger is disclosed, the light is again at once extinguished. It may be observed that the largest of these organs is situated just under the eye, so that the fish is actually provided with a bull's eye lantern. In other cases

* *Nuovi Ann. dei Sci. Nat.*, 1838.

the light may rather serve as a defence, some having—
as, for instance, in the genus Scopelus—a pair of large
ones in the tail, so that "a strong ray of light shot
forth from the stern-chaser may dazzle and frighten an
enemy." * In other cases they probably serve as lures.
The "sea-devil," or "angler," of our coasts has on
its head three long, very flexible, reddish filaments,
while all round its head are fringed appendages, closely
resembling fronds of seaweed. The fish conceals itself
at the bottom, in the sand or among seaweed, and
dangles the long filaments in front of its mouth.
Other little fishes, taking them for worms, unsuspect-
ingly approach, and themselves fall victims.

Several species of the same family live at great

Fig. 115.—*Ceratius bispinosus* ("Challenger Reports," vol. xxvii.).

depths, and have very similar habits. A mere red
filament would, however, be invisible in the dark, and
therefore useless. They have, however, developed
(Fig. 115) a luminous organ, a living "glow-lamp," at

* Günther, "Challenger Reports," vol. xxvii.

the end of the filament, which doubtless proves a very effective lure.*

These cases, however, though very interesting, throw little light on the use of the muciferous system in ordinary fish, which, I think, still remains an enigma.

In some of the lower animals, the nerves terminate on reaching the skin at the base of rod-like structures similar, in many respects, to the rods of the retina, or the auditory rods of the ear, and of which it is very difficult to say whether they are organs of touch or of some higher sense.

Round the margin of the common sea-anemone is a circle of bright blue spots, or small bladders. If a section be made, there will be found a number of cylindrical organs, each containing a fine thread, and terminating in a "cnidocil (Fig. 14);" and, secondly, fibres very like nerve-threads, swelling from time to time with ganglionic expansions, and also terminating in a cnidocil. These structures, in all probability, serve as an organ of sense, but what impressions they convey it is impossible to say.

Some jelly-fishes (Trachynemadæ) have groups of long hairs arranged in pairs at the base of the tentacles (Fig. 116), which have been regarded as organs of touch, and it is certainly difficult to suggest any other function for them. They are obviously sense-hairs, but I see no reason for attributing to them the sense of touch.

The so-called eyes of the leech, in Leydig's † opinion,

---

* Günther, " Study of Fishes."

† " Die Augen und neue Sinnesorgane der Egel.," *Reichert's Arch.*, 1861.

which is confirmed by Ranke,* are also developed from
the supposed special organs of touch.   The latter are
much more numerous, as many as sixty being developed

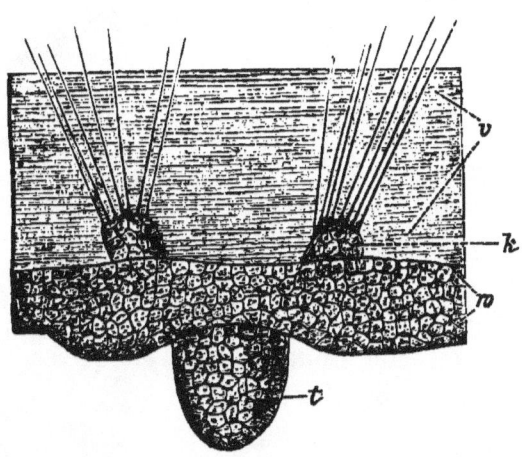

Fig. 116.—Edge of a portion of the mantle of *Aglaura hemistoma*, with a pair of sense-
organs (after Hertwig).   *v*, Velum; *k*, sense-organ; *ro*, layer of nettle cells; *t*,
tentacle.

on the head alone.   They are cylindrical organs, lined
with large nucleated refractive cells, which occupy
nearly all the interior.   A special nerve penetrates
each, and, after passing some way up, appears to
terminate in a free end.

I may also allude to the very varied bristles and
cirrhi of worms, with their great diversity of forms.

Among Insects and Crustacea, there are a great
number of peculiarly formed skin appendages, for
which it is very difficult to suggest any probable
function.

The lower antennæ of the male in Gammarus, for
instance, bear a very peculiar slipper-shaped organ,
situated on a short stalk : this was first mentioned by

* " Beit. zu der Lehre. von den Uebergangs Sinnesorganen," *Zeit.*
für Wiss. Zool., 1875.

Milne Edwards, and subsequently by other authors, especially by Leydig.* The short stalk contains a canal, which appears to divide into radiating branches on reaching the "slipper," which itself is marked by a series of rings.

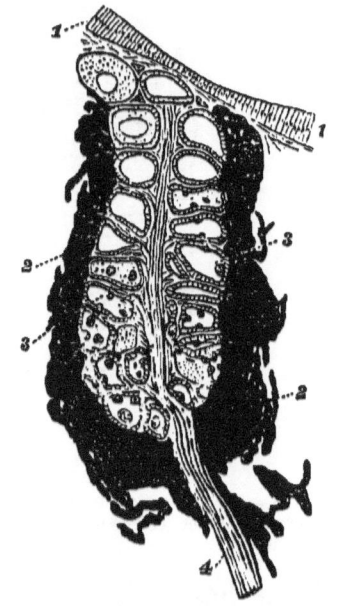

Among other problematical organs, I might refer to the remarkable pyriform sensory organs on the antennæ of Pleuromma,† the appendages on the second thoracic leg of Serolis, those on the maxillipeds of Eurycopa, on the metatarsus of spiders, the finger-shaped organ on the antennæ of Polydesmus, the singular pleural eye (?) of Pleuromma, and many others.

Fig. 117.—Sense-organ of leech (from Carrière, after Ranke). 1, Epithelium; 2, pigment; 3, cells; 4, nerve. The longer axis equals ·4 mm.

There is every reason to hope that future studies will throw much light on these interesting structures. We may, no doubt, expect much from the improvement in our microscopes, the use of new reagents, and of mechanical appliances, such as the microtome; but the ultimate atoms of which matter is composed are so infinitesimally minute, that it is difficult to foresee any manner in which we may hope for a final solution of these problems.

Loschmidt, who has since been confirmed by Stoney and Sir W. Thomson, calculates that each of the

---

* *Zeit. für Wiss. Zool.*," 1878.

† Brady, " On the Copepoda of the *Challenger* Expedition," vol. viii.

ultimate atoms of matter is at most $\frac{1}{50.000.000}$ of an inch in diameter. Under these circumstances, we cannot, it would seem, hope at present for any great increase of our knowledge of atoms by improvements in the microscope. With our present instruments we can perceive lines ruled on glass which are $\frac{1}{50.000}$ of an inch apart. But, owing to the properties of light itself, the fringes due to interference begin to produce confusion at distances of $\frac{1}{74.000}$, and in the brightest part of the spectrum, at little more than $\frac{1}{50.000}$, they would make the obscurity more or less complete. If, indeed, we could use the blue rays by themselves, their waves being much shorter, the limit of possible visibility might be extended to $\frac{1}{120.000}$; and, as Helmholtz has suggested, this perhaps accounts for Stinde having actually been able to obtain a photographic image of lines only $\frac{1}{100.000}$ of an inch apart. This, however, would appear to be the limit, and it would seem, then, that, owing to the physical characters of light, we can scarcely hope for any great improvement so far as the mere visibility of structure is concerned, though in other respects, no doubt, much may be hoped for. At the same time, Dallinger and Royston Pigott have shown that, as far as the mere presence of simple objects is concerned, bodies of even smaller dimensions can be perceived. According to the views of Helmholtz, the smallest particle that could be distinctly defined, when associated with others, is about $\frac{1}{80.000}$ of an inch in diameter. Now, it has been estimated that a particle of albumen of this size contains 125,000,000 of molecules. In the case of such a simple compound as water, the number would be no less than 8,000,000,000. Even then, if we could construct microscopes far more powerful than any we now possess, they could not enable us to obtain by direct vision any idea of the ultimate molecules of matter. The smallest sphere of organic matter which could be clearly defined with our most powerful microscopes may be, in reality, very complex; may be built up of many millions of molecules, and it follows that there may be an almost infinite number of structural characters in organic tissues which we can at present foresee no mode of examining.

Again, it has been shown that animals hear sounds which are beyond the range of our hearing, and that they can perceive the ultra-violet rays, which are invisible to our eyes.*

Now, as every ray of homogeneous light which we can perceive at all, appears to us as a distinct color, it becomes probable that these ultra-violet rays must make themselves apparent to the ants as a distinct and separate color (of which we can form no idea), but as different from the rest as red is from yellow, or green from violet. The question also arises whether white light to these insects would differ from our white light in containing this additional color. At any rate, as few of the colors in nature are pure, but almost all arise from the combination of rays of different wavelengths, and as in such cases the visible resultant would be composed not only of the rays we see, but of these and the ultra-violet, it would appear that the colors of objects and the general aspect of nature must present to animals a very different appearance from what it does to us.

These considerations cannot but raise the reflection

* " Ants, Bees, and Wasps."

how different the world may—I was going to say must
—appear to other animals from what it does to us.
Sound is the sensation produced on us when the vibrations of the air strike on the drum of our ear. When
they are few, the sound is deep; as they increase in
number, it becomes shriller and shriller; but when they
reach 40,000 in a second, they cease to be audible.
Light is the effect produced on us when waves of light
strike on the eye. When 400 millions of millions of
vibrations of ether strike the retina in a second, they
produce red, and as the number increases the color
passes into orange, then yellow, green, blue, and violet.
But between 40,000 vibrations in a second and 400
millions of millions we have no organ of sense capable
of receiving the impression. Yet between these limits
any number of sensations may exist. We have five
senses, and sometimes fancy that no others are possible.
But it is obvious that we cannot measure the infinite
by our own narrow limitations.

Moreover, looking at the question from the other
side, we find in animals complex organs of sense, richly
supplied with nerves, but the function of which we are
as yet powerless to explain. There may be fifty other
senses as different from ours as sound is from sight;
and even within the boundaries of our own senses there
may be endless sounds which we cannot hear, and
colors, as different as red from green, of which we have
no conception. These and a thousand other questions
remain for solution. The familiar world which surrounds us may be a totally different place to other
animals. To them it may be full of music which we
cannot hear, of color which we cannot see, of sensations
which we cannot conceive. To place stuffed birds and

beasts in glass cases, to arrange insects in cabinets, and dried plants in drawers, is merely the drudgery and preliminary of study; to watch their habits, to understand their relations to one another, to study their instincts and intelligence, to ascertain their adaptations and their relations to the forces of nature, to realize what the world appears to them; these constitute, as it seems to me at least, the true interest of natural history, and may even give us the clue to senses and perceptions of which at present we have no conception.

CHAPTER IX.

ON BEES AND COLORS.

IN my book on "Ants, Bees, and Wasps," [*] I have recorded a number of observations which seemed to me to prove that bees possess the power of distinguishing colors—a power implied, of course, in the now generally accepted views as to the origin of the colors of flowers, but which had not up to that time been proved by direct experiment.

Amongst other experiments, I brought a bee to some honey which I placed on a slip of glass laid on blue paper, and about three feet off I placed a similar drop of honey on orange paper. With a drop of honey before her a bee takes two or three minutes to fill herself, then flies away, stores up the honey, and returns for more. My hives were about two hundred yards from the window, and the bees were absent about three minutes, or even less; when working quietly they fly very quickly, and the actual journeys to and fro did not take more than a few seconds. After the bee had returned twice, I transposed the papers; but she returned to the honey on the blue paper. I allowed her to continue this for some time, and then again transposed the papers. She

---

[*] "Ants, Bees, and Wasps," International Scientific Series. Kegan Paul, Trench & Co.

returned to the old spot, and was just going to alight, when she observed the change of color, pulled herself up, and without a moment's hesitation darted off to the blue. No one who saw her at that moment could have the slightest doubt about her perceiving the difference between the two colors.

I also made a number of similar observations with red, yellow, green, and white. But I was anxious to carry the matter further, and ascertain, if possible whether they have any preference for one color over another, which had been denied by M. Bonnier. To test this I took slips of glass of the size used for slides for the microscope, viz. three inches by one, and pasted on them slips of paper of the same size, coloured respectively blue, green, orange, red, white, and yellow. I then put them on a lawn, in a row, about a foot apart, and on each put a second slip of glass with a drop of honey. I also put with them a slip of plain glass with a similar drop of honey. I had previously trained a marked bee to come to the place for honey. My plan then was, when the bee returned and had sipped for about a quarter of a minute, to remove the honey, when she flew to another slip. This I then took away, when she went to a third, and so on. In this way, as bees generally suck for three or four minutes, I induced her to visit all the drops successively before returning to the nest. When she had gone to the nest, I transposed all the upper glasses with the honey, and also moved the colored glasses. Thus, as the drop of honey was changed each time, and also the position of the colored glasses, neither of these could influence the selection by the bee.

In recording the results, I marked down successively

the order in which the bee went to the different coloured glasses. For instance, in the first journey from the nest, as recorded below, the bee lit first on the blue, which accordingly I marked 1; when the blue was removed, she flew about a little, and then lit on the white; when the white was removed, she settled on the green, and so on successively on the orange, yellow, plain, and red. I repeated the experiment a hundred times, using two different hives—one in Kent and one in Middlesex—and spreading the observations over some time, so as to experiment with different bees, and under varied circumstances.

I believe that the precautions taken placed the colors on an equal footing, and that the number of experiments is sufficient to give a fair average. Moreover, they were spread over several days, and the daily totals did not differ much from one another. The result shows a marked preference for blue, then white, then successively yellow, red, green, and orange. The red I used was a scarlet; pink would, I believe from subsequent observations, have been more popular. I may also observe that the honey on plain glass was less visited than that on any of the colors, which was the more significant because when I was not actually observing, the colors were removed, and some drops of honey left on plain glass, which naturally gave the plain glass an advantage.

Another mode of testing the result is to take the number of times in which the bee went first to each color, for instance, in a hundred visits she came to the blue first thirty-one times, and last only four; while to the plain glass she came first only five times, and last twenty-four times. It may be worth while to add that I by no means expected such a result.

A recent number of *Kosmos* contains a very courteous and complimentary notice of these observations by Dr. H. Müller, which, coming from so high an authority, is especially gratifying. Dr. Müller, however, criticizes some of the above-mentioned experiments, and remarks that, in order to make the test absolutely correct, the seven glasses should have been arranged in every possible order, and that this would give no less than 5040 combinations. I did not, however, suppose that I had attained to mathematical accuracy, or shown the exact degree of preference; all I claimed to show was the existence, and order, of preference, and I think that, as in my experiments the position of the colors was continually being changed, the result in this respect would have been substantially the same.

Dr. Müller also observes that when a bee has been accustomed to come to one place for honey, she returns to it, and will tend to alight there whatever the color may be; and he shows, by the record of his own experiences, that this has a considerable influence. This is so. Of course, however, it applies mainly to bees which had been used for some time, and were accustomed to a particular spot. I was fully alive to this tendency of the bees, and neutralized it to a considerable extent, partly by frequently changing the bee, and partly by moving the glasses. While, however, I admit that it is a factor which has to be taken into consideration, I do not see that it affords any argument against my conclusions. The tendency would be to weaken the effect of preference for any particular color, and to equalize the visits to all the glasses. This tendency on the part of the bees was, as my experiments show, overborne by the effect produced upon them

by the color. So far, then, from weakening my conclusions, the fact, so far as it goes, tends to strengthen
them, because it shows that notwithstanding this
tendency the blue was preferred, and the honey on
colorless glass neglected. The legitimate conclusion
to be drawn seems, I confess, to me, not that my mode
of observation was faulty, but rather that the preference of the bees for particular colors is even somewhat greater than the numbers would indicate.

Next, Dr. Müller objects that when disturbed from
one drop of honey, the bees naturally would, and that
in his experiments they actually did, fly to the next.
As a matter of fact, however, this did not happen in
mine, because, to avoid this source of error, when I
removed the color I gave the bee a good shake, and so
made her take a flight before settling down again.

According to my experience, bees differ considerably
in character, or, I should rather perhaps say, in humour.
Some are much shyer and more restless than others.
When disturbed from the first drop of honey, some are
much longer before they settle on the next than others.
Much also, of course, depends on how long the bee has
been experimented on. Bees, like men, settle down to
their work. Moreover, it is no doubt true that, *cæteris
paribus*, a bee in search of honey will go to the nearest
source.

But, as a matter of fact, in my hundred experiments
I had but very few cases like those quoted above from
Dr. Müller. This arose partly from the fact that my
bees were frequently changed, and partly because, as
already mentioned, I took care, in removing the color,
to startle the bee enough to make her take a little
flight before alighting again. Dr. Müller says that in

his experiments, when the bee did not go to the next
honey, it was when he shook her off *too* vigorously. I
should rather say that in his observations he did not
shake the bee off vigorously enough. The whole
objection, however, is open to the same remark as the
last. The bee would have a tendency, of course, like
any one else, to go to its goal by the nearest route.
Hence I never supposed that the figures exactly indicate the degree of preference. The very fact, however,
that there would naturally be a tendency on the part
of the bees to save themselves labour by going to the
nearest honey, makes the contrast shown by my
observations all the more striking.

I have never alleged that it was possible, in the case
of bees (or, for that matter, of men either), to get any
absolute and exact measure of preference for one color
over another. It would be easy to suggest many considerations which would prevent this. For instance,
something would probably depend on the kind of
flower the bee had been in the habit of visiting. A
bee which had been sucking daisies might probably
behave very differently from one which had been
frequenting a blue flower.

So far, however, as the conclusions which I ventured
to draw are concerned, I cannot see that they are in
any way invalidated by the objections which Dr.
Müller has urged, which, on the other hand, as it seems
to me, rather tend to strengthen my argument.

I may perhaps be asked, If blue is the favourite
color of bees, and then pink, and if bees have had so
much to do with the origin of flowers, how is it there
are so few blue and pink ones?

The explanation I believe to be that all blue flowers

have descended from ancestors in which the flowers were red, these from others in which they were yellow, while originally they were all green—or, to speak more precisely, in which the leaves immediately surrounding the stamens and pistil were green; that they have passed through stages of yellow, and generally if not always red, before becoming blue.

It is, of course, easy to see that the possession of color is an advantage to flowers in rendering them more conspicuous, more easily seen, and less readily overlooked, by the insects which fertilize them ; but it is not quite so clear why, apart from brilliancy and visibility at a distance, one color should be more advantageous than another. These experiments however, which show that insects have their preference, throw some light on the subject.

Where insects are beguiled into visits, as is the case especially with flies, they are obviously more likely to be deceived if the flowers not only, as is often the case, smell like decaying animal substance, but almost resemble them in appearance. Hence many fly flowers not only emit a most offensive smell, but also are dingy yellow or red, often mottled, and very closely resemble in color decaying meat.

There remains another case in which allied flowers, and species, moreover, which are fertilized by very much the same insects, are yet characterized by distinct colors. We have, for instance, three nearly allied species of dead nettle—one white (*Lamium album*), one red (*Lamium maculatum*), and one yellow (*Lamium galeobdolon* or *luteum*).

Now, if we imagine the existence in a single genus of three separate species, similar in general habit and

appearance, and yet mutually infertile, it is easy to
see that it would be an advantage to them to have
their flowers differently colored. The three species
of Lamium above mentioned may be growing together,
and yet the bees, without difficulty or loss of time, can
distinguish the species from one another, and collect
pollen and honey without confusing them together. On
the other hand, if they were similarly colored, the
bees could only distinguish them with comparative
difficulty, involving some loss of time and probably
many mistakes.

I have not yet alluded especially to white flowers.
They seem to stand in a somewhat special position.
The general sequence, as I have suggested, is from
green, through yellow and red, to blue. Flowers
normally yellow seldom sport into red or blue; those
normally red often sport into yellow, but seldom into
blue. On the other hand, flowers of almost any color
may sport into white. White is produced by the
absence of color, may therefore appear at any stage,
and will be stereotyped if for any reason it should prove
to be an advantage.*

* The genesis of the color is a large and interesting question. It
may be due to various causes, and is by no means always owing to the
presence of a different coloring matter. For instance, as Professor
Foster has observed to me, many species of Iris occur in blue and
yellow forms. The yellow is largely, or wholly, produced by chroma-
toplacts, the purple or blue to cell-sap, and if the latter is absent the
yellow becomes apparent.

CHAPTER X.

ANTS AND COLORS.

I HAVE elsewhere * recorded a series of experiments on ants with light of different wave-lengths, in order, if possible, to determine whether ants have the power of distinguishing colors. For this purpose I utilized the dislike which ants, when in their nest, have for light. Not unnaturally, if a nest is uncovered, they think they are being attacked, and hasten to carry their young away to a darker and, as they suppose, a safer place. I satisfied myself, by hundreds of experiments, that if I exposed to light the greater part of a nest, but left any of it covered over, the young would certainly be conveyed to the dark part. In this manner I satisfied myself that the various rays of the spectrum act on them in a different manner from that in which they affect us; for instance, that ants are specially sensitive to the violet rays.

But I was anxious to go beyond this, and to attempt to determine whether, as M. Paul Bert supposed, their limits of vision are the same as ours. We all know that

* " Ants, Bees, and Wasps."

if a ray of white light is passed through a prism, it is broken up into a beautiful band of colors, known as the spectrum. To our eyes this spectrum, like the rainbow, which is, in fact, a spectrum, is bounded by red at the one end and violet at the other, the edge being sharply marked at the red end, but less abruptly at the violet But a ray of light contains, besides the rays visible to our eyes, others which are called, though not with absolute correctness, heat-rays and chemical rays. These, so far from falling within the limits of our vision, extend far beyond it, the heat-rays at the red end, the chemical or ultra-violet rays at the violet end.

I made a number of experiments which satisfied me that ants are sensitive to the ultra-violet rays, which lie beyond the range of our vision. I was also anxious to see how two colors identical to our eyes, but one of which transmitted and the other intercepted the ultra-violet rays, would affect the ants.

Mr. Wigner was good enough to prepare for me a solution of iodine in bisulphide of carbon, and a second of indigo, carmine, and roseine mixed so as to produce the same tint. To our eyes the two were identical both in color and capacity; but of course the ultra-violet rays were cut off by the bisulphide-of-carbon solution, while they were, at least for the most part, transmitted by the other. I placed equal amounts in flat-sided glass bottles, so as to have the same depth of each liquid. I then laid them, as in previous experiments, over a nest of *Formica fusca.* In twenty observations the ants went seventeen times in all under the iodine and bisulphide, twice under the solution of indigo and carmine, while once there were some under each. These observations, therefore, show that the solutions,

though apparently identical to us, appeared to the ants
very different, and that, as before, they preferred to
rest under the liquid which intercepted the ultra-violet
rays.   In two or three cases only they went under the
other bottle ; but I ought to add that my observations
were made in winter, when the ants were rather
sluggish.   I am disposed to think that in summer
perhaps these exceptional cases would not have
occurred.

Professor Graber, however, while admitting the
accuracy of my observations, has attempted to prove
that the perception of the ultra-violet rays is not a
case of sight in the ordinary acceptation of the words,
but is due to the general sensitiveness of the skin.

It has long been known that some of the lower
animals which do not possess eyes are, nevertheless,
sensitive to light.   Hoffmeister,* in his work on earthworms, states that, with some exceptions, they are
very sensitive to light.   Darwin, perhaps, experimented
with a different species (for there are many different
kinds); at any rate, his specimens seemed to be less
keenly affected, though if one was suddenly illuminated it dashed "like a rabbit into its burrow."   He
observed, however, that some individuals were more
sensitive to light than others, and that the same individuals by no means always acted in the same way.
Moreover, if they "were employed in dragging leaves
into their burrows or in eating them, and even during
the short intervals when they rested from their work,
they either did not perceive the light or were regard-
less of it."†   He observes, however, that it is only the

* "Familie der Regenwürmer," 1845.
† Darwin's "Earthworms."

anterior extremity of the body, where the cerebral ganglia lie, which is affected by light, and he suggests that the light may pass through the skin and acts directly on the nervous centres.

Lacaze-Duthiers, Haeckel, Engelmann, Graber, Plateau, and other naturalists have abundantly proved the sensitiveness to light of other eyeless animals.

There has, indeed, long been a vague idea that blind people have some faint perception of light through the general surface of the skin. So far as I am aware there is not the slightest evidence or foundation for this belief; nor, indeed, has it been advocated by any competent authority. It seems *à priori* improbable that an animal with complex eyes should still retain a power which would be almost entirely useless.

On the other hand, it is unquestionable that light can, and often does, act directly on the nerve terminations without the intermediate operation of any optical-apparatus.

Some of them might, perhaps, be open to criticism. The effect of heat may not have been always sufficiently guarded against. Again, it is quite true that, as Plateau observes "Lorsque les Myriapodes chilopodes aveugles ou munis d'yeux, déposés sur le sol, s'introduisent avec empressement dans la première fente qu'ils rencontrent, cet acte n'est pas déterminé par le seul besoin de fuir la lumière, ces animaux cherchent en même temps un milieu humide et avec lequel la plus grande partie de la surface de leur corps soit en contact direct." * But though this is no doubt true, and though, perhaps, the moisture may be some help, still, whatever be their

---

* Plateau, " Rech. sur la perception de la lumière par les Myriapodes aveugles," *Jour. de l'Anatomie*, etc., T. xxii. 1886.

object, we can hardly doubt that the absence of light is the principal guide.

Professor Graber,* in his interesting memoir on this subject confirms the observations on ants and Daphnias, in which I showed that they are sensitive to the ultra-violet rays, by similar observations on earthworms, newts, etc. It is interesting, moreover, that the species examined by him showed themselves, like the ants, specially sensitive to the blue, violet, and ultra-violet rays. Graber, however, states that he differs from me inasmuch as I attribute the sensitiveness to the ultra-violet rays exclusively to vision;—that it is "ausschliesslich durch die Augen vermittelt." I am not, however, of that opinion as a general expression, though I believe it to be true of ants, where the opacity of the chitine renders it unlikely that the light could be perceived except by the medium of the eyes or ocelli.

Graber has shown in earthworms and newts, and Plateau † in certain Myriapods, that these animals perceive the difference between light and darkness by the general surface of the skin. But more than this, Graber seems to have demonstrated that earthworms and newts distinguish not only between light of different intensity, but also between rays of different wavelengths, preferring red to blue or green, and green to blue. He found, moreover, as I did, that they are sensitive to the ultra-violet rays. Earthworms, of course, have no eyes; but, thinking that the light might

* "Fundamental Versuche über die Helligkeits und Farben Empfindlichkeit augenloser und geblendeter Thiere," *Sitz. Kais. Akad. d. Wiss.* Wien: 1883.

† *Journ. de l'Anatomie et de la Physiologie,* 1886.

act directly on the cephalic ganglia, Graber decapitated a certain number, and found that the light still acted on them in the same manner, though the differences were not so marked. He also covered over the eyes of newts, and found that the same held good with them.

Hence he concludes that the general surface of the skin is sensitive to light. These results are certainly curious and interesting, but even if we admit the absolute correctness of his deductions, I do not see that they are in opposition to those at which I had arrived. My main conclusions were that ants, Daphnias, etc., were able to perceive light of different wave-lengths, and that their eyes were sensitive to the ultra-violet rays much beyond our limits of vision. His observations do not in any way controvert these deductions; indeed, the argument by which he endeavours to prove that the effect is due to true light, and not to warmth, presupposes that sensations which can be felt by the general surface of the skin, would be still more vividly perceived by the special organs of vision.

In connection with this subject, I may add that I do not at all doubt the sensitiveness to light of eyeless animals. In experimenting on this subject, I have always found that though the blind woodlice (Platyarthrus), which live with the ants, have no eyes, yet if part of the nest be uncovered and part kept dark, they soon find their way into the shaded part. It is, however, easy to imagine that in unpigmented animals, whose skins are more or less semi-transparent, the light might act directly on the nervous system, even though it could not produce anything which could be called vision.

11

Forel, in some recent experiments, varnished over the eyes of fifteen ants (*Camponotus ligniperdus*) and put them with fifteen others, which were left in their normal condition, in a flat box with a glass top and divided in the middle into two halves by a cardboard division, which, however, left room enough underneath for the ants to pass freely from one half to the other. After some other experiments, in the course of which one of the varnished ants was accidentally killed, at 1 p.m. all the varnished ants and thirteen of the unvarnished were in the right half of the box, and two unvarnished in the left. He then placed over the whole box two flat bottles containing water to intercept heat-rays—over the right half a piece of cobalt (violet) glass; and over the left, a flat bottle containing a solution of esculine, which is quite transparent, but cuts off the ultra-violet rays. At 1.55 the result was as follows :—

Under the esculine.	Under the cobalt.
5 varnished.	9 varnished.
13 normal.	2 normal.

The esculine and cobalt were then transposed. At 2.3 the position was—

Under the cobalt.	Under the esculine.
4 varnished.	13 varnished.
3 normal.	12 normal.

The esculine and cobalt were again transposed, and one normal ant was accidentally wounded and removed. At 3.8—

Under the esculine.	Under the cobalt.
3 varnished.	12 varnished.
11 normal.	3 normal.

The esculine and cobalt were once more transposed, and at 3.13 there were—

Under the cobalt.	Under the esculine.
3 varnished.	11 varnished.
1 normal.	13 normal.

Thus the number of ants which followed the esculine and moved from one half of the box to the other at each transposition of the esculine and cobalt, was as follows :—

	Varnished.	Normal.
First change	5	11
Second „	1	10
Third „	0	9
Fourth „	0	10
	6	40

And the number remaining under the cobalt and esculine respectively was—

	Under the cobalt.		Under the esculine.	
	Varnished.	Normal.	Varnished.	Normal
First experiment	9	2 ...	... 5	13
Second „	4	3 ...	... 10	12
Third „	12	3 ...	... 3	11
Fourth „	3	1 ...	... 12	13
	28	9	30	49

These experiments clearly showed that, while the normal ants moved from side to side so as to be under the esculine and consequently protected from the ultra-violet rays, those in which the eyes had been varnished remained unaffected by the transposition of the esculine and the cobalt, showing that the difference was perceived, not by the general surface of the skin, but by the eyes, and that when these were covered the ants were unaffected by the change.

It might be suggested that possibly the ants had been injured or stupefied by the varnishing. M. Forel accordingly, on the following day at 8 a.m., placed over one half of the box a layer of water six centimetres deep, and on the other a piece of red glass, which, while intercepting some of the light, allows almost all the heat to pass through. At 9.25 there were—

Under the red glass.	Under the layer of water.
3 varnished.	11 varnished.
12 normal.	2 normal.

Here, it seems that the ants which could see preferred the shade, even though they were rather too warm; while the hoodwinked ants went under the cool water.

This indicated that the varnished ants remained sensitive to heat, though not to light. Indeed, Forel states that they were just as lively, just as sensitive to currents of air, as the normal ants.[*]

These experiments, then, entirely confirm those I had made. "C'est une confirmation entière," says Forel, "des resultats de Lubbock †" and he sums up as follows:—The ants "paraissent percevoir l'ultra-violet principalement avec leurs yeux, c'est-à-dire qu'elles le voient, car lorsque leurs yeux sont vernis elles s'y montrent presque indifférentes; elles ne réagissent alors nettement qu'à une lumière solaire directe ou moins forte. Les expériences ci-dessus semblent indiquer que les sensations dermatoptiques sont plus faibles chez les fourmis que chez les animaux étudiés par Graber."

From these and other experiments M. Forel comes

[*] *Loc. cit.*, p. 167.　　　　　† Ibid., p. 174.

to the same conclusion as I did, that the ants perceive the ultra-violet rays with their eyes, and not as suggested by Graber, by the skin generally. It is very gratifying that my experiments and conclusions should thus be entirely confirmed by an observer so careful and so experienced as M. Forel.

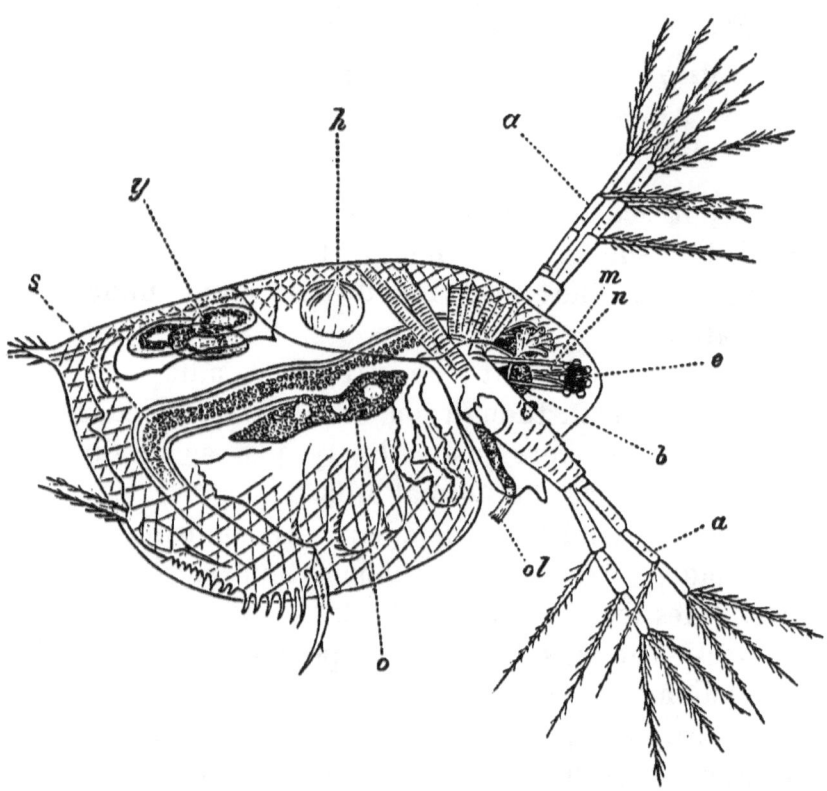

Fig. 118.—*Daphnia pulex.* *a*, Antennæ; *b*, brain; *e*, eye; *h*, heart; *m*, muscle of eye; *n*, nerve of eye; *o*, ovary; *ol*, olfactory organ; *s*, stomach; *y*, three eggs deposited in the space between the back and the shell.

EXPERIMENTS WITH DAPHNIAS.

The late M. Paul Bert made some very interesting experiments on a small fresh-water crustacean belonging to the genus *Daphnia* (Fig. 118), from which he concludes that they perceive all the colors known to us, being, however, especially sensitive to the yellow and green, and that their limits of vision are the same as ours.

Nay, he even goes further than this, and feels justified in concluding, from the experience of two species —Man and Daphnia—that the limits of vision would be the same in all cases.

His words are—

1. "Tous les animaux voient les rayons spectraux que nous voyons."

2. "Ils ne voient aucun de ceux que nous ne voyons pas."

3. "Dans l'étendue de la région visible, les différences entre les pouvoirs éclairants des différents rayons colorés sont les mêmes pour eux et pour nous."

He also adds, "Puisque les limites de visibilité semblent être les mêmes pour les animaux et pour nous, ne trouvons-nous pas là une raison de plus pour supposer que le rôle des milieux de l'œil est tout à fait secondaire, et que la visibilité tient à l'impressionnabilité de l'appareil nerveux lui-même ?"

These generalizations would seem to rest on a very narrow foundation. I have already attempted to show that the conclusion does not appear to hold good in the case of ants; and I determined, therefore, to make some experiments myself on Daphnias, the results of which are here embodied.*

Professor Dewar was kind enough to arrange for me, at the Royal Institution, a spectrum, which, by means of a mirror, was thrown on to the floor. I then placed some

---

* These observations were published in the *Journal of the Linnean Society* for 1881.

Daphnias in a shallow wooden trough fourteen inches by four inches, and divided by cross partitions of glass into divisions, so that I could isolate the parts illuminated by the different coloured rays. The two ends of the trough extended somewhat beyond the visible spectrum. I then placed fifty specimens of *Daphnia pulex* in the trough, removing the glass partitions so that they could circulate freely from one end of the trough to the other. Then, after scattering them equally through the water, I exposed them to the light for ten minutes, after which I inserted the glass partitions, and then counted the Daphnias in each division. The results were as follows :—

NUMBER OF DAPHNIAS.

	Beyond the red.	In the red and yellow.	In the greenish yellow and green.	In the blue.	In the violet.	Beyond the violet.
Obs. 1 ...	0	20	28	2	0	0
„ 2 ...	1	21	25	3	0	0
„ 3 ...	2	21	24	3	0	0
„ 4 ...	1	19	29	1	0	0
„ 5 ...	0	20	27	3	0	0
	4	101	133	12	0	0

I may add that the blue and violet divisions were naturally longer than the red and green.

May 25.—Tried again the same arrangement, but separating the yellow, and giving the Daphnias the choice between red, yellow, green, blue, violet, and dark :—

	Dark.	Violet.	Blue.	Green.	Yellow.	Red.
Exp. 1	0	0	3	39	5	3
„ 2	0	1	2	37	7	3
„ 3	0	0	4	31	10	5
„ 4	0	1	5	30	8	6
„ 5	0	1	4	33	6	6
	0	3	18	170	36	23

Of course, it must be remembered that the yellow band is much narrower than the green. I reckoned as yellow a width of three-quarters of an inch, and the width of the green two inches.

Again—

	Dark.	Violet.	Blue.	Green.	Yellow.	Red.
Exp. 1	0	0	4	30	6	10
„ 2	0	1	3	25	8	13
„ 3	0	0	2	24	9	15
„ 4	1	0	3	25	8	13
„ 5	0	1	2	24	7	16
	1	2	14	128	38	67
Adding them together, we get	1	5	32	298	74	90

M. Paul Bert observes (*loc. cit.*) that in his experiments the Daphnias followed exactly the brilliance of the light. It will be observed, however, that in my experiments this was not the case, as there were more Daphnias in proportion, as well as absolutely, in the green, although the yellow is the brightest portion of the spectrum. In fact, they follow the light up to a certain brightness; but, as will be seen presently, they do not like direct sunshine.

I then arranged the trough so that the yellow fell in the middle of one of the divisions. The result was—

NUMBER OF DAPHNIAS.

	Ultra-red and lower red.	Upper edge of red, yellow, and lower green.	Greenish blue and blue.	Violet.	Ultra-violet.
Exp. 1	8	38	4	0	0
„ 2	9	36	5	0	0
„ 3	8	39	3	0	0
	25	113	12	0	0

May 18.—In order to test the limits of vision at the

red end of the spectrum, I used the same arrangement as before, placing the trough so that the extreme division was in the ultra-red, and the second in the red. I then placed sixty Daphnias in the ultra-red. After five minutes' exposure, I counted them. There were in the—

	Red.	Ultra-red.
Exp. 1	54 ...	5
„ 2	56 ...	4

I now gave them four divisions to select from—dark, red, ultra-red, and dark again. The numbers were—

	Dark.	Red.	Ultra-red	Dark.
Exp. 1	5	47	6	2
„ 2	9	41	7	3

I then shut them off from all the colors excepting red, giving them only the option between red and ultra-red :—

	Red.	Ultra-red.
Exp. 1	46	4
„ 2	47	3
„ 3	44	6

I then left them access to a division on the other side of the red, which, however, I darkened by interposing a piece of wood. This enabled me better to compare the ultra-red rays with a really dark space :—

	Dark.	Red.	Ultra-red.
Exp. 1	4	43	3
„ 2	3	45	2

These observations appear to indicate that their limits of vision at the red end of the spectrum coincide approximately with ours.

I then proceeded to examine their behaviour with reference to the other end of the spectrum.

In the first place, I shut them off from all the rays

except the blue, violet, and ultra-violet. The result was as follows:—

NUMBER OF DAPHNIAS.

				Ultra-violet.	Violet.	Blue.	Dark.
Exp. 1	...	...	...	1	9	38	2
„ 2	...	...	...	4	6	38	2
„ 3	...	...	...	0	2	46	2
				5	17	122	6

This shows that they greatly prefer blue and violet to darkness or ultra-violet.

I afterwards gave them only the option of ultra-violet, violet, and darkness:—

					Ultra-violet.	Violet.	Dark.
Exp. 1	...	...	...	...	8	48	4
„ 2	...	...	...	...	6	48	6
„ 3	...	...	...	...	12	47	1
„ 4	...	...	...	...	15	42	3
„ 5	...	...	...	...	4	53	3
					45	238	17

They preferred the violet; but there were many more in the ultra-violet than in the dark.

I then tried ultra-violet and dark. The width of the violet was two inches; and I divided the ultra-violet portion again into divisions each of two inches, which we may call ultra-violet, further ultra-violet, and still further ultra-violet. The results were—

NUMBER OF DAPHNIAS.

			Still further ultra-violet.	Further ultra-violet.	Ultra-violet.	Dark.
Exp. 1	...	...	0	6	52	2
„ 2	...	...	0	5	52	3
„ 3	...	...	0	6	50	4
„ 4	...	...	0	4	53	3
„ 5	...	...	0	4	54	2
				286		14

In this case the preference for ultra-violet over dark was very marked.

May 18.—I again tried them with the ultra-violet rays, using three divisions—namely, further ultra-violet, ultra-violet, and dark. The numbers were as follows, viz. under the—

	Further ultra-violet.	Ultra-violet.	Dark.
Exp. 1	6	50	4
„ 2	3	55	2
	9	105	6

To my eye there was no perceptible difference between the further ultra-violet and the ultra-violet portion; but slightly undiffused light reached the two extreme divisions. It may be asked why the still further ultra-violet division should have been entirely deserted, while in each case two or three Daphnias were in the darkened one. This, I doubt not, was due to the fact that, the darkened division being next to the ultra-violet, one or two in each case straggled into it.

Not satisfied with this, I tried another test. There are some liquids which, though transparent to the rays we see, are quite opaque to the ultra-violet rays. Bisulphide of carbon, for instance, is quite colourless and transparent: it looks just like water, but it entirely cuts off the ultra-violet rays. If, then, we place the trough containing Daphnias, as I had previously done my nest of ants, in the ultra-violet part of the spectrum, and then place over one half of it a flat bottle containing water, and over the other half a similar bottle containing bisulphide of carbon, both halves will seem equally dark to us, but the ultra-violet rays reach one half of the vessel, while they are cut off from the other.

To our eyes both, as I say, are equally dark, and so they would be to the Daphnias if their limits of vision were the same as ours. As a matter of fact, however, the Daphnias all collected in the part of the trough under the water, and avoided that under the bisulphide of carbon, showing that this, therefore, was to them darker than the other. I varied the experiments in several ways, but always with similar results. Bichromate of potash is also impervious to the ultra-violet rays, and had the same effect.

Not satisfied with this, I tried to test it in another way.

I took a cell, in which I placed a layer of five-percent. solution of chromate of potash less than an eighth of an inch in depth, and which, though almost colourless to our eyes, completely cut off the ultra-violet rays. I then turned my trough at right angles, so that I could cover one side of the ultra-violet portion of the spectrum with the chromate and leave the other exposed. The numbers were as follows :—

	Side of the ultra-violet covered with chromate of potash.	Side uncovered.	Dark.
Exp. 1	5 ...	55 ...	0

I now covered up the other side.

Exp. 2	3 ...	57 ...	0

Again covered up the same side as at first.

Exp. 3	4 ...	56 ...	0

Again covered up the other side.

Exp. 4	3 ...	57 ...	0

May 19.—I again tried the same arrangement, reducing the chromate of potash to a mere film, which,

however, still cut off the ultra-violet rays. I then placed it, as before, over one half of the ultra-violet portion of the spectrum ; and over the other half I placed a similar cell containing water. Between each experiment I reversed the position of the two cells. The numbers were—

	Under the film of chromate of potash.	Under the water.
Exp. 1	8	52
„ 2	4	56
„ 3	10	50
„ 4	7	53

Evidently, then, even a film of chromate of potash exercises a very considerable influence ; and, indeed, I doubt not that, if a longer time had been allowed, the difference would have been even greater.

It seems clear, therefore, that a five-per cent. solution of chromate of potash only one-eighth of an inch in thickness, which cuts off the ultra-violet rays, though absolutely transparent to our eyes, is by no means so to the Daphnias.

These observations seem to prove, though I differ with great reluctance from so eminent an authority as M. Paul Bert, that the limits of vision of Daphnias do not, at the violet end of the spectrum, coincide with ours, but that the Daphnia, like the ant, is affected by the ultra-violet rays.

Since these observations were published, M. Merejkowski has experimented on the subject, and come to the conclusion that the Daphnias are attracted wherever there is most light, that they are conscious only of the intensity of the light, and that they have no power of distinguishing colors. It is no doubt true that in ordinary diffused daylight the Daphnias generally congregate wherever the light is strongest. Their eyes are, however, so delicate that one would naturally expect, *à priori*, that there would be a limit to this; and, in fact, direct sunshine is somewhat too strong for their comfort.

For instance, I took a porcelain trough, seven and a half inches long, two and a half broad, and one deep, and put in it some water containing fifty Daphnias. One half I exposed to direct sunlight, and the other I shaded, counting the Daphnias from time to time, and transposing the exposed and shaded halves. The numbers were as follows:—

					In the sun.			In the shade.
At 10.40 a.m.	...	...	...	4	...	...	46
„ 12.50 „	...	...	...	8	...	...	42
„ 1.10 „	...	...	...	7	...	...	43
„ 1.35 „	...	...	...	7	...	...	43
„ 1.50 „	...	...	...	4	...	...	46
„ 2 5 „	...	...	...	3	...	...	47
„ 2.40 „	...	...	...	4	...	...	46
„ 3.0 „	...	...	...	5	...	...	45
„ 4.0 „	...	...	...	7	...	...	43
„ 4 30 „	...	...	...	4	...	...	46
				53			447

This seems clearly to show that they avoid the full sunlight.

I believe, then, that in some of my previous experiments the yellow light was too brilliant for them; and the following experiments seem to show that, when sufficiently diffused, they prefer yellow to white light.

M. Merejkowsky, however, denies to the crustacea any sense of color whatever. His experiments were made with larvæ of *Balanus* and with a marine copepod, *Dias longiremis*. These, if I understand him correctly, have given identical results. He considers that they perceive all the luminous rays, and can distinguish very slight differences of intensity; but that they do not distinguish between different colors. He sums up his observations as follows :—

"Il résulte de ces expériences que ce qui agit sur les Crustacés, ce n'est point la qualité de la lumière, c'est exclusivement sa quantité. Autrement dit, les Crustacés inférieurs ont la perception de toute onde *lumineuse* et de toutes les différences, même très légères, dans son intensité; mais ils ne sont point capables de distinguer la nature des ondes, de différentes couleurs. Ils distinguent très bien l'intensité des vibrations éthérées, leur amplitude, mais point leur nombre. Il y a donc, dans le mode de perception de la lumière, une grande différence entre les Crustacés inférieurs et l'Homme, et même entre eux et les Fourmis; tandis que nous voyons les différentes couleurs et leurs différentes intensités, les Crustacés inférieurs ne voient qu'une seule couleur dans ses différentes variations d'intensité. Nous percevons des couleurs comme couleurs; ils ne les perçoivent que comme lumière." *

It is by no means easy to decide such a question absolutely; but the subject is of much interest, and accordingly I made some further experiments, as it did not seem to me that those of M. Merejkowsky bore out the conclusion he has deduced from them.

Professor Dewar most kindly arranged the apparatus for me again. He prepared a normal diffraction-spectrum, produced by a Rutherfurd grating with 17,000 lines to the inch; the spectrum of the first order was thrown on the trough. In this case the distribution of

---

* M. C. Merejkowsky, " Les Crustacés inférieurs distinguent-ils les couleurs ? "

luminous intensity has been shown to be uniform on each side of the line having the mean wave-length, *i.e.* a little above the line D in the yellowish green of the spectrum.

I then took a long shallow trough in which were a number of Daphnias, and placed it so that the centre of the trough was at the brightest part of the spectrum, a little, however, if anything, towards the green end. After scattering the Daphnias equably I left them for five minutes, and then put a piece of blackened cardboard over the brightest part. After five minutes more, there were at the green end, 410; in the dark, 14; at the red end, 76. Here the two ends of the trough were equally illuminated; but the preference for the green over the red side was very marked.

I then took five porcelain vessels, seven and a half inches long, two and a half broad, and one deep, and in each I put water containing fifty Daphnias. One half of the water I left uncovered; the other half I covered respectively with an opaque porcelain plate, a solution of aurine (bright yellow), of chlorate of copper (bright green), a piece of red glass, and a piece of blue glass. Every half-hour I counted the Daphnias in each half of every vessel, and then transposed the coverings, so that the half which had been covered was left exposed, and *vice versâ*. I also changed the Daphnias from time to time.

Here, then, in each case the Daphnias had a choice between two kinds of light. It seemed to me that this would be a crucial test, because in every case the colored media act by cutting off certain rays. Thus the aurine owes its yellow color to the fact that it cuts off the violet and blue rays. The light beneath it contains no more yellow rays than elsewhere; but those rays produce the impression of yellow, because the yellow is not neutralized by the violet and blue. In each case, therefore, there was less light in the covered than in the uncovered part.

After every five experiments I added up the number of the Daphnias; and the following table gives twenty such totals, each containing the result of five observations, making in all one hundred.

My reason for adding one vessel in which one half had an opaque cover was to meet the objection that possibly the light might have been too strong for the Daphnias; so that when they went under the sheltered part they did so, not for color, but for shade. I was not very sanguine as to the result of this arrangement, because I had expected that the preference of the Daphnias for light would overcome their attachment to yellow.

The numbers were as in the following table (p. 224).

The result was very marked. The first two columns show the usual preference for light. If the covered half had been quite dark, no doubt the difference in numbers would have been greater; but a good deal of light found its way into the covered half. Still the result clearly shows that the Daphnias preferred the lighter half. The numbers were 2048 in the dark to 2952 in the light; and it will be seen that the preference for the light was shown, though in different degrees, in almost every series.

The result in the blue gives, I think, no evidence as to color-sense. The numbers were respectively 2046 against 2954, and were therefore practically the same

NUMBER OF DAPHNIAS.

	1. In the Opaque.	Uncovered.	2. In the Yellow.	Uncovered.	3. In the Red.	Uncovered.	4. In the Green.	Uncovered.	5. Blue.	In the Uncovered.
Feb. 5	126	124	175	75	66	184	83	167	112	138
,, 5	141	109	140	110	97	153	164	86	115	135
,, 6	130	120	191	59	67	183	115	135	100	150
,, 7	102	148	174	76	66	184	87	163	110	140
,, 8	110	140	172	78	76	174	104	146	82	168
,, 8	117	133	183	67	80	170	110	140	94	156
,, 9	92	158	135	115	126	124	116	134	108	142
,, 9	124	126	182	68	120	130	153	97	135	115
,, 10	89	161	126	124	113	137	87	163	57	193
,, 11	126	124	138	112	116	134	127	123	106	144
	1157	1343	1616	884	927	1573	1146	1354	1019	1481
Feb. 11	131	119	153	97	114	136	137	113	91	159
,, 13	112	138	164	86	100	150	106	144	78	172
,, 17	106	144	126	124	114	136	139	111	69	181
,, 18	114	136	159	91	118	132	137	113	130	120
,, 18	59	191	133	117	116	134	112	138	102	148
,, 18	54	196	146	104	109	141	126	124	106	144
,, 18	69	181	174	76	75	175	121	129	102	148
,, 18	50	200	146	104	66	184	120	130	95	155
,, 19	99	151	138	112	94	156	114	136	117	133
,, 19	97	153	141	109	95	155	148	102	137	113
	891	1609	1480	1020	1001	1499	1260	1240	1027	1473
Total ...	2048	2952	3096	1904	1928	3072	2406	2594	2046	2954

as in the preceding set.   Since, however, a certain quantity of light was transmitted through the blue, the result may indicate a want of sensitiveness to the blue rays.

In the red the numbers were 1928 as against 3072.

As regards the yellow, the results were very different, the numbers being, under the yellow, 3096; in the uncovered part, 1904.   Here, therefore, we see a very distinct preference, all the more remarkable because the amount of light was really less than in the uncovered part.

In the green the numbers were much more equal, namely, 2406 against 2594.   Here also the love for green neutralized the preference for light.   I do not, however, wish for the moment to draw any conclusion from these last figures, though I give them for what they are worth. The coloured medium was, I believe, somewhat too opaque.   With a more transparent green, as will be seen subsequently, the result would have been very different.

At any rate, the above observations seemed to show a marked preference for yellow.   Still, I thought it might be objected that, though the Daphnias obviously preferred the uncovered to the shaded half of the vessel, and the yellow to the uncovered half of the vessel, perhaps in the former the uncovered water was rather too bright, and in the latter the shaded part was rather too dark, and that after all the yellow was chosen, not because it was yellow, but because it hit off the happy medium of intensity.   The suggestion is very improbable, because the observations were made on several successive, and very different, days, and at very different hours.   I also thought that the green was perhaps too dark; I took, therefore, a lighter tint, and rearranged my little apparatus as follows:—

I placed (March 26) fifty Daphnias in a trough (1), covering over one half of it with a pale green, and another fifty in a trough (2) half of which was covered with yellow (aurine). On one side was a similar trough (3), one end of which was shaded by a porcelain plate; and on the other side a fourth trough (4), one end of which had a little, though but little, extra light thrown on it by means of a mirror. As before, I counted the Daphnias from time to time, and turned the troughs round. All four were in a light room, but not actually in direct sunshine. Thus, then, in one trough I had half the water in somewhat green light; in the second trough, half the water in yellow light; in the third, one half was exposed and the other somewhat darkened; while the fourth, on the contrary, gave me a contrast with somewhat more vivid light. If, then, the Daphnias went under the green and yellow glass, not on account of the color, but for the sake of shade, then in trough 3 a majority of them would have gone under the porcelain plate. On the other hand, if the porcelain plate darkened the water too much, and yet the open water was rather too light for the Daphnias, then in the fourth trough they would, of course, have avoided the illuminated half. The results show that the third trough was unnecessary, still, I may as well give the figures; the fourth proves that the Daphnias preferred a light somewhat brighter than the ordinary diffused light of the room. Of course, it does not follow that the effect of color is the same as with us.

	Trough 1.		Trough 2.		Trough 3.		Trough 4.	
	Green light.	White light.	Yellow light.	White light.	Exposed half.	Darkened half.	Illuminated half.	Unilluminated half.
March 27.								
12 ...	35	15	33	17	35	15	28	22
12.25 ...	32	18	28	22	37	13	36	14
12.50 ...	27	23	33	17	36	14	25	25
1.40 ...	33	17	33	17	38	12	30	20
2.5 ...	26	24	42	8	35	15	26	24
	153	97	169	81	181	69	145	105
2.25 ...	36	14	36	14	26	24	35	15
3.0 ...	41	9	13	32	24	26	23	27
3.25 ...	31	19	34	16	36	14	35	15
5.15 ...	35	15	25	25	31	19	28	22
5 40 ...	30	20	35	15	32	18	27	23
	173	77	148	102	149	101	148	102
March 28.								
7.30 ...	33	17	34	16	35	15	30	20
7.50 ...	32	18	37	13	27	23	32	18
8.10 ...	34	16	33	17	29	21	30	20
8.35 ...	36	14	35	15	26	24	33	17
9.5 ...	26	24	27	23	33	17	35	15
	161	89	166	84	150	100	160	90
March 29.								
9.10 ...	36	20	25	25	29	21	32	18
9.25 ...	30	20	27	23	35	15	30	20
9.40 ...	19	31	25	25	29	21	29	21
9.55 ...	20	30	34	16	37	13	29	21
10.30 ...	30	14	34	16	20	30	26	24
	135	115	145	105	150	100	146	104
Total ...	622	378	628	372	630	370	599	401

It may be said that perhaps in the previous experiments the red and blue were too dark. I therefore took a very pale solution, and counted the number twenty times for the red and ten for the blue, placing the yellow in another trough, as before, for comparison. The preference for the yellow was as marked as ever. In the experiments with the red and yellow the numbers were respectively

Trough 1.		Trough 2.	
Under the yellow.	In the uncovered half.	Under the red.	In the uncovered half.
670	330	498	502

When, therefore, the red solution was sufficiently light, the Daphnias were indifferent to it. In the experiments with light blue the numbers were—

Trough 1.		Trough 2.		Trough 3.	
Under the yellow.	In the uncovered half.	Under the blue.	In the uncovered half.	Under the porcelean plate.	In the uncovered half.
687	313	286	714	336	664

One other possible objection also suggested itself to me. I thought it might be said that the Daphnias went under the yellow and the green not on account of any preference for yellow or green light, but on account of the shelter afforded by the covering. To test this, I covered one half of a trough over with transparent glass, leaving the other uncovered; but after twenty observations I found the number of Daphnias in each half to be practically identical. The mere fact of the covering, therefore, made no difference. In this way I was able to test the preference of the Daphnias for various colours, and the result made it abundantly clear that Daphnias have the power of distinguishing between light of different wave-lengths, and that they prefer the light which we call yellow and green. Whether it actually appears to them as it does to us is, of course, another and a more difficult question—one, moreover, not yet solved even for the higher animals. Nor would I necessarily claim for them any æsthetic sense of beauty; it must be remembered that they feed on minute algæ and other minute vegetables, the prevalent colors of which are yellow, yellowish green, and green. There is, therefore, nothing improbable, à *priori*, but rather the reverse, in their preference for these colors.

It will be observed that though in these vessels the Daphnias made their preference unmistakable, there were always a certain number in the least popular part. This is natural, because, as the position of the light half was reversed every observation, the Daphnias had to swim across the vessel, and some naturally did not find their way to the favourite part. Then, again, in any considerable numbers of Daphnias some are changing, or have recently changed, their skin, and are, therefore, more or less inactive. Moreover, in pure water the desire for food must often overpower any preference for one colour over another. To such causes as these we must, I think, attribute the presence of so many Daphnias in the first vessel at the opaque end, and in the second in the uncovered part.

Still, it was of course not impossible that the presence, for instance, of a certain number under the red and blue was due to a difference of taste; that, though the majority preferred yellow, there might be some preferring blue or red. To test this I tried the following experiment. I placed, as before, fifty Daphnias in three of the vessels, covering one half of one with the yellow, of a second with blue, and the third with red. I then from time to time, at intervals of not less than half an hour, removed these which were in the uncovered part and replaced them with an equal number of fresh ones. If, then, some Daphnias preferred red or blue, I ought thus to eliminate the others, and gradually to get together fifty agreeing in this taste. This, however, was not the case. In the first experiment, an hour after the Daphnias were placed in the vessels there were, out of 50, 41 under the yellow, 16 under the red, and 15 under the blue, the remaining 9, 34, and 35 respectively being in the uncovered portions. These, then, I removed and replaced by others. After doing this five times, and thus adding 80 in the yellow division, 187 in the red, and 209 in the blue, the numbers were 37 under the yellow, 15 under the red, and 6 under the blue.

In the second experiment, the numbers after the first hour were 32 under the yellow, 10 under the red, and 11 under the blue. After five observations, during which 86 were added to the yellow division, 188 to the red, and 180 to the blue, the numbers were—under the yellow, 35 ; red, 11 ; blue, 15.

In the third experiment, the numbers after half an hour were 40 under the yellow, 14 under the red, and 8 under the blue. After five observations, during which 73 were added to the yellow, 186 to the red, and 206 to the blue, there were—under the yellow, 43 ; under the red, 15 ; and under the blue, 7.

In the fourth experiment, the numbers after half an hour were 38 under the yellow, 15 under the red, and 14 under the blue. After six observations, during which 89 were added to the yellow, 166 to the red, and 176 to the blue, the numbers were—under the yellow, 30 ; under the red, 19 ; and under the blue, 10.

In the fifth experiment, the numbers after half an hour were 40 under the yellow, 14 under the red, and

13 under the blue. After seven observations, during which 86 were added to the yellow, 263 to the red, and 272 to the blue, the numbers were—under the yellow, 38; under the red, 13; and under the blue, 15.

	Yellow.	Red.	Blue.
First observation.			
At the beginning	41	16	15
„ end	37	15	6
Second observation.			
At the beginning	32	10	11
„ end	35	11	15
Third observation.			
At the beginning	40	14	8
„ end	43	15	7
Fourth observation.			
At the beginning	38	15	14
„ end	30	19	10
Fifth observation.			
At the beginning	40	14	13
„ end	38	13	15

I conclude, then, that the presence of some of the Daphnias in the red, blue, and violet is more or less due to the causes above indicated, and not to any individual preference for those colors.

My experiments, I think, show that, while the Daphnias prefer light to darkness, there is a certain maximum of brilliancy beyond which the light becomes inconveniently bright to them, and that they can distinguish between light of different wave-lengths. I suppose it would be impossible to prove that they actually perceive colours; but to suggest that the rays of various wave-lengths produce on their eyes a different impression from that of color, is to propose an entirely novel hypothesis.

At any rate, I think I have shown that they do distinguish between rays of different wave-lengths, and prefer those which to our eyes appear green and yellow.

12

CHAPTER XI.

ON RECOGNITION AMONG ANTS.

DURING the many years that I have had ants under observation, I have never on any occasion seen anything like a quarrel between any two ants belonging to the same community. This is certainly very much to their credit. The experience of Huber, Forel, McCook, and others who have watched ants, is, moreover, the same as mine. I have also shown* that they recognize one another even after a separation of a year and nine months.

On the other hand, every community of ants is hostile to every other. I am not now speaking of ants belonging to different kinds, but of ants belonging to the same species. Some species, indeed, are more intolerant of strangers than others; but, as regards most species of ants, it may be said that if an individual be taken from its own nest and introduced into another, even though belonging to the same species, it will be at once attacked and driven, or rather dragged, out.

These facts, then, show that the ants of a community all recognize one another. But when we consider the immense number of ants in a nest, amounting in some cases to over 500,000, this is indeed a wonderful fact.

* See " Ants, Bees, and Wasps."

It may be remembered that my nests have enabled me to keep ants under observation for long periods, and that I have thus identified workers of *Lasius niger* and *Formica fusca* which were at least seven years old, but my oldest ants have been two queens of *Formica fusca*, which I took in a nest in December, 1874. They must then have been nine months old, and of course may have been more. One of these queens, after ailing for some days, died on July 30, 1887. She must then have been more than thirteen years old. I was at first afraid that the other one might be affected by the death of her companion. She is, however, still alive (May, 1888), and, though a little stiff in the joints, as far as I can judge, in her usual health. Still, there are only a few queens in a nest, and no doubt the majority of the workers, at least in the summer and when the community is most active, are very young, which adds greatly to the difficulty of supposing that they are personally known to one another.

It has been suggested that each nest has, perhaps, a special signal or pass-word. To test this I took, as I have already mentioned in my book on " Ants, Bees, and Wasps," a number of ants, half from one nest and half from another, and made them very drunk, so as to be thoroughly insensible. I then marked them with spots of different colours, so as to distinguish the two lots, and put them on a table near where some ants belonging to the nest from which one half of them had been taken, were feeding on some honey. The table was surrounded by a moat containing water to prevent the ants from wandering away. The sober ants were rather puzzled; but, after examining the intoxicated individuals, they picked up the strangers and threw them into the ditch, while they carried their own friends into the nest, where no doubt they slept off the effects of the spirits. This experiment seemed to show that the recognition was not effected by means of any sign; but I thought the suggestion might be tested in another way.

I made, therefore, the following experiment. I took a few specimens of *Formica fusca* from two different nests, which I will call A and B, and placed them together. At first they were rather shy; but after a while they fraternized. After they had lived amicably together for three months, I put two of these ants from nest A into nest B; but they were soon attacked vigorously and driven out of the nest. I thought it desirable to repeat and extend this test. Accordingly, on June 16 I put three specimens of *F. fusca* from my nest No. 81 with the same number from nest No. 71. Then on September 19, one of the six having died in the interval, I put the two from nest 81 into nest 71, and the three from nest 71 into 81. They were all attacked, though not very quickly or vigorously, but eventually all five were expelled.

Again, on September 25 I took three ants from each of these nests and put the six together. Then on March 19 following (one having died), I put the two from 71 into 81, and the three from 81 into 71. They were all attacked, so that they were evidently recognized as strangers; but it seemed to me that the attack was less vigorous, and I could not be sure that they were either killed or driven out. In the course of the week three or four dead ants were brought out of each of the nests; but I could not feel certain that they were those experimented with.

Lastly, on April 9 I again put twelve ants, six from each of these nests, together, and kept them so till October. I then took four of those from 71, put three into 81 and the fourth into 71. I also took four of those from 81, and put three into 71, and the fourth back into 81 among her old friends. The two ants thus restored respectively to their old nests were as usual recognized as friends and left quite unmolested. As regards the other six, the results were as follows. The ants were introduced into the nests at 8.15 a.m.

Nest 71.		Nest 81.	
8.45.	One was being attacked.	One was being attacked.	
9.15.	None were ,,	,,	,,
9.45.	Two were ,,	,,	,,
10.15.	One was ,,	,,	,,
10.45.	None were ,,	,,	,,
12.30.	Two were ,,	,,	,,
1.30.	Two were ,,	None were	,,
2.30.	One was ,,	,,	,,

I do not give these results as by any means proving that ants do not recognize their friends by means of smell. They do seem, however, at any rate, to show that not even six months of close companionship under precisely similar conditions will so far assimilate the odour as to lead to confusion. If the recognition *is* due in any degree to this cause, the odour is therefore probably an hereditary characteristic.

In the interesting memoir already cited, Forel says,* " Lubbock (*loc. cit.*) a cru démontrer que les fourmis enlevées de leur nid à l'état de nymphe et écloses hors de chez elles étaient néanmoins reconnues par leurs

* *Recueil Zool. Suisse,* 1887.

compagnes lorsqu'on les leur rendait. Dans mes
Fourmis de la Suisse, j'avais cru démontrer le contraire.
Voici une expérience que j'ai faite ces jours-ci : Le 7
août, je donne des nymphes de *Formica pratensis* près
d'éclore à quelques *Formica sanguinea* dans une boîte.
Le 9 août quelques-unes éclosent. Le 11 août, au
matin, je prends l'une *de jeunes pratensis* âgée de deux
ou trois jours seulement et je la porte à sa fourmilière
natale dont elle était sortie comme nymphe seulement
4 jours auparavant. Elle y est fort mal reçue. Ses
nourrices d'il y a 4 jours l'empoignent qui par la tête,
qui par le thorax, qui par les pattes en recourbant leur
abdomen d'un air menaçant. Deux d'entre elles la
tinrent longtemps en sens inverse chacune par une
patte en l'écartelant. Enfin cependant on finit par la
tolérer, comme on le fait aussi pour de si jeunes fourmis
(encore blanc jaunâtre) provenant de fourmilières différentes. J'attends encore deux jours pour laisser durcir
un peu mes nouvelles écloses. Puis j'en reporte deux
sur leur nid. Elles sont violemment attaquées. L'une
d'elles est inondée de venin, tiraillée et tuée. L'autre
est longtemps tiraillée et mordue, mais finalement
laissée tranquille (tolérée ?). On m'objectera l'odeur
des *sanguinea* qui avait vécu 4 jours avec la première
et 6 jours avec les deux dernières. A cela je répondrai
simplement par l'expérience de la page 278 à 282 de
mes *Fourmis de la Suisse*, où des *F. pratensis* adultes
séparées depuis deux mois de leurs compagnes par une
alliance forcée avec des *F. sanguinea*, alliance que j'avais
provoquée, reconnurent immédiatement leurs anciennes
compagnes et s'allièrent presque sans dispute avec elles.
Je maintiens donc mon opinion : les fourmis apprennent
à se connaître petit à petit à partir de leur éclosion.

Je crois du reste que c'est au moyen de perceptions olfact:ves de contact." *

I have, however, repeated my previous observations, with the same results.

At the beginning of August I brought in a nest of *Lasius niger* containing a large number of pupæ. Some of these I placed by themselves, in charge of three ants belonging to the same species, but taken from a nest I have had under observation for rather more than ten years. On August 28 1 took twelve of the young ants, which in the mean time had emerged from the separated pupæ, selecting some which had almost acquired their full colour. Four of them I placed in their old nest, and four in that from which their nurses were taken.

At 4.30 in their own nest none were attacked.
,, ,, ,, nurses' nest one was attacked.
,, 5.0 ,, own nest none were attacked.
,, ,, ,, nurses' nest all four were attacked.
,, 8.0 ,, own nest none were attacked.
,, ,, ,, nurses' nest three were attacked.

The next day I took six more and marked them with a spot of paint as usual, and at 7.30 replaced them in their own nest.

At 8.0 I found 5 quite at home; the others I could not see, but none were attacked.

,,	8.30	,,	5	,,	,,	,,	,,
,,	9.0	,,	8	,,	,,	,,	,,
,,	10.0	,,	4	,,	,,	,,	,,
,,	11.0	,,	5	,,	,,	,,	,,
,,	12.0	,,	8	,,	,,	,,	,,
,,	1.0	,,	8	,,	,,	,,	,,
,,	4.0	,,	4	,,	,,	,,	,,
,,	7.0	,,	1	,,	,,	,,	,,
,,	9.0	,,	2	,,	,,	,,	,,

* "Forel. Exp. et Rem. crit. sur les Sensations des Insectes," *Recueil Zool. Suisse.*, 1887.

The next morning I could only see two, but none were being attacked, and there were no dead ones. It is probable that the paint had been cleaned off the others, but it was not easy to find them all among so many. At any rate, none were being attacked, nor had any been killed.

These observations, therefore, quite confirm those previously made, and seem to show that if pupæ are taken from a nest, kept till they become perfect insects, and then replaced in the nest, they are recognized as friends.

As regards the mode of recognition, Mr. McCook considers that it is by scent, and states that if ants are more or less soaked in water, they are no longer recognized by their friends, but are attacked. He mentions a case in which an ant fell accidentally into some water: "She remained in the liquid several moments, and crept out of it. Immediately she was seized in a hostile manner, first by one, and then another, then by a third, the two antennæ and one leg were thus held. A fourth one assaulted the middle thorax and petiole. The poor little bather was thus dragged helplessly to and fro for a long time, and was evidently ordained to death. Presently I took up the struggling heap. Two of the assailants kept their hold, one finally dropped; the other I could not tear loose, and so put the pair back upon the tree, leaving the doomed immersionist to her hard fate."

His attention having been called to this, he noticed several other cases, always with the same result. I have not myself been able to repeat the observation with the same species, but with two at least of our native ants the results were exactly reversed. In one case five specimens of *Lasius niger* fell into water and remained immersed for three hours. I then took them out and put them into a bottle to recover themselves. The following morning I allowed them to return. They were received as friends, and, though we watched them from 7.30 till 1.30 every hour, there was not the slightest sign of hostility. The nest was, moreover, placed in a closed box, so that if any ant were killed we could inevitably find the body, and no ant died. In this case, therefore, it is clear that the immersion did not prevent them from being recognized. Again, three specimens of *Formica fusca* dropped into water. After three hours I took them out, and, after keeping them by themselves for the night to recover, I put them back into the nest. They were unquestionably received as friends, without the slightest sign of hostility or even of doubt. I do not, however, by any means intend to express the opinion that smell is not the mode by which recognition is effected.

It will be remembered, perhaps, that my ants (*Formica fusca*) recognized one another after a separation of a year and nine months, though "after some months' separation they were occasionally attacked, as some of the ants, perhaps the young ones, did not recognize them. Still, they were never killed or driven out of the nest, so that evidently when a mistake was made it was soon discovered." Hence it would appear that there are differences in the memory of different species.

In one case Forel had taken some ants from a large nest of *Componotus*, for the experiments on their sensibility to the ultra-violet rays, to which I have already referred. After his observations were concluded, he returned them to the nest, some after eight, some after forty-one days. Those which were returned after eight days were at once recognized, while as regards those which had been forty-one days away from home. "On reculait de part et d'autre, se menaçait des mandibules, s'examinait à fond avec les antennes, se mordait même. Plusieurs même allèrent dans leur irritation jusqu' à essayer de décapiter et même à décapiter quelques-unes de leurs anciennes compagnes et sœurs avec leurs mandibules (c'est le mode de combat des Camponotus)! Les fourmis vernies prirent part à ces rixes aussi bien que les non vernies; je les vis même attaquer, et elles étaient à peine moins adroites. Les combats ne cessèrent entièrement qu'au bout d'un ou deux jours, et, à part les quelques victimes du premier jour, l'incident se termina par une alliance."

Forel seems to entertain no doubt that the recognition is effected by a form of smell, which he terms "odorat au contact." He says, "Beaucoup d'insectes ont en outre une sorte d'odorat au contact que nous ne possédons pas et qui permet entre autres aux fourmis de distinguer leurs compagnes de leurs ennemies."

His observations, however, do not favour the hypothesis that the recognition may be by smell. If the ants recognized their companions by any odour characteristic of the community, the lapse of thirty days could not have made any difference. Here the question of memory would not enter, because the perception of the odour would in both cases be continually before them. M. Forel is so excellent an observer, and has so great a knowledge of the ways of ants, that his opinion is entitled to great weight. It would be very interesting to repeat similar observations, for if it turn out to be the case that separations of comparatively few days lead, in some species, to a want of recognition, it would be a strong argument against the hypothesis that this recognition is due to smell.

It certainly seems as if the recognition was effected to a great extent by the antennæ. Not only do the ants cross and recross them, almost, so to say, as two deaf mutes conversing by their fingers; but, as M. Forel has shown, if ants of different species are brought together after the removal of their antennæ they show no signs of hostility. That this latter statement is correct I am quite content to take on M. Forel's authority; but it is not so conclusive as might seem at first sight, because in ants, as in men, "a fellow-feeling makes us wondrous kind," and ants when isolated, and especially when suffering, are much less pugnacious than they are under normal conditions.

CHAPTER XII.

THE hive bee and the common wasps are so familiar and so interesting that they have to a great extent diverted attention from the so-called solitary species of the same groups. Few, for instance, are aware that about 4500 species of wild bees are known, and of wasps 1100, of which some 170 and 16 respectively live in Britain.

These insects often live in association, but do not form true communities. Speaking generally, we may say that each female constructs a cell, every species having its own favourite site, sometimes underground, sometimes in a hollow stick, in an empty snail-shell, or built against a wall, a stone, or the branch of a tree. Having completed her cell, the female stores up in it a sufficient supply of food, which in the case of bees consists of pollen and honey; while the wasps select small animals, such as beetles, caterpillars, spiders, etc., each species generally having one kind of prey. The mother then lays an egg, after which she closes up the cell, and commences another. Having thus provided sufficiently for her offspring, she generally takes no further heed of it. This is not, however, an invariable rule: in the genus Bembex, for instance, the mother, instead of provisioning her cell once for all, brings food to the young grub from day to day.

This, however, is an exceptional case, and the mode of life of the solitary wasps raises one of the most interesting questions in connection with instinct. The Ammophila, for instance, having built her cell, places in it, as food for her young, the full-grown caterpillar of a moth, *Noctua segetum*. Now, if the caterpillar were uninjured, it would struggle to escape and almost inevitably destroy the egg; nor would it permit itself to be eaten. On the other hand, if it were killed, it would decay and soon become unfit for food. The wasp, however, avoids both horns of this dilemma. Having found her prey, she pierces with her sting the membrane between the head and the first segment of the body, thus nearly disabling the caterpillar, and then proceeds to inflict eight more wounds between the following segments; lastly crushing the head, and thus completely paralyzing her victim, but not actually killing it; so that it lies helpless and motionless, but, though living, let us hope insensible. M. Fabre, to whom we are indebted for a most interesting and entertaining series of essays on this group of insects, argues that this remarkable instinct cannot have been gradually acquired.

The spots selected are, he says, exactly those occupied by the ganglia. No others among the innumerable points which might have been chosen would have answered the purpose; not one wound is misplaced or without effect. M. Fabre truly observes that chance offers no explanation.* Moreover, he unhesi-

---

* In the case of other insects, such as Mutilla, Chrysis, Leucospis, Anthrax, etc., which do not possess the instinct of paralyzing their victims, the young feed on the chrysalis, which is normally without power of movement.

tatingly asserts that "Si de son côté l'hyménoptère excelle dans son art, c'est qu'il est fait pour l'exercer ; c'est qu'il est doué, non seulement d'outils, mais encore de la manière de s'en servir. Et ce don est originel, parfait dès le début ; le passé n'y a rien ajouté, l'avenir n'y ajoutera rien."* But how was it acquired? M. Fabre cuts the Gordian knot. "Et tout naïvement je me dis : Puisqu'il faut des Araignées aux Pompiles, de tout temps ceux-ci ont possédé leur patiente astuce et les autres leur sotte audace. C'est puéril, si l'on veut, peu conforme aux visées transcendantes des théories à la mode ; il n'y a là ni objectif ni subjectif, ni adaptation ni différentiation, ni attavisme ni transformisme ; soit, mais du moins je comprends."

"Je comprends!" M. Fabre says he understands, and no doubt he thinks so ; but I confess that his explanation seems to me to leave us just where we were. To my mind, I confess, it seems to me to throw no light whatever on the matter. M. Fabre asserts that the habits of these insects have been "de tout temps" exactly what they are now. I pass by the fact that the Hymenoptera are, geologically speaking, of comparatively recent appearance. But is it the case that habits are so invariable? Quite the reverse. The cases of variation are innumerable.

Romanes† refers to a criticism of the same nature by Kirby and Spence. "Why," they ask, "if instincts are open to modification by experience and intelligence, are not bees sometimes found to use mud or mortar instead of wax or propolis? Show us," they say, "but one instance of their having substituted mud for

---

* J. H. Fabre, "Nouveaux Souvenirs Entomologiques."
"Mental Evolution in Animals."

propolis, . . . and there could be no doubt of their having been guided by reason." Such cases have, however, been observed. Andrew Knight found that his bees collected some wax and turpentine with which he had covered some decorticated trees, and used it instead of propolis, the manufacture of which they discontinued. Nay, M. Fabre has himself placed on record some cases of the same kind, and shown that the instincts of these animals are not absolutely unalterable. Thus one solitary wasp, *Sphex flavipennis*, which provisions its nest with small grasshoppers, when it returns to the cell, leaves the victim outside, and goes down for a moment to see that all is right. During her absence M. Fabre moved the grasshopper a little. Out came the Sphex, soon found her victim, dragged it to the mouth of the cell, and left it as before. Again and again M. Fabre moved the grasshopper, but every time the Sphex did exactly the same thing, until M. Fabre was tired out. All the insects of this colony had the same curious habit; but on trying the same experiment with a Sphex of the following year, after two or three disappointments she learned wisdom by experience, and carried the grasshopper directly down into the cell.

Eumenes pomiformis builds, as already mentioned, a cell in the open air. If attached to a broad base, " C'est un dôme avec goulot central, évasé en embouchure d'urne. Mais quand l'appui se réduit à un point, sur un rameau d'arbuste par exemple, le nid devient une capsule sphérique, surmontée toujours d'un goulot, bien entendu." *

Again, he has shown good reason for believing that, although the *Tachytes nigra* generally makes its

* *Loc cit.*, p. 66.

own burrow and stores it with paralyzed prey for its
own larvæ to feed on, yet that, when this insect finds a
burrow already made and stored by another Sphex, it
takes advantage of the prize, and becomes for the
occasion parasitic.   On which Mr. Darwin has justly
observed that he could see no difficulty in natural
selection making an occasional habit permanent, if of
advantage to the species, and if the insect whose nest
and stored food are thus feloniously appropriated be
not thus exterminated.

The problem is certainly one of great difficulty, and
it is with diffidence that I would suggest to M. Fabre
certain considerations which may perhaps throw some
light on it.   Let us examine some of the other solitary
wasps, and see whether their habits afford us any clue.
That an animal of prey knows where its victim is
most vulnerable, has not in itself anything unusual or
unaccountable.

The genus Bembex kills the insects on which its
young are fed, and supplies the cell with a fresh
victim from time to time.   Eumenes, like Ammophila
and Sphex, stores up the victims once for all.   They
are grievously wounded, but not altogether paralyzed.
Here, then, we have the very condition which M. Fabre
considers would be fatal to the tender egg of the wasp.
But not necessarily so.   The wretched caterpillars lie
in a wriggling mass at the bottom of the cell; a clear
space is left above them, and from the summit of the
cell the delicate egg is suspended by a fine thread, so
that, even if touched by a caterpillar in one of its con-
vulsive struggles, it would simply swing away in safety.
When the young grub is hatched, it suspends itself to
this thread by a silken sheath, in which it hangs head

downwards over its victims. Does one of them struggle? quick as lightning it retreats up the sheath out of harm's way.

In Odynerus the arrangement is very similar, but the grub simply attaches itself to the support, and does not construct a tube. Moreover, while in the solitary bees and wasps the laying of the egg is generally the final operation before the closing of the cell, in Odynerus, on the contrary, or at least in *Odynerus reniformis*, the egg is laid before the food is provided. This, perhaps, may have reference to the different condition of the victims.

According to Marchal,[*] *Cerceris ornata* practically kills her victim; moreover, she stings it not in, but between, the ganglia, and though the first sting is planted between the head and thorax, the following ones do not always follow the same order.

At present the Ammophila supplies each cell with one large caterpillar; but was this always so? One species of Odynerus deposits in each cell no less than twenty-four victims, another only eight. *Eumenes Amedei* regulates the number according to the sex: ten for the female grub, five only for the smaller male.

Moreover, while phytophagous larvæ will not generally eat any plants but those to which they are accustomed, it has been proved that, as a matter of fact, these larvæ will feed and thrive on other insects almost, if not quite, as well as on their natural food.

Is it, then, impossible that in far bygone ages the larvæ may have grown more rapidly, so that the victims had not time to decay; or that the ancestors

* Marchal, "Sur l'Instinct du *Cerceris ornata*," *Arch. d. Zool. Exper.*, 1887.

of our present Ammophilas may have fed their young from day to day with fresh food, as Bembex does even now ; that they may then have gradually brought the provisions at longer intervals, choosing small and weak victims, and laying the egg in a special part of the cell, as Eumenes does? that during these long ages they may have gradually learnt the spots where their sting would be most effective, and, thus saving themselves the trouble of capturing a number of victims, have found that it involved less labour to select a fine fat common caterpillar, such as that of *Noctua segetum,* and so have gradually acquired their present habits? Wonderful doubtless they are ; but, though I hint the suggestion with all deference, such a sequence does not seem to me to present any insuperable difficulty.

This suggestion was made in the *Contemporary Review* for 1885, and I was much interested to find in Mr. Darwin's life that he had made a similar suggestion in a letter to M. Fabre. He refers to the great skill of the Gauchos in killing cattle, and suggests that each young Gaucho sees how the others do it, and with a very little practice learns the art. "I suppose that the sand-wasps originally merely killed their prey by stinging them in many places (see p. 129 of Fabre's 'Souvenirs,' and p. 241), and that to sting a certain segment was found by far the most successful method, and was inherited like the tendency of a bulldog to pin the nose of a bull, or of a ferret to bite the cerebellum. It would not be a very great step in advance to prick the ganglion of its prey only slightly, and thus to give its larvæ fresh meat instead of only dried meat." *

* "Life and Letters of Charles Darwin."

Perhaps, however, it may be asked, Why should the insect change its habits? Several reasons might be suggested. The prey first selected might be exterminated, or at any rate diminish in numbers, and, though each species as a general rule confines itself to one special victim, some exceptions have already been noticed. For instance, *Sphex flavipennis* habitually preys on a species of grasshopper, but on the banks of the Rhone M. Fabre found it, on the contrary, attacking a field cricket, whether from the absence of the grasshopper or not he was unable to determine.

Take another case. M. Fabre denies * that the different species of Sphex can ever have been derived from one source. Every species now, he observes, has some one victim, some one insect on which it preys, to which it restricts itself, and which the other species do not attack. But "Que chassait, je vous prie, ce prototype des Sphégiens? Avait il régime varié ou régime uniforme? Ne pouvant décider, examinons les deux cas."

He begins by supposing that with the ancestor of the Sphex, "Le régime était varié. J'en félicite hautement ce premier né des Sphex. Il était dans les meilleures conditions pour laisser descendance prospère." Is it likely then, he says, that they would have limited themselves to one prey, and thus have foolishly diminished their chances in life? "Mais non," he adds, in his lively style, "mes beaux Sphex, vous n'avez pas été aussi idiots que cela. Si vous êtes de nos jours cantonnés chacun dans un mets de famille, c'est que votre ancêtre ne vous a pas enseigné la variété."

He then discusses the alternative whether the

* "Souv. Entom., troisième série."

ancestral Sphex restricted itself to one victim, and that its descendants "subdivisés en groupes et constitués enfin en autant d'espèces distinctes par le lent travail des siècles, se sont avisés qu'en dehors du comestible des ancêtres il y avait une foule d'autres aliments."

This, he says, supposes that they experimented on various victims, found several of them to their liking, and then, after a period of varied and plentiful diet, voluntarily abandoned so great an advantage.

"Avoir découvert, par vos essais d'âge en âge, la variété de l'alimentation; l'avoir pratiquée, au grand avantage de votre race, et finir par l'uniformité, cause de décadence; avoir connu l'excellent et le répudier pour le médiocre, 'Oh! mes Sphex, ce serait stupide si le transformisme avait raison.'"

"J'estime," then he concludes, "que votre ancêtre commun, votre précurseur, à goûts simples ou bien à goûts multiples, est une pure chimère."

No doubt the habits of Hymenoptera present many difficulties, and have undoubtedly many surprises in store for us, and I cannot think the matter is so clear as M. Fabre imagines, or that he has exhausted the possible cases. It is possible, though it is, I admit, only a supposition, that the ancestral Sphex hunted some species which does not now exist—at least not in the south of France—and which might have disappeared gradually. As it became rarer, they might be driven to attack other prey, and M. Fabre has himself shown by a variety of most ingenious experiments that the larvæ are by no means fastidious as to their food. The Hymenoptera vary considerably in size, and the larger individuals might be able to overmaster some large insect, while the feebler specimens were compelled to content themselves with humbler fare.

This is no purely imaginary case. M. Fabre himself distinguishes three races—or are they species?—of Leucospis which live on the three species of Chalicodomas.

"Venu du Chalicodome des galets ou des murailles, dont l'opulente larve le sature de nourriture, il mérite par sa grosseur le nom le *Leucospis gigas,* que lui donne Fabricius; venu du Chalicodome des hangars, il ne mérite plus que le nom de *Leucospis grandis,* que lui octroie Klug. Avec une ration moindre, le géant baisse d'un degré et n'est plus que le grand. Venu du Chalicodome des arbustes, il baisse encore, et si quelque nomenclateur s'avisait de le qualifier, il n'aurait plus droit qu'au titre de médiocre.

The Anthrax, again, differs considerably according to the species on which it has fed, those coming from the cocoons of *Osmia tricornis* being much larger from those from *O. cyanea.*

Or it might well happen that while the victim was from some cause or other, say for instance the absence of food elsewhere, limited to a particular district, the region beyond was suited to the ancestress Sphex. In that case, would she not naturally try whether she could not find some other suitable food? This again, is not a purely imaginary case. M. Fabre himself tells us that while " la Scolie interrompue avait pour gibier aux environs d'Avignon, la larve de l'Anoxie velue (*Anoxia villosa*). Aux environs de Sérignan, dans un sol sablonneux semblable, sans autre végétation que quelques maigres gramens, je lui trouve pour vivres l'Anoxie matutinale (*Anoxia matutinalis*), qui remplace ici la velue."

That bees soon take to newly introduced flowers is a familiar case which every one must have noticed, and which it is surely not logical to dismiss by the convenient process of referring it to " instinct." It is indeed difficult for any one who watches these insects to deny to bees the possession of a higher and conscious faculty.

In considering the question whether these remarkable instincts were originally, so to say, engrafted in the insect, or whether they were the result of innumerable repetitions of similar actions carried on by a long series of ancestors, we may perhaps be aided by the consideration that, though the results would in either case be in many respects the same, there are some in which they would altogether differ. In the former, for instance, we might expect that the insect would be so gifted that no slight obstacle should interfere with the great end in view: in the latter, on the contrary, the very repetition which gave such remarkable results would tend to incapacitate the insect from dealing with any unusual conditions.

LIMITATION OF INSTINCT.

We should, in fact, find side by side with these wonderful instincts almost equally surprising evidence of stupidity. Now, one species of Sphex preys on a large grasshopper (Ephippigera). Having disabled her victim, she drags it along by one of the antennæ, and M. Fabre found that if the antennæ be cut off close to the head, the Sphex, after trying in vain to get a grip, gives the matter up as a bad job, and leaves her victim in despair, without ever think'ng of dragging it by one of its legs. Again, when a Sphex had provisioned her cell, laid her egg, and was about to close it up, M.

Fabre drove her away, and took out both the Ephippigera and the egg. He then allowed the Sphex to return.
She went down into the empty cell, and though she
must have known that the grasshopper and the egg
were no longer there, yet she proceeded calmly to stop
up the orifice just as if nothing had happened.

The genus Sphex paralyzes its victims and provisions
its cell once for all. Bembex, on the contrary, as
already mentioned, kills the insects on which its young
are to feed, and, perhaps on this account, brings its
young fresh food (mainly flies) from time to time.
But while the Bembex thus preys on some flies, there
are others which avenge their order. The genus
Miltogramma lays its eggs in the cell of the Bembex;
and, though there seems no reason why the Bembex,
which is by far the stronger insect, should tolerate this
intrusion, which, moreover, she shows unmistakably to
be most unpalatable, she never makes any attack on
her enemy. Nay, when the young of the Miltogramma
are hatched, so far from being killed or removed, these
entomological cuckoos are actually fed until they reach
maturity. Nevertheless, it seems contrary to etiquette
for the fly to enter the cell of the Bembex; she watches
the opportunity when the latter is in the cell and is
dragging down the victim. Then is the Miltogramma's
opportunity; she pounces on the victim, and almost
instantaneously lays on it two or three eggs, which are
then transferred, with the insect on which they are to
feed, to the cell.

It is remarkable how the Bembex remembers (if one
may use such a word) the entrance to her cell, covered
as it is with sand, exactly to our eyes like that all
round. On the other hand, M. Fabre found that if he

removed the surface of the earth and the passage, exposing the cell and the larva, the Bembex was quite at a loss, and did not even recognize her own offspring. It seems as if she knew the door, the nursery, and the passage, but not her child.

Another ingenious experiment of M. Fabre's was made with a mason bee (Chalicodoma). This genus constructs an earthen cell, through which at maturity the young insect eats its way. M. Fabre found that if he pasted a piece of paper round the cell, the insect had no difficulty in eating through it; but if he enclosed the cell in a paper case, so that there was a space even of only a few lines between the cell and the paper, in that case the paper formed an effectual prison. The instinct of the insect taught it to bite through one enclosure, but it had not wit enough to do so a second time.

One of the most striking instances of stupidity (may I say) is mentioned by M. Fabre, in the case of one of his favourite bees, the *Chalicodoma pyrenaica*. This species builds cells of masonry, which she fills with honey as she goes on, raising the rim a little, then making a few journeys for honey, then raising the rim again, and so on until the cell is completed. She then prepares a last load of mortar, brings it in her mandibles, lays her egg, and immediately closes up the cell; having doubtless provided the mortar beforehand, lest during her absence an enemy should destroy the egg or any parasitic insect should gain admittance. This being so, M. Fabre chose a cell which was all but finished, and during the absence of the bee he broke away part of the cell-covering. Again, in some half-finished cells he broke away a little of the wall. In all these cases the bee, as might be expected, repaired

the mischief, the operation being in the natural order
of her work.   But now comes the curious fact.   In
another series of cells M. Fabre pierced a hole in the cell
below the part where the bee was working, and through
which the honey at once began to exude.   The poor
stupid little bee, however, never thought of repairing
the breach.   She worked on as if nothing had happened.
In her alternate journeys she brought first mortar and
then honey, which, however, ran out again as fast as it
was poured in.   This experiment he repeated over and
over again with various modifications in detail, but
always with the same result.   It may be suggested that
possibly the bee was unable to stop up a hole once
formed.   But that could not have been the case.   M.
Fabre took one of the pellets of mortar brought by the
bee, and successfully stopped the hole himself.   The
omission, therefore, was due, not to a want of power,
but of intellect.   But M. Fabre carried his experiment
still further.   Perhaps the bee had not noticed the injury.
He chose, therefore, a cell which was only just begun
and contained very little honey.   In this he made a
comparatively large hole.   The bee returned with a
supply of honey, and, seeming much surprised to find
the hole in the bottom of the cell, examined it carefully,
felt it with her antennæ, and even pushed them through
it.   Did she then, as might naturally have been expected,
stop it up?   Not a bit.   The unexpected catastrophe
transcended the range of her intellect, and she calmly
proceeded to pour into this vessel of the Danaides load
after load of honey, which of course ran out of the bottom
as fast as she poured it in at the top.   All the afternoon
she laboured at this fruitless task, and began again
undiscouraged the next morning.   At length, when she

13

had brought the usual complement of honey, she laid her egg, and gravely sealed up the empty cell. In another case, he made a large hole in the cell just above the level of the honey—a hole so large that through it he was able to see the bee lay her egg. Having done so, she carefully closed the top of the cell, but though she closely examined the hole in the side, it did not enter into the range of her ideas that such an accident could take place, and it never occurred to her to cover it up.

Another curious point raised by these ingenious experiments has reference to the quantity of honey. The cell is by no means filled; a space is always left between the honey and the roof of the cell. The usual depth of the honey in a completed cell is ten milli- metres. But the bee is not guided by this measure- ment, for in the preceding cases she sometimes closed the cell when the honey had a depth of only five milli- metres, of three, or even when the cell was almost empty. No; in some mysterious manner the bee feels when she has provided as much honey as her ancestress had done before her, and regards her work as accomplished. What a wonderful, but what a narrow, nature! She has built the cell and provided the honey, but there her instinct stops: if the cell is pierced, if the honey is removed, it does not occur to her to repair the one or fill up the other. M. Fabre not unnaturally asks, "Avec la moindre lueur rationnelle, l'insecte déposerait- il son œuf sur le tiers, sur le dixième des vivres néces- saires; le déposerait-il dans une cellule vide; laisserait- il le nourrisson sans nourriture, incroyable aberration de la maternité? J'ai raconté, que le lecteur décide."

The family of bees is generally reckoned to be one of great intelligence, but these and many other similar instances which might be recorded seem to show great limitation of intelligence.

Let me give one other, which any person may easily test for himself. I took a glass shade or jar eighteen inches long, and with a mouth six and a half inches wide, turning the closed end to the window, and put in a common hive bee. She buzzed about for an hour, when, as there seemed no chance of her getting out, I put her back into the hive. Two flies, on the contrary, which I put in with her, got out at once. Again I put another bee and a fly into the same glass; the latter flew out at once. For half an hour the bee tried to get out at the closed end; I then turned the glass with its open end to the light when she flew out at once. To make sure, I repeated the experiment once more, with the same result.

And yet there is, no doubt, ample foundation for the ordinary view which attributes considerable intelligence to the bee, within the sphere of her own operations.

Several other points of resemblance between instincts and habits could be pointed out. As in repeating a well-known song, so in instincts, one action follows another by a sort of rhythm. If a person be interrupted in a song, or in repeating anything by rote, he is often forced to go back to recover the habitual train of thought; so P. Huber found it was with a caterpillar, which makes a very complicated hammock; for if he took a caterpillar which had completed its hammock up to, say, the sixth stage of construction, and put it into a hammock completed up only to the third stage, the caterpillar simply re-performed the fourth, fifth, and sixth stages of construction. " If, however, a caterpillar were taken out of a hammock made

up, for instance, to the third stage, and were put into
one finished up to the sixth stage, so that much of its
work was already done for it, far from feeling the
benefit of this, it was much embarrassed, and, in order
to complete its hammock, seemed forced to start from
the third stage, where it had left off, and thus tried to
complete the already finished work."*

Another very interesting series of observations which
we owe to M. Fabre has reference to the question of
sex, and it would really seem that the mother can
regulate the sex of the egg at will. In many of our
wild bees, the females are much larger than the males.
The male lives a life of pleasure, idle but short.
"Quinze jours de bombance dans un magasin à miel,
un an de sommeil sous terre, une minute d'amour au
soleil, puis la mort."

But the female "C'est la mère, la mère seule qui,
péniblement, creuse sous terre des galeries et des
cellules, pétrit le stuc pour enduire les loges, maçonne
la demeure de ciment et de graviers, taraude le bois et
subdivise le canal en étages, dé·oupe des rondelles de
feuilles qui seront assemblées en pots à miel, malaxe
la résine cueillie en larmes sur les blessures des pins
pour édifier des voûtes dans la rampe vide d'un es-
cargot, chasse la proie, la paralyse et la traîne au
logis, cueille la poussière pollinique, élabore le miel
dans son jabot, emmagasine et mixtionne la pâtée.
Ce rude labeur, si impérieux, si actif, dans lequel se
dépense toute la vie de l'insecte, exige, c'est évident,
une puissance corporelle bien inutile au mâle, l'amou-
reux désœuvré."

In the hive bee the drone cells differ materially in
shape from those of the queens and workers.

* Darwin, " Origin of Species."

In the solitary wasps, where the females are much larger than the males, the mother builds a larger cell and provides more food for the former than for the latter.

The Chalicodoma (one of the mason bees) often lays her eggs in old cells of the previous year. These are of two sizes—large ones, originally built for the females, and small ones for the males. Now, in utilizing old cells, the bee always places male eggs in male cells and female eggs in female cells. If, however, a female cell be cut down so as to reduce the size, then indeed the bee deposits in it a male egg.

The bees belonging to the genus Osmia* arrange their cells in a row in a hollow stick, or some other similar situation, and it has long been known that in these and similar cases the cells first provisioned, and which are therefore furthest from the entrance, always contain females, while the outer cells always contain males.

There is an obvious advantage in this, because the males come out a fortnight or more before the females, and it is, of course, convenient that those which have to come out first should be in the cells nearest the door. The bee does not, however, lay all the female eggs first, and then all the male eggs. By no means. She produces altogether from fifteen to thirty eggs, but seldom arranges them in one row; generally they are in several series, and in every one the same sequence occurs—females further from, and males nearest to, the door.

For instance, one of M. Fabre's marked bees—one, moreover, of exceptional fertility—occupied some glass

---

* *Osmia tridentata* constitutes an exception to the general rule in this respect, as in some others.

tubes, which he arranged conveniently for her. From the 1st to the 10th of May she constructed, in one tube, eight cells—first seven female, and then one male. From the 10th to the 17th, in a second tube, she built first three female and then three male cells; from the 17th to the 25th, in a third, three female and then two male; on the 26th, in a fourth, one female; and, finally, from the 26th to the 30th, in a fifth, two female and three male: altogether twenty-five, seventeen female and eight male cells.

The advantage of this is clear, but the manner in which it is secured is not so obvious. It might be suggested that the quantity of food was not regulated by the sex of the young one, but that the sex depended on the quantity of food. This would be very improbable, and M. Fabre attempted to disprove it by some very ingenious experiments. He found that if he took some of the food from a female cell, the bee or wasp produced was still a female, though a starveling; while if he added food to a male cell, the larva still produced a male, though a very large and fine one.

M. Fabre then made some of his most ingenious experiments. He brought into his room a large number of cocoons of Osmia. When the perfect insects were about to emerge, he arranged for them a number of glass tubes, of which the Osmias gladly availed themselves, and in which they proceeded to construct their cells. The usual arrangement, as already mentioned, is that the males are placed nearest to, and the female furthest from, the door. But M. Fabre so arranged the tubes that each was in two parts, an outer wider portion having a diameter of eight to twelve millimetres, which is sufficient for a female cell; and an inner narrower portion with a diameter of five to five and a half millimetres, which is too small for a female, but just large enough for a male. This arrangement placed the Osmias in a difficulty. They could not follow their natural instinct and construct at the end of the tube cells large enough for females.

What happened? Some of the Osmias shut off the narrow ends, and used only the outer wider portion. Others, reluctant, as it were, to throw away a chance, built also in the narrow part of the tube, and under these circumstances, contrary to the otherwise invariable rule, the inner and first constructed cells contained males.

M. Fabre concludes then, and it seems to me has given very strong reasons for thinking so, that these privileged insects not only know the sex of the insect which will emerge from the egg they are about to lay, but that at their own will they can actually control it! Certainly a most curious and interesting result!

He concludes his charming work as follows :—" Mes chèrs insectes, dont l'étude m'a soutenu et continue à me soutenir au milieu de mes plus rudes épreuves, il faut ici, pour aujourd'hui, se dire adieu. Autour de moi les rangs s'eclaircissent et les longs espoirs ont fui. Pourrai-je encore parler de vous ? " and every lover of nature will, I am sure, echo the wish.

CHAPTER XIII.

ON THE SUPPOSED SENSE OF DIRECTION.

ONE of the most interesting questions connected with the instincts and powers of animals has reference to the manner in which they find their way back, after having been carried to a distance from, home. This has by some been attributed to the possession of a special " sense of direction."

Mr. Darwin suggested that it would be interesting to try the effect of putting animals " in a circular box with an axle, which could be made to revolve very rapidly, first in one direction and then in another, so as to destroy for a time all sense of direction in the insects. I have sometimes," he said, " imagined that animals may feel in which direction they were at the first start carried." In fact, in parts of France it is considered that if a cat is carried from one house to another in a bag, and the bag is whirled round and round, the cat loses her direction and cannot return to her old home.

On this subject M. Fabre has made some interesting and amusing experiments. He took ten bees belonging to the genus Chalicodoma, marked them on the back with a spot of white, and put them in a bag. He then carried them half a kilometre in one direction, stopping at a point where an old cross stands by the wayside, and whirled the bag rapidly round his head. While he was doing so a good woman came by, who was not a little surprised to find the professor standing in front of the old cross, solemnly whirling a bag round his head, and, M. Fabre fears, strongly suspected him of some satanic practice. However this may be, M. Fabre, having sufficiently whirled his bees, started off back in the opposite direction, and carried his prisoners to a distance from their home of three kilometres. Here he again whirled them round, and then let them go one by one. They made one or two turns round him, and then flew off in the direction of home. In the meanwhile his daughter Antonia was on the watch. The first bee did the mile and three-quarters in a quarter of an hour. Some hours after two more returned; the other seven did not reappear.

The next day he repeated this experiment with ten other bees. The first returned in five minutes, and two more in about an hour. In this case, again, seven out of ten failed to find their way home.

In another experiment he took forty-nine bees. When let out, a few started wrong, but he says that "lorsque la rapidité du vol me laisse reconnaître la direction suivie;" the great majority flew homewards. The first arrived in fifteen minutes. In an hour and a half eleven had returned, in five hours six more, making seventeen out of forty-nine. Again he experimented with twenty, of which seven found their way home. In the next experiment he took the bees rather further—to a distance of about two and a quarter miles. In an hour and a half two had returned, in three hours and a half seven more; total, nine out of forty. Lastly, he took thirty bees: fifteen marked rose he took by a roundabout route of over five miles; the other fifteen marked blue he sent straight to the rendezvous, about one and a half miles from home. All the thirty were let out at noon; by five in the evening seven "rose" bees and six "blue" bees had returned, so that the long détour had made no appreciable difference. These experiments seem to M. Fabre conclusive. "La démonstration," he says, "est suffisante. Ni les mouvements enchevêtrés d'une rotation comme je l'ai décrite; ni l'obstacle de collines à franchir et de bois à traverser; ni les embûches d'une voie qui s'avance, rétrograde et revient par un ample circuit, ne peuvent troubler les Chalicodomes dépaysés et les empêcher de revenir au nid." *

I am not ashamed to confess that, charmed by M. Fabre's enthusiasm, dazzled by his eloquence and ingenuity, I was at first disposed to adopt this view. Calmer consideration, however, led me to doubt, and though M. Fabre's observations are most ingenious, and are very amusingly described, they do not carry conviction to my mind. There are two points specially to be considered—

1. The direction taken by the bees when released.

2. The success of the bees in making good their return home.

As regards the first point, it will be observed that the successful bees were in the following proportion, viz.:—

3	out of	10
4	,,	10
17	,,	49
7	,,	20
9	,,	40
7	,,	15
Or altogether 47	,,	144

* J. H. Fabre, "Nouveaux Souvenirs Entomologiques."

This is not a very large proportion. Out of the whole number no less than ninety-seven appear to have lost their way. May not the forty-seven have found theirs by sight or by accident? Instinct, however inferior to reason, has the advantage of being generally unerring. When two out of three bees went wrong, we may, I think, safely dismiss the idea of instinct. Moreover, the distance from home was only one and a half to two miles. Now, bees certainly know the country for some distance round their home; how far they generally forage I believe we have no certain information, but it seems not unreasonable to suppose that if they once came within a mile of their nest they would find themselves within ken of some familiar landmark. Now, if we suppose that 150 bees are let out two miles from home, and that they flew away at random, distributing themselves equally in all directions, a little consideration will show that some twenty-five of them would find themselves within a mile of home, and consequently would know where they were. I have never myself experimented with Chalicodomas, but I have observed that if a hive bee is taken to a distance, she behaves as a pigeon does under similar circumstances; that is to say, she flies round and round, gradually rising higher and higher and enlarging her circle, until I suppose her strength fails or she comes within sight of some known object. Again, if the bees had returned by a sense of direction, they would have been back in a few minutes. To fly one and a half or two miles would not take five minutes. One bee out of the 147 did it in that time; but the others took one, two, three, or even five hours. Surely, then, it is reasonable to suppose that these lost some time before they came in sight of any object known to them. The second result of M. Fabre's observations is not open to these remarks. He observes that the great majority of his Chalicodomas at once took the direction home. He confesses, however, in the sentence I have already quoted, that it is not always easy to follow bees with the eye. Admitting the fact, however, it seems to me far from impossible that the bees knew where they were ; and, at any rate, this does not seem so improbable that we should be driven to admit the existence of a new sense, which we ought only to assume as a last resource.

Moreover, M. Fabre himself says, " Lorsque la rapidité du vol me laisse reconnaître la direction suivie," which seems to imply a doubt. Indeed, some years previously he had made a similar experiment with the same species, but taking them direct to a point rather over two miles (four kilometres) from the nest, and not whirling them round his head. I looked back, there, fore, to his previous work to see how these behaved, and I found that he says—

"Aussitôt libres, les Chalicodomes fuient, comme effarés, qui dans une direction, qui dans la direction tout opposée. Autant que le permet leur vol fougueux, je crois néanmoins reconnaître un prompt retour des abeilles lancées à l'opposé de leur demeure, et la majorité me semble se diriger du côté de l'horizon où se trouve le nid. Je laisse ce point avec des doutes, que rendent inévitables des insectes perdus de vue à une vingtaine de mètres de distance."

In this case, then, some went in one direction, some in another. It certainly would be remarkable if bees which were taken direct missed their way, while those which were whirled round and round went straight home.

Moreover, it appears that after all, as a matter of fact, they did not fly straight home. If they had done so they would have been back in three or four minutes, whereas they took far longer. Even then, if they started in the right direction, it is clear that they did not adhere to it. I have myself tried experiments of the same kind with hive bees and ants. For instance, I put down some honey on a piece of glass close to a nest of *Lasius niger*, and when the ants were feeding I placed it quietly on the middle of a board one foot square, and eighteen inches from the nest. I did this with thirteen ants, and marked the points at which they left the board. Five of them did so on the half of the board nearest the nest, and eight on that turned away from it. I then timed three of them. They all found the nest eventually, but it took them ten, twelve, and twenty minutes respectively. Again, I took forty ants which were feeding on some honey, and put them down on a gravel-path about fifty yards from the nest, and in the middle of a square eighteen inches in diameter, which I marked out on the path by straws.

I prepared a corresponding square on paper, and, having indicated by the arrow the direction of the nest, I marked down the spot where each ant passed the boundary. They crossed it in all directions; and dividing the square into two halves, one towards the nest and one away from it, the number in each were almost exactly the same.

After leaving the square, they wandered about with every appearance of having lost themselves, and crossed the boundary backwards and forwards in all directions. Two of them, however, we watched for an hour each. They meandered about, and at the end of the time one was about two feet from where she started, but scarcely any nearer home; the other about six feet away, and nearly as much further from home. I then took them up and replaced them near the nest, which they at once joyfully entered.

I mentioned some of the foregoing facts in a paper which I read at the meeting of the British Association at Aberdeen, and they have since been confirmed by Mr. Romanes.[*]

"In connection," he says, "with Sir John Lubbock's paper at the British Association, in which this subject is treated, it is perhaps worth while to describe some experiments which I made last year. The question to be answered is whether bees find their way home merely by their knowledge of landmarks, or by means of some mysterious faculty usually termed a sense of direction. The ordinary impression appears to have been that they do so in virtue of some such sense, and are therefore independent of any special knowledge of the district in which they may be suddenly liberated; and, as Sir John Lubbock observes, this impression was corroborated by the experiments of M. Fabre. The conclusions drawn from these experiments, however, appeared to me, as they appeared to Sir John, unwarranted by the facts; and therefore, like him, I repeated them with certain variations. In the result I satisfied myself that the bees depend entirely upon their special knowledge of district or landmarks, and it is because my experiments thus fully corroborate those

[*] *Nature*, October 29, 1886.

which were made by Sir John that it now occurs to me
to publish them.

"The house where I conducted the observations is
situated several hundred yards from the coast, with
flower-gardens on each side, and lawns between the
house and the sea. Therefore bees starting from the
house would find their honey on either side of it, while
the lawns in front would be rarely or never visited—
being themselves barren of honey, and leading only to
the sea. Such being the geographical conditions, I
placed a hive of bees in one of the front rooms on the
basement of the house. When the bees became
thoroughly well acquainted with their new quarters by
flying in and out of the open window for a fortnight, I
began the experiments. The *modus operandi* consisted
in closing the window after dark when all the bees were
in their hive, and also slipping a glass shutter in front
of the hive door, so that all the bees were doubly im-
prisoned. Next morning I slightly raised the glass
shutter, thus enabling any desired number of bees to
escape. When the desired number had escaped, the
glass shutter was again closed, and all the liberated
bees were caught as they buzzed about the inside of the
shut window. These bees were then counted into a box,
the window of the room opened, and a card well smeared
over with birdlime placed upon the threshold of the
beehive, or just in front of the closed glass shutter.
The object of all these arrangements was to obviate the
necessity of marking the bees, and so to enable me not
merely to experiment with ease upon any number of
individuals that I might desire, but also to feel confident
that no one individual could return to the hive unnoticed. For whenever a bee returned it was certain

to become entangled in the bird-lime, and whenever I found a bee so entangled, I was certain that it was one which I had taken from the hive, as there were no other hives in the neighbourhood.

"Such being the method, I began by taking a score of bees in the box out to sea, where there could be no land-marks to guide the insects home. Had any of these insects returned, I should next have taken another score out to sea (after an interval of several days, so as to be sure that the first lot had become permanently lost), and then, before liberating them, have rotated the box in a sling for a considerable time, in order to see whether this would have confused their sense of direction. But, as none of the bees returned after the first experiment, it was clearly needless to proceed to the second. Accordingly, I liberated the next lot of bees on the sea-shore, and, as none of these returned, I liberated another lot on the lawn between the shore and the house. I was somewhat surprised to find that neither did any of these return, although the distance from the lawn to the hive was not above two hundred yards. Lastly, I liberated bees in different parts of the flower-garden, and these I always found stuck upon the bird-lime within a few minutes of their liberation. Indeed, they often arrived before I had had time to run from the place where I had liberated them to the hive. Now, as the garden was a large one, many of these bees had to fly a greater distance, in order to reach the hive, than was the case with their lost sisters upon the lawn, and therefore I could have no doubt that their uniform success in finding their way home so immediately was due to their special knowledge of the flower-garden, and not to any general sense of direction.

"I may add that, while in Germany a few weeks ago, I tried on several species of ant the same experiments as Sir John Lubbock describes in his paper as having been tried by him upon English species, and here also I obtained identical results; in all cases the ants were hopelessly lost if liberated more than a moderate distance from their nest.

M. Romanes' experiments, therefore, as he himself says, entirely confirm the opinion I have ventured to express—that there is no sufficient evidence among insects of anything which can justly be called a "sense of direction."

CHAPTER XIV.

ON THE INTELLIGENCE OF THE DOG.

CONSIDERING the long ages during which man and the other animals have shared this beautiful world, it is surely remarkable how little we know about them. We have recently had various interesting works on the intelligence and senses of animals, and yet I think the principal impression which they leave on the mind is that we know very little indeed on the subject.

THE DOG.

As to the intelligence of the dog, a great many people, indeed, seem to me to entertain two entirely opposite and contradictory opinions. I often hear it said that the dog, for instance, is very wise and clever. But when I ask whether a dog can realize that two and two make four, which is a very simple arithmetical calculation, I generally find much doubt expressed.

That the dog is a loyal, true, and affectionate friend must be gratefully admitted, but when we come to consider the psychical nature of the animal, the limits of our knowledge are almost immediately reached. I have elsewhere suggested that this arises in great measure from the fact that hitherto we have tried to teach animals, rather than to learn from them—to convey our ideas to

them, rather than to devise any language or code of
signals by means of which they might communicate
theirs to us.   The former may be more important
from a utilitarian point of view, though even this is
questionable, but psychologically it is far less interesting.   Under these circumstances, it occurred to me
whether some such system as that followed with deaf
mutes, and especially by Dr. Howe with Laura Bridgman, might not prove very instructive if adapted to the
case of dogs.

A very interesting account of Laura Bridgman has
been published by Wright, compiled almost entirely from
reports of the Perkins Institution, and the Massachusetts
Asylum for the Blind, in which Dr. Howe, the director
of the establishment, details the history of Laura Bridgman, who was deaf, dumb, and blind, almost without the
power of smell and taste, but who, nearly alone among
those thus grievously afflicted, possessed an average, if
not more than an average, amount of intelligence,
although, until brought under Dr. Howe's skilful treat-
ment and care, her physical defects excluded her from
all social intercourse.

Laura Bridgman was born of intelligent and respect-
able parents, in Hanover, New Hampshire, U.S., in
December, 1829.   She is said to have been a sprightly,
pretty infant, but subject to fits, and altogether very
fragile.   At two years old she was fairly forward, had
mastered the difference between A and B, and, indeed,
is said to have displayed a considerable degree of
intelligence.   She then became suddenly ill, and had
to be kept in a darkened room for five months.   When
she recovered she was blind, deaf, and had nearly lost
the power both of smell and taste.

"What a situation was hers! The darkness and silence of the tomb were around her; no mother's smile gladdened her heart, or 'called forth an answering smile;' no father's voice taught her to imitate his sounds. To her, brothers and sisters were but forms of matter, which resisted her touch, but which differed not from the furniture of the house, save in warmth and in the power of locomotion, and in these respects not even from the dog or cat."

Her mind, however, was unaffected, and the sense of touch remained. "As soon as she was able to walk, Laura began to explore the room, and then the house; she became familiar with the form, density, weight, and heat of every article she could lay her hands on.

"She followed her mother, felt her hands and arms, as she was occupied about the house, and her disposition to imitate led her to repeat everything herself. She even learnt to sew a little, and to knit. Her affections, too, began to expand, and seemed to be lavished upon the members of her family with peculiar force.

"The means of communication with her, however, were very limited. She could only be told to go to a place by being pushed, or to come to one by a sign of drawing her. Patting her gently on the head signified approbation; on the back, the contrary."

The power of communication was thus most limited, and her character began to suffer, when fortunately Dr. Howe heard of her, and in October, 1837, received her into the institution.

"For a while she was much bewildered, till she became acquainted with her new locality, and somewhat familiar with the inmates; the attempt was made to give her knowledge of arbitrary signs, by which she could interchange thoughts with others.

"The first experiments were made by taking the articles in common use, such as knives, forks, spoons, keys, etc., and pasting upon them labels, with their names embossed in raised letters. These she felt carefully, and soon, of course, distinguished that the crooked lines s-p-o-o-n differed as much from the crooked lines k-e-y, as the spoon differed from the key in form. Then small detached labels with the same words printed upon them were put into her hands; she soon observed that they were the same as those pasted upon the articles. She showed her perception of this similarity by laying the label k-e-y upon the key, and the label s-p-o-o-n upon the spoon.

"Hitherto, the process had been mechanical, and the success about as great as that of teaching a very knowing dog a variety of tricks.

"The poor child sat in mute amazement, and patiently imitated everything her teacher did. But now her intellect began to work, the truth flashed upon her, and she perceived that there was a way by which she could herself make a sign of anything that was in her own mind, and show it to another mind. At once her countenance lighted up with a human expression. It was no longer as a mere instinctive animal; it was an immortal spirit, eagerly seizing upon a new link of union with other spirits. I could almost fix upon the moment when this truth dawned upon her mind, and spread its beams upon her countenance; I saw that the great obstacle was overcome, and that henceforth nothing but patient and persevering, but plain and straightforward, efforts were necessary.

"The result, thus far, is quickly related and easily conceived; but not so was the process, for many weeks of apparently unprofitable labour were spent before it was effected.

" The next step was to procure a set of metal types, with the different letters of the alphabet cast separately on their ends; also a board, in which were square holes, into which she could set the types, so that the letters could alone be felt above the surface.

" Thus, on any article being handed to her, as a pencil or watch, she would select the component letters and arrange them on the board, and read them with apparent pleasure, assuring her teacher that she understood by taking all the letters of the word and putting them to her ear, or on the pencil."

It is unnecessary, from my present point of view, to carry the narrative further, interesting as it is. I will only observe that even in the case of Laura Bridgman the process was one of much difficulty and requiring great patience. For a long while it was found impossible to make her realize the use of adjectives; she could not "understand any general expression of quality." Again, we are told that "Some idea of the difficulty of teaching her common expressions may be derived from the fact that a lesson of two hours upon the words 'right' and 'left' was deemed very profitable if she had in that time really mastered the idea."

Now, it seemed to me that the ingenious method devised by Dr. Howe, and so successfully carried out in the case of Laura Bridgman, might be adapted to the case of dogs, and I have tried this in a small way with a black poodle named Van.

VAN AND HIS CARDS.

I took two pieces of cardboard about ten inches by three, and on one of them printed in large letters the word

$$\boxed{F \ O \ O \ D}$$

leaving the other blank. I then placed the two cards over two saucers, and in the one under the "food" card put a little bread and milk, which Van, after having his attention called to the card, was allowed to eat. This was repeated over and over again till he had had enough. In about ten days he began to distinguish between the two cards. I then put them on the floor and made him bring them to me, which he did readily enough. When he brought the plain card I simply threw it back, while when he brought the "food" card I gave him a piece of bread, and in about a month he had pretty well learned to realize the difference. I then had some other cards printed with the words "out," "tea," "bone," "water," and a certain number also with words to which I did not intend him to attach any significance, such as "nought," "plain," "ball," etc. Van soon learned that bringing a card was a request, and soon learned to distinguish between the plain and printed cards; it took him longer to realize the difference between words, but he gradually got to recognize several, such as "food," "out," "bone," "tea," etc. If he was asked whether he would like to go out for a walk, he would joyfully fish up the "out" card, choosing it from several others, and bring it to me, or run with it in evident triumph to the door.

I need hardly say that the cards were not always put in the same places. They were varied quite indiscriminately and in a great variety of positions. Nor could the dog recognize them by scent. They were all alike, and all continually handled by us. Still, I did not trust to that alone, but had a number printed for each word. When, for instance, he brought a card with "food" on it, we did not put down the same identical card, but another bearing the same word; when he had brought that, a third, then a fourth, and so on. For a single meal, therefore, eighteen or twenty cards would be used, so that he evidently is not guided by scent. No one who has seen him look down a row of cards and pick up the one he wanted could, I think, doubt that in bringing a card he felt that he is making a request, and that he could not only distinguish one card from another but also associate the word and object.

I used to leave a card marked "water" in my dressing-room, the door of which we used to pass in going to or from my sitting-room. Van was my constant companion, and passed the door when I was at home several times in the day. Generally he took no heed of the card. Hundreds, or I may say thousands, of times he passed it unnoticed. Sometimes, however, he would run in, pick it up, and bring it to me, when of course I gave him some water, and on such occasions I invariably found that he wanted to drink.

I might also mention, in corroboration, that one morning he seemed unwell. A friend, being at breakfast with us, was anxious to see him bring his cards, and I therefore pressed him to do so. To my surprise he brought three dummy cards successively, one marked "ham," one "bag," and one "brush." I said reproachfully, "Oh, Van! bring "food," or "tea;" on which he looked at me, went very slowly, and brought the "tea" card. But when I put some tea down as usual, he would not touch it. Generally he greatly enjoyed a cup of tea, and, indeed, this was the only time I ever knew him refuse it.

A definite numerical statement always seems to me clearer and more satisfactory than a mere general assertion. I will, therefore, give the actual particulars of certain days. Twelve cards were put on the floor, one marked "food" and one "tea." The others had more or less similar words. I may again add that every time a card was brought, another similarly marked was put in its place. Van was not pressed to bring cards, but simply left to do as he pleased.

1	Van brought "food"	4 times.	"Tea" 2 times.				
2	"	"	6	"			
3	"	"	8	"	"	2	"
4	"	"	7	"	"	3	"
5	"	"	6	"	"	4	"
6	"	"	6	"	"	3	"	"Nought" once.
7	"	"	8	"	"	2	"
8	"	"	5	"	"	3	"
9	"	"	4	"	"	2	"
10	"	"	10	"	"	4	"	"Door" once.
11	"	"	10	"	"	3	"
12	"	"	6	"	"	3	"
			80			31	

Thus out of 113 times he brought food 80 times, tea 31 times, and the other 10 cards only twice. Moreover, the last time he was wrong he brought a card—namely, "door"—in which three letters out of four were the same as in "food."

14

This is, of course, only a beginning, but it is, I venture to think, suggestive, and might be carried further, though the limited wants and aspirations of the animal constitute a great difficulty. My wife has a beautiful and charming collie, Patience, to whom we are much attached. This dog was often in the room when Van brought the "food" card and was rewarded with a piece of bread. She must have seen this thousands of times, and she begged in the usual manner, but never once did it occur to her to bring a card. She did not touch, or, indeed, even take the slightest notice of them.

I then tried the following experiment:—I prepared six cards about ten inches by three, and coloured in pairs—two yellow, two blue, and two orange. I put one card of each colour on the floor, and then, holding up one of the others, endeavoured to teach Van to bring me the duplicate. That is to say, that if the blue was held up, he should fetch the corresponding colour from the floor; if yellow, he should fetch the yellow, and so on. When he brought the wrong card he was made to drop it and return for another, until he brought the right one, when he was rewarded with a little food.

We continued the lessons for nearly three months, but as a few days were missed, we may say for ten weeks, and yet at the end of the time I cannot say that Van appeared to have the least idea what was expected of him. It seemed a matter of pure accident which card he brought. There is, I believe, no reason to doubt that dogs can distinguish colours; but as it was just possible that Van might be colour-blind, we then repeated the same experiment, only substituting for the coloured cards others marked respectively with one, two, and three dark bands. This we continued for another three months, or, say, allowing for intermissions, ten weeks ; but, to my surprise, entirely without success, for we altogether failed to make Van understand what we wanted. I was rather disappointed at this, as, if it had succeeded, the plan would have opened out many interesting lines of inquiry. Still, in such a case one ought not to wish for one result more than another as, of course, the object of all such experiments is merely to elicit the truth, and our result in the present case, though negative, is very interesting. I do not, however, regard it as by any means conclusive, and should be glad to see it repeated. If the result proved to be the same, it would certainly imply very little power of combining even extremely simple ideas.

Can Animals count ?

I then endeavoured to get some insight into the arithmetical condition of the dog's mind. On this subject I have been able to find but little in any of the standard works on the intelligence of animals. Considering, however, the very limited powers of savage men in this respect—that no Australian language, for instance, contains numerals even up to four, no Australian being able to count his own fingers even on one hand—we cannot be surprised if other animals have made but little progress. Still, it is curious that so little attention should have been directed to this subject. Leroy, who, though he expresses the opinion that " the nature of the soul of animals is unimportant," was an excellent observer, mentions a case in which a man was anxious to shoot

a crow. " To deceive this suspicious bird, the plan was
hit upon of sending two men to the watch-house, one
of whom passed on, while the other remained ; but the
crow counted, and kept her distance. The next day
three went, and again she perceived that only two
retired. In fine, it was found necessary to send five or
six men to the watch-house to put her out in her
calculation. The crow, thinking that this number of
men had passed by, lost no time in returning." From
this he inferred that crows could count up to four.
Lichtenberg mentions a nightingale which was said to
count up to three. Every day he gave it three meal-
worms, one at a time ; when it had finished one it
returned for another, but after the third it knew that
the feast was over. I do not find that any of the recent
works on the intelligence of animals, either Buchner,
or Peitz, or Romanes in either of his books, give any
additional evidence on this part of the subject. There
are, however, various scattered notices.

According to my bird-nesting recollections, which I
have refreshed by more recent experience, if a nest
contains four eggs, one may safely be taken ; but if
two are removed, the bird generally deserts. Here, then,
it would seem as if we had some reason for supposing
that there is sufficient intelligence to distinguish three
from four.

An interesting consideration rises also with reference to the number of the victims allotted to each
cell by the solitary wasps. Ammophila considers one
large caterpillar of *Noctua segetum* enough ; one species
of Eumenes supplies its young with five victims ;
one ten, another fifteen, and one even as many as
twenty-four. The number is said to be constant in

each species. How, then, does the insect know when her task is fulfilled? Not by the cell being filled, for if some be removed she does not replace them. When she has brought her complement she considers her task accomplished, whether the victims are still there or not. How, then, does she know when she has made up the number twenty-four? Perhaps it will be said that each species feels some mysterious and innate tendency to provide a certain number of victims. This would not under any circumstances be an explanation, nor is it in accordance with the facts. In the genus Eumenes the males are much smaller than the females. Now, in the hive bees, humble bees, wasps, and other insects where such a difference occurs, but where the young are directly fed, it is, of course, obvious that the quantity can be proportioned to the appetite of the grub. But in insects with the habits of Eumenes and Ammophila the case is different, because the food is stored up once for all. Now, it is evident that if a female grub was supplied with only food enough for a male, she would starve to death; while if a male grub were given enough for a female it would have too much. No such waste, however, occurs. In some mysterious manner the mother knows whether the egg will produce a male or female grub, and apportions the quantity of food accordingly. She does not change the species or size of her prey; but if the egg is male she supplies five, if female ten, victims. Does she count? Certainly this seems very like a commencement of arithmetic. At the same time, it would be very desirable to have additional evidence before we can arrive at any certain conclusion.

Considering how much has been written on instinct,

it seems surprising that so little attention has been
directed to this part of the subject.   One would fancy
that there ought to be no great difficulty in determining
how far an animal can count; and whether, for instance, it could realize some very simple sum, such as
that two and two make four.   But when we come to
consider how this is to be done, the problem ceases to
appear so simple.   We tried our dogs by putting a
piece of bread before them, and preventing them from
touching it until we had counted seven.   To prevent
ourselves from unintentionally giving any indication,
we used a metronome (the instrument used for marking
time when practising the pianoforte), and to make the
beats more evident we attached a slender rod to the
pendulum.   It certainly seemed as if our dogs knew
when the moment of permission had arrived ; but their
movement of taking the bread was scarcely so definite
as to place the matter beyond a doubt.   Moreover,
dogs are so very quick in seizing any indication given
them, even unintentionally, that, on the whole, the
attempt was not satisfactory to my mind.   I was the
more discouraged from continuing the experiment in
this manner by an account Mr. Huggins gave me of a
very intelligent dog belonging to him.   A number of
cards were placed on the ground, numbered respectively
1, 2, 3, and so on up to 10.   A question was then asked :
the square root of 9 or 16, or such a sum as $6+55-3$.
Mr. Huggins pointed consecutively to the cards, and
the dog always barked when he came to the right one.
Now, Mr. Huggins did not consciously give the dog any
sign, yet so quick was the dog in seizing the slightest
indication, that he was able to give the correct answer.

"The mode of procedure is this.   His master tells

him to sit down, and shows him a piece of cake. He is then questioned, and barks his answers. Say he is asked what is the square root of 16, or of 9; he will bark four or three times, as the case may be. Or such a sum as $\frac{6+1.2-3}{5}$ he will always answer correctly. The piece of cake is, of course, the meed of such cleverness. It must not be supposed that in these performances any sign is consciously made by his questioner. None whatever. We explain the performance by supposing that he reads in his master's expression when he has barked rightly; certainly he never takes his eyes from his master's face." *

This observation seems to me of great interest in connection with the so-called "thought-reading." No one, I suppose, will imagine that there was in this case any "thought-reading" in the sense in which this word is generally used. Evidently "Kepler" seized upon some slight indication unintentionally given by Mr. Huggins. The observation, however, shows the great difficulty of the subject.

The experiments I have made are, I feel, very incomplete, but I have ventured to place them on record, partly in hope of receiving some suggestions, and partly in hope of inducing others with more leisure and opportunity to carry on similar observations, which I cannot but think must lead to interesting results.

* M. L. Huggins, "Kepler: a Biography."

INDEX.

A

Acalles, 66
Acanthopleura, 15, 145
Acheta, 61, 63, 97, 117
Acridiidæ, 100, 106
Actinia, 13
Ageronia, 73
Aglaura, 188
Alciopidæ, 14, 22, 137
Ammophila, 243, 282
Amphibia, 32, 129
Amphicora, 87
Amphioxus, 129
Angler, 186
Anguis, 126
Annelides, touch, 13; taste, 22; smell, 34; hearing, 87; sight, 134; problematical organs, 189
Anobium, 67
Anoxia, 251
Anthidium, 71
Anthrax, 251
Ants, 24, 31, 43, 56, 69, 107, 115, 178, 202
Apion, 94
Apis, 26, 29, 58, 69, 70, 115, 150, 172, 194, 258, 283
Arca, 141
Arenicola, 87
Arithmetic of animals, 281
Arthropods, touch, 16; taste, 23; smell, 35; hearing, 88; sight, 146; problematical organs, 188
Articulata. See Annelides, Insects

Ascidians, 129
Asellus, 48
Astacus, 23, 51, 88
Asteracanthion, 133
Asterope, 22
Astropecten, 132
Ateuches, 66
Auditory hairs, 16, 79, 85, 88, 116
—— organs, 77
—— rods, 18, 104, 111

B

Balanus, 220
Bee, hive. See Apis
Bee, solitary, 242
Beetles. See Coleoptera
Bembex, 242, 246
Birds, 129, 282
Blatta, 46, 152
Blethisa, 68
Blind spot in eye, 125
Bohemilla, 13, 134
Bombardier beetle, 65
Bombus, 28, 70, 73, 178, 283
Bostrychida, 67
Brachinus, 64, 68
Brachyura, 90
Butterfly. See Lepidoptera

C

Calanella, 159
Calotis, 127
Callianassa, 50

Camponotus, 208
Capitellidæ, 34
Capricorn beetle, 96
Carcinus, 92
Cards, Van and his, 277
Carinaria, 87
Caterpillars, 23, 243, 259
Cats, 262
Centipedes, 49, 74
Cephalopoda, 34, 141
Cerambyx, 67, 95, 96
Ceratius, 186
Ceratophyus, 68
Chalcididæ, 27
Chalicodoma, 251, 262
Chiasognathus, 68
Chitons, 15, 144
Cicadas, 61, 64, 151
Cicadidæ, 151
Clepsine, 134
Cockchafer. *See* Melolontha
Cockroach, 46, 152
Cœlenterata, touch, 11; taste, 22; smell, 33; hearing, 82; sight, 131
Coleoptera, 58, 67, 111, 151
Collie, 280
Color of deep-sea fish, 185
—— of flowers, 199
——, sense of, 190, 194, 202, 230
Componotus, 239
Compound eyes, 163
Copepoda, 48
Copilia, 158
Copris, 68, 95
Corephium, 145
Corethra, 18, 113, 117, 151
Corixa, 75
Corti, the organ of, 80, 105
Corycæus, 157
Cossus, 148
Count? can animals, 281
Crabs, 90, 92
Crayfish. *See* Astacus
Cricket. *See* Acheta
Crioceris, 68
Crow, 282
Crustacea, touch, 16; taste, 23; smell, 46; hearing, 88; sight, 156; sense of color, 211; problematical organs, 188
Crystalline cone, 168

Culex, 68, 115
Curculionidæ, 68
Cychrus, 68
Cyclostoma, 140
Cymbulia, 88

D

Daphnia, 48, 206, 212
Dead-nettle, 200
Death-watch, 66
Dias, 220
Dinetus, 39
Diptera, 52, 69, 110, 149, 151
Direction, sense of, 262
Dog, intelligence of the, 272
Dragon-fly. *See* Libellula
Dytiscus, 5, 6, 112, 131, 146, 167

E

Ear. *See* Auditory organs
—— in tail of Mysis, 92
——, structure of the human, 78, 101
Earthworms, 206
Elaphrus, 68
Elaterida, 67
Empusa, 176
Endosmosis, 25
Englena, 130
Epeira, 146
Ephippigera, 103
Epithelial cells, 14, 20
Epithelium, 11, 19
Eristalis, 69, 174, 176
Eucopidæ, 85
Eucorybar, 74
Eumenes, 245, 282
Euphausia, 161
Eurycopa, 189
Eutima, 83
Evaneadæ, 27
Eye, compound, 163
—— of man, 121
——, pineal, 126
——, simple, 170

F

Fish, 182
Flowers, 200

Fly. *See* Musca
Forficula, 151, 167
Formica. *See* Ants

G

Gammarus, 49, 188
Gasteropods, 86
Geotrupes, 68
Geryonia, 86
Glomeris, 50
Glossopharyngeal nerves, 19
Gnat, 68, 115
Gryllotalpa, 102
Gryllus, 63, 98, 106, 108

H

Hairs, auditory, 16, 79, 85, 88, 116
——, depressed, 17
——, flattened, 56
——, glandular, 29
——, hollow, 17
—— in insects, 16
—— of touch. *See* Tactile
——, olfactory, 16, 25
——, ordinary surface, 16, 56
——, plumose natatory, 16, 94
——, simple, 18
——, solid, 17, 82
——, tactile, 16, 18, 28, 29, 56
——, taste, 16, 28
Haliotis, 5, 139
Hattaria, 127
Hearing, organs of, in Vertebrata, 77;
    Cœlenterata, 82; Mollusca, 86;
    Annelida, 87; Arthropods, 88
——, sense of, 60, 97
Helix, 14, 139
Hemiptera, 112, 151
Hesione, 135
Humble-bee. *See* Bombus
Hydaticus, 40
Hydrachna, 28
Hydromedusæ, 86
Hydrophilus, 168
Hydrozoa, 13
Hylœus, 58
Hymenoptera, 23, 25, 56, 57, 58, 69,
    70, 96, 151, 181, 250

Hyperia, 171
Hypoderm, 5, 16

I

Ichneumon, 54, 58
Ichthyosaurus, 129
Infusoria, 11
Insects, touch, 16; taste, 23; smell,
    35, 52; hearing, 61, 94; sight,
    146; problematical organs, 188
Instinct—
    Ant, 202, 232, 267
    Bee, hive, 194, 253
    ——, solitary, 255, 260, 262
    Birds, 282
    Bombardier beetle, 64
    Change in, 244
    Crustacea, 90
    Daphnia, 229
    Dog, 272
    Fish, 186
    Fly, 174, 177
    Limitation of, 253
    Of direction, 262
    Onchidium, 144
    Paussus, 65
    Wasp, solitary, 243, 282
Isopteryx, 109

J

Jelly-fish. *See* Medusæ
Julus, 49

L

Labyrinthodons, 129
Lacerta, 126, 128
Lamellibranchiata, 14, 141
Lamellicornia, 37, 52
Lamium, 200
Lampyris, 167
Lancelet, 129
Lasius. *See* Ants
Laura Bridgman, 273
Leech, 189
Lema, 68
Lepidoptera, 37, 71, 94, 111, 148,
    151, 168, 181
Leptodora, 156

Leucospis, 251
Libellula, 69, 70, 149, 152, 171
Light-organs, 161, 185
Ligia, 167
Limitation of instinct, 253
Limpet, 4, 138
Limulus, 159
Lithobius, 155
Lizzia, 132
Lobster, 90, 91
Locusts, 62, 99, 106, 111, 149, 176
Longicorn beetles, 66, 95
Lucanus, 43, 52
Lucilia, 177
Lycosa, 179
Lyda, 58

M

Mammals, 129
Maxillæ, 25
Meconema, 102, 105
Medusæ, 6, 22, 82, 83, 84, 85, 86, 117
Meissner's corpuscles, 7
Melolontha, 52, 58, 67, 68, 148, 152, 168
Mesonotum, 67
Metronome, 284
Miltogramma, 254
Mollusca, 14, 22, 34, 61, 86, 120, 137, 140
Mordella, 148
Mosaic vision, 163
Mosquito. See Culex
Moths. See Lepidoptera
Murex, 139
Musca, 17, 29, 30, 45, 53, 58, 68, 71, 110, 113, 148, 153, 165, 172, 174, 177, 254
Mutilla, 69, 70
Myriapods, 155, 205
Myrmica. See Ants
Mysis, 92, 98, 157, 161

N

Nautilus, 140
Necrophorus, 66, 68
Needle cells, 21
Nematocera, 151

Nematocysts, 12
Nereis, 12, 135
Nesticus, 180
Neuroptera, 111, 151
Newts, 207
Noctua, 73, 243, 282

O

Oceanidæ, 86
Ocypoda, 61
Odynerus, 247
Œstrus, 148
Olfactory organs. See Organs of smell
Omaloplia, 68
Onchidium, 14, 131, 143
Oniscoidæ, 170
Ontorchis, 6, 84
Organs of hearing, 17, 19, 77, 81, 93, 109, 114
—— of sight, 19, 130, 146
—— of smell, 17, 88
—— of taste, 17, 19, 21
—— of temperature, 6, 10
—— of touch, 11, 14, 17, 19, 131
——, problematical, 182
Origin of organs of sense, 3
Orthoptera, 37, 99, 107, 112, 131, 176
Oryctes, 68
Osmia, 251
Otolithes, 52, 82, 84, 85, 89, 90, 91, 92
——, possible origin of, 3

P

Pacinian corpuscle, 8
Pagurus, 51
Palæmon, 51
Palinurus, 61
Palpi, 30, 37, 38, 39, 41, 73
Paludina, 140
Pamphila, 184
Paniscus, 58
Patella, 138, 140
Paussus, 65
Pectens, 61, 141
Pectunculus, 141
Pelagia, 86

Pelobius, 68
Periplaneta, 152
Perophthalmus, 144
Pheidole, 108
Phialidium, 85
Photichthys, 185
Pineal eye, 127
Pinnotheres, 51
Piscicola, 134
Platyarthrus, 207
Plesiosaurus, 129
Pleuromona, 189
Podophthalmata, 50, 156
Polydesmus, 189
Polyophthalmus, 33, 98, 134
Pompilus, 58
Ponera, 69
Pontella, 47, 48
Pontinia, 51
Poodle dog, 276
Pressure-point, 10
Prionus, 67
Proctotrupidæ, 27
Pronotum, 67
Prosobranchiata, 138
Protoplasm, 21
Protozoa, 32, 61
Pteropods, 87
Ptychoptera, 113

R

Recognition among ants, 234
Reptilia, 127, 130
Respiration in insects, 35
Retina, 123
Rhopalonema, 85
Rods, auditory, 18, 104, 111, 187
——, olfactory, 55
——, retinal, 124

S

Salivary gland, 30
Sarcophaga, 111
Schizochiton, 145
Scolopendra, 155
Scopelus, 186
Scorpions, 179
Sea-anemone, 12, 187

Sense-hairs. *See* Hairs
Sense of direction, 262
Sense-organs, origin of, 3, 86, 111
Senses, unknown, 192
Serolis, 189
Setæ. *See* Hairs
Sex, power of regulating, 262
Sight, organs of, in Vertebrata, 121;
    Cœlenterata, 131 ; Annelida, 133;
    Mollusca, 137 ; Arthropods, 146
——, sense of, 118
——, three possible modes of, 118
Silpha, 38, 41
Sirex, 58
Skin, termination of nerves in, 18
Smell, organs of, in Vertebrata, 32;
    Protozoa, 33 ; Cœlenterata, 33;
    Annelida, 33; Mollusca, 34; Arthro-
    pods, 35
Smerinthus, 73
Solaster, 133
Sound, organs of, not known in Pro-
    tozoa or Cœlenterata, 61; Mollusca,
    61 ; Crustacea, 61 ; Insects, 62
Sphex, 245
Sphinx, 73, 148
Sphœrotherium, 74
Spiders, 74, 146, 155, 170, 178
Spondylis, 67, 141
Squilla, 51
Stag-beetle, 43, 52
Staphylinus, 50
Stenobothrus, 62, 63
Stratiomys, 167
Syrphus, 69, 170

T

Tachytes, 246
Taste, organs of, in Vertebrata, 19;
    Annelida, 22 ; Mollusca, 22 ; Ar-
    thropods, 23
Telephorus, 112
Temperature, organs of, 10
Tenebrionida, 68
Tenthredo, 27, 58
Theridium, 75
Touch, organs of, in Vertebrata, 7 ;
    Protozoa, 11 ; Cœlenterata, 11 ;
    Medusæ, 12 ; Annelida, 13 ; Mol-
    lusca, 14; Arthropods, 16

Touch, sense of, 7
Tracheæ, 29, 30, 101
Trachymedusæ, 85
Trachynemadæ, 187
Tritonia, 87
Trochus, 138
Trox, 68
Tunicata, 129
Turbellaria, 133

V

Van, 276
Vanessa, 73, 174

Varanus, 127
Vaterian corpuscles, 7
Vertebrata, 7, 19, 32, 77
Vespa, 28, 55, 58, 175, 178, 283

W

Wagner's corpuscles, 7
Warmth organs, 6, 10
Wasp. *See* Vespa
———, solitary, 242, 282
Weevils, 67, 94
Wolffian glands, 27
Worms. *See* Annelides

THE END.